IMAGES
of America

WASHOUGAL

I0812412

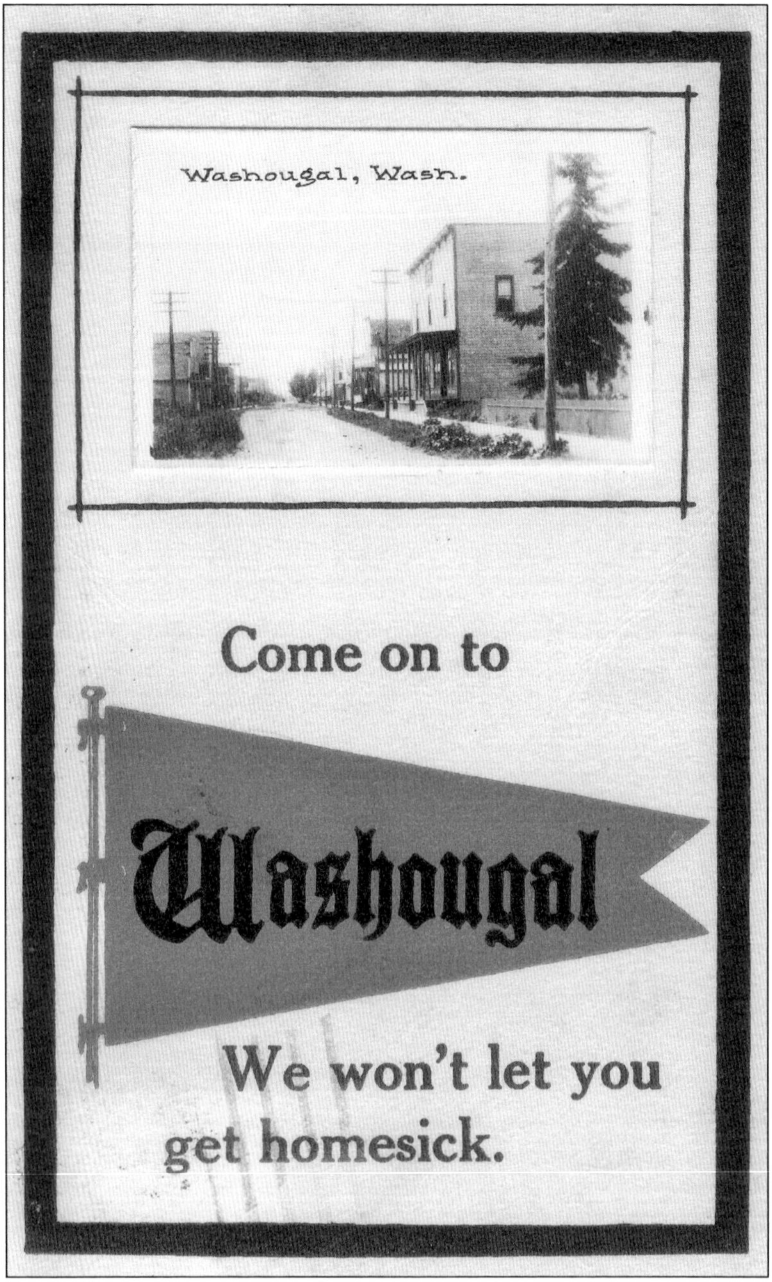

Washougal and the Columbia Gorge have long been popular destinations for tourists. This 1916 promotional postcard invites visitors to see Washougal. It is aimed in particular at those driving newfangled automobiles. Pennants, such as the one depicted on the postcard, served as bragging rights for travelers. Tourists would hang the pennants on the flaps and windows of early touring cars, such as the Mitchell.

ON THE COVER: The waterways of the Pacific Northwest were primary corridors for moving goods and passengers throughout the West. The *Bailey Gatzert*, built in 1890 in Ballard, Washington, had few equals in size and accommodation. The *Dalles City* made daily trips to Portland and The Dalles, stopping at the many landings along the way. In the 1900s, a round-trip ticket from Washougal to Portland cost 25¢. (Photograph by H. Egan.)

IMAGES
of America

WASHOUGAL

Richenda Fairhurst

ARCADIA
PUBLISHING

ISBN 978-0-7385-3134-2

Published by Arcadia Publishing
Charleston, South Carolina

Printed in the United States of America

Library of Congress Catalog Card Number: 2006921512

For all general information contact Arcadia Publishing at:
Telephone 843-853-2070
Fax 843-853-0044
E-mail sales@arcadiapublishing.com
For customer service and orders:
Toll-Free 1-888-313-2665

Visit us on the Internet at www.arcadiapublishing.com

This book is dedicated to the many photographers who worked in an emerging West. These men and women are now largely unknown, but thanks to their efforts we may better know our history. Photographs within this book include works by Darius Kinsey, Helfrich DeVere, Edward and Asahel Curtis, Fred Froesschle of Cape Horn, Veil Studio in Camas, Leo's Studio and Goff's Studio in Washougal, J. F. Ford of Portland, and Dr. Charles Meredith of Cape Horn.

Contents

Acknowledgments 6

Introduction 7

1. Early Settlement and Discovery 9

2. A Town Springs Up 19

3. At Work in a River Town 37

4. Life in Town and Country 57

5 Port to Port along the Gorge 81

6. Growing Up and Moving Out 95

7. Washougal Today 123

Acknowledgments

The author is grateful to the many people who contributed to this story of Washougal, most especially to the Two Rivers Heritage Museum and photograph archivist Beverly Burris Hughey. All the photographs in this book that are not otherwise credited belong to Two Rivers Heritage Museum and their collections. Thanks also to Betty Ramsey, Two Rivers director, for her help and especially for the Sasquatch story. Thanks to the many knowledgeable museum volunteers and to Curtis Hughey, Two Rivers chairman. Curtis's many reference books are a terrific resource for those interested in Washougal. I would also like to thank Rick McClure, CCC guru for the Gifford Pinchot National Forest, Sharon Tiffany of the Skamania County Historical Society, Karen Spilman at the National Cowboy and Western Heritage Museum in Oklahoma, Debbie Coryell of Pendleton Woolen Mills, Jeffrey Smith at the Clark County Maritime Museum, Dr. Chuck Cardinell of the Oregon Maritime Museum, Carla Wulfsberg of the Henderson House Museum, Elaine Miller of the Washington State Historical Society, and Nicolette Bromberg, special collections librarian at the University of Washington.

In researching Washougal, a few sources in particular were consistently helpful. Those include *Washougal, Washington: Gateway to the Gorge* by Mildred Piontek and *Clark County Pioneers, A Centennial Salute* and *Clark County Pioneers through the Turn of the Century* by Rose Marie Harshman, Clark County Genealogical Society Publications. Also helpful was Two Rivers Heritage Museum's collection of oral histories, including Emily Webber Bright's *The Record of the Webber Family*. Thanks also to Thomas Gentry and Edward Margeson.

INTRODUCTION

A mythical West has fueled the imagination for hundreds of years. Those who made it by sea or overland found a near-tropical landscape in a temperate zone. Forests of towering ancients grew right up to the river's edge. Ferns stuffed between tree trunks grew seven feet high, with not a blackberry thorn to be seen in any direction. This is what Washougal looked like to the native tribes who had lived along the Columbia River for thousands of years.

In the 1700s, Spain, Britain, and the United States vied for ownership of the land. It was an eruption of discovery fueled by the myth of abundance. Fur traders and explorers recognized the potential of the land and, to claim it, charted what they saw. Capt. Robert Gray, of the *Columbia Rediviva*, was the first American explorer to push across the sandbar that hid the mouth of the fabled Northwest Passage. He entered the Columbia River and drew a map. That chart, that little slip of paper, eventually helped determine who would succeed in their claim for the land and who would fail.

British Royal Navy captain George Vancouver followed Gray into the mouth of the Columbia River. Or at least he tried to. But his ship, the *Discovery*, was too large to cross the sandbar. Instead he sent Lieutenant Broughton across in the *Chatham*, instructing him to find the headwaters of the river. Broughton would journey for more than 100 miles but never even get close. In 1792, the British lieutenant brought his boat to within sight of the place that would someday be Washougal. He was sure the headwaters must be close. The Chinook Indians, sympathetic perhaps to this confounded white man on the river, nodded politely and sent him on his way.

Though the British would try to claim it, the mighty Columbia River became part of Oregon Territory in 1846. Huge numbers of settlers came west. The Cascade, Chinook, and Yakima tribes would spar with them but lose the battle. Decimated by new diseases, their numbers were too few. The incoming settlers, exhausted and overwrought yet brimming with a desperate hope, swept away all before them. In just a few generations, the native tribes' influence along the river would diminish. American enterprise would forge a whole new "West," and Washougal would be part of it.

Washougal was founded in 1880, nine years before Washington was a state. The first white child born in Washington, Christopher Columbus Simmons entered the world on what would become Washougal soil. The first settlers were from New York, Norway, Minnesota, Britain, Germany, and Ohio. Trappers and sailors became farmers, staking donation land claims in 1850. Some fell in love with Native American women, or even princesses, and started families. Washougal was at the core of such a family. Betsey White Wing was a Chinook princess whose ancestral homeland was part of what became Washougal. She fell in love and married a British sailor stationed at the Hudson's Bay Company's Fort Vancouver. Part of their 633 acres of shore and woodland became a town, and their children peopled Washougal for generations.

All along the Columbia River, the towns cropped up. Each town thrust wooden pilings into the soft river soil and built landings, one after another, up and down the shore: Fisher Landing, Gentry's Landing, Parker's Landing, Steam Boat Landing, Mount Pleasant, Cape Horn, Cascade,

Stevenson, and on and on. Steamboats traveled from one to the other, and eventually the North Bank Railroad would link them all the way down to the Pacific Ocean.

Despite bitter winters and ravaging floods, Washougal flourished. First-generation immigrants became parents, grandparents, and great-grandparents. Their descendents would build roads, found schools, and make a history that would be remembered. Washougal's history. It is a story of spirit, enterprise, enthusiasm, forbearance, survival, pluck, and no small amount of good humor.

One

Early Settlement and Discovery

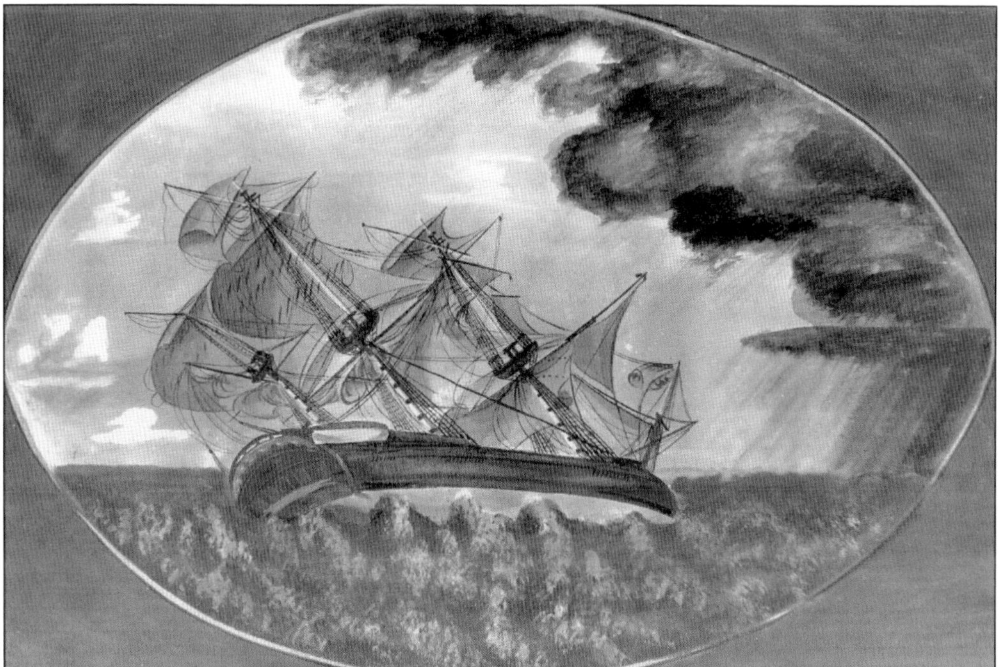

In 1792, Capt. Robert Gray was the first white explorer to sail into the Columbia River. The entrance was hidden by a sandbar and many had missed it, including British Royal Navy captain George Vancouver, who hoped to claim the river for Britain. This painting of Gray's ship, the *Columbia Rediviva*, by George Davidson, a member of the crew, records the perils of their voyages. (Courtesy Columbia River Maritime Museum.)

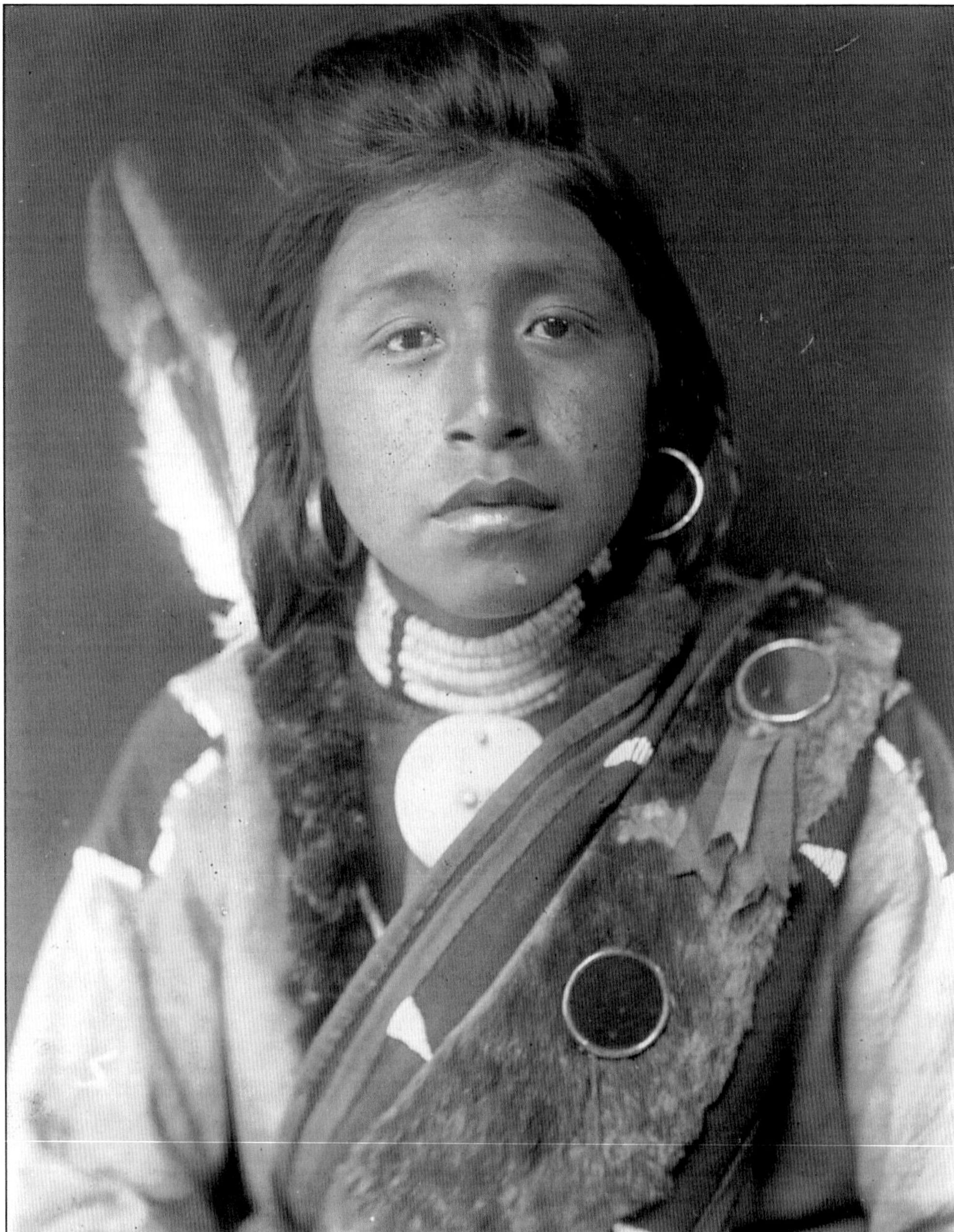

The Columbia River Robert Gray "discovered" was not new to the Chinook people. For at least 11,000 years, the Chinook, such as this man photographed in 1910, lived along the *Wimahl*, or Columbia River. Europeans first came into contact with them during the fur trade. The Chinook were vigorous traders and traded locally and regionally in salmon, pottery, and slaves, as well as furs. In the 1800s, a *hyas tyee*, or Chinook chief, named Concomly held power over a wide geographical area. Catholic missionary Father De Smet reported that, on ceremonial occasions, Concomly commanded a processional of 300 slaves. As he walked, the path ahead of him was spread with beaver and otter skins. (Photograph by Edward Curtis; courtesy Library of Congress.)

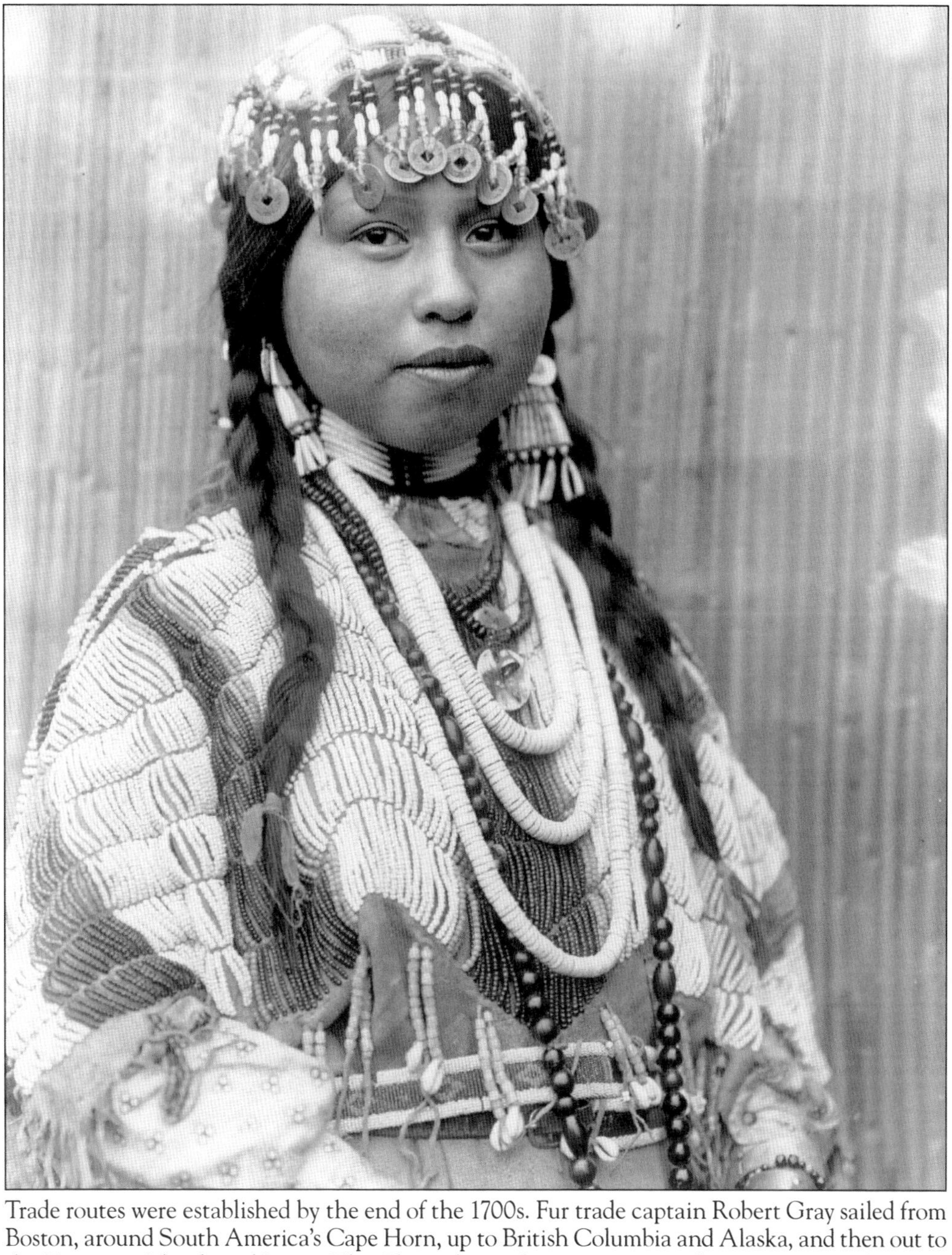

Trade routes were established by the end of the 1700s. Fur trade captain Robert Gray sailed from Boston, around South America's Cape Horn, up to British Columbia and Alaska, and then out to the Hawaiian Islands and Japan. The Chinook people were active trading partners, exchanging with the Europeans for goods and currency with either shells or coins. This Chinook woman, photographed in 1910, displays her wealth and status with a headdress decorated with Chinese coins. The Chinook spoke a trade language, Wawa, known to the fur traders as Jargon. Edward H. Thomas compiled a dictionary of Chinook Wawa in 1935. According to Thomas, the numbers 1 to 10 in Wawa were *ikt* (1), *mokst* (2), *klone* (3), *lakit* (4), *kwinnim* (5), *taghum* (6), *sinamokst* (7), *stotekin* (8), *kwaist* (9), and *tahtlum* (10). Wawa included English words also, such as "musket" and "get up." (Photograph by Edward Curtis; courtesy Library of Congress.)

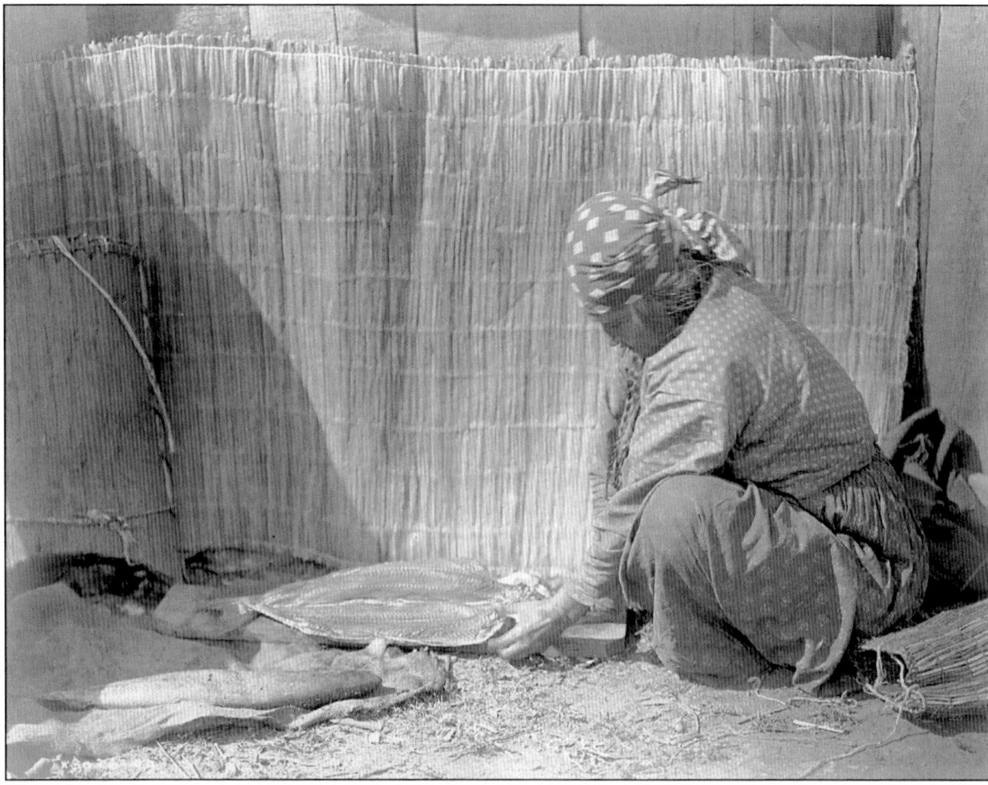

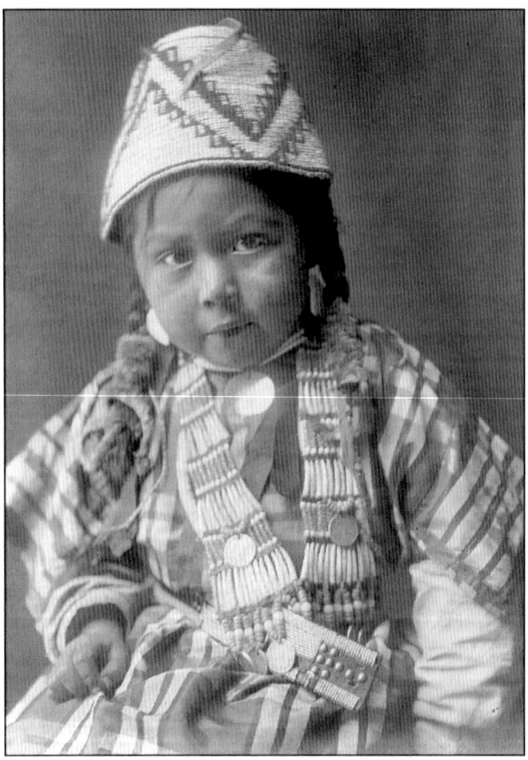

Traditionally Chinook men and women wore only a loincloth. They also practiced tattooing and wore a shell through their noses. Clothing changed by the 1870s and men and women wore garments of deerskin, which they elaborately decorated. This woman, processing salmon in 1910, wears a western-style fabric dress. Dried salmon was stored in cedar bark baskets for winter. (Photograph by Edward Curtis; courtesy Library of Congress.)

This infant, pictured in 1910, dealt with a harsh past and an uncertain future. Diseases like cholera and smallpox proved catastrophic for the Chinooks. The population, estimated at over 16,000 in 1800, dipped to 2,500 by 1825. Then in 1830, "intermittent fever" left as few as 40 survivors, though some may have fled. Following an uprising in 1856, the Chinook people were placed on reservations. (Photograph by Edward Curtis; courtesy Library of Congress.)

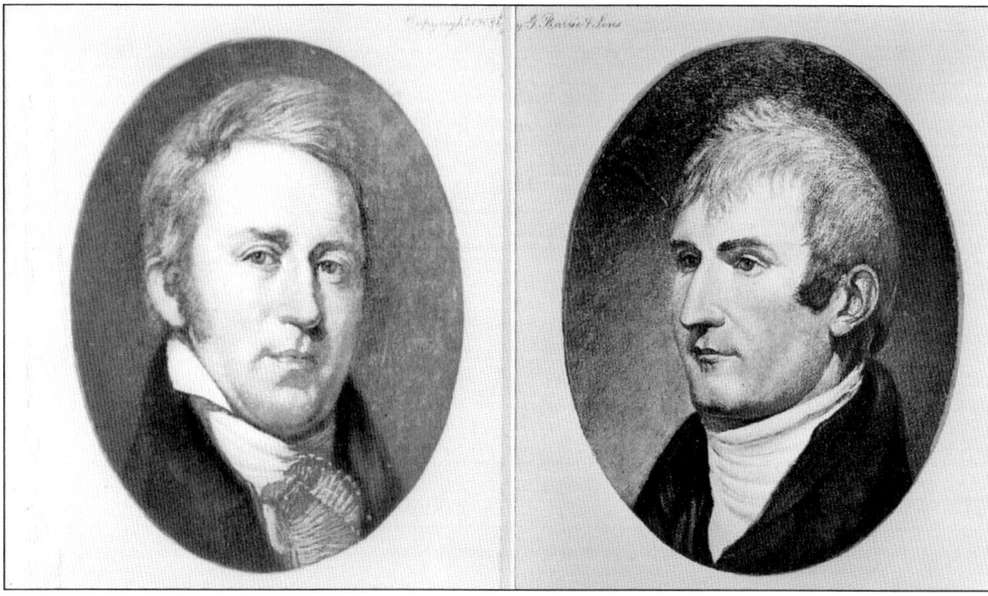

In the race to claim the West, Briton Sir Alexander Mackenzie reached the Pacific Ocean overland first in 1793. Capt. William Clark (left) and Meriwether Lewis (right) followed in 1805, spending six days at Cottonwood Beach near Washougal in 1806. Their careful notes and charts would open the West for settlement and lay claim to the land for the United States. (Portraits by Charles Wilson Peale; courtesy Library of Congress.)

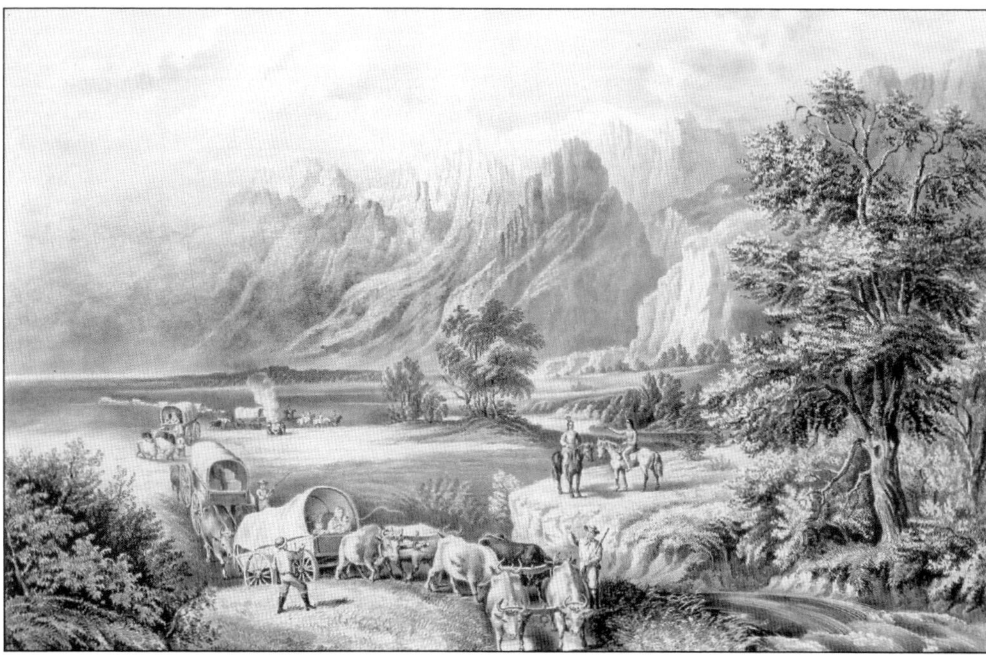

As the cry "Westward ho" echoed across the land, men and women from America and Europe did just that. Of those who came by wagon, a journey of 2,000 miles, an estimated 34,000 people died. This 1866 Currier and Ives print by Fanny Palmer shows a wagon train near the Rocky Mountains and illustrates the optimism of many who embarked on the trail west. (Courtesy Library of Congress.)

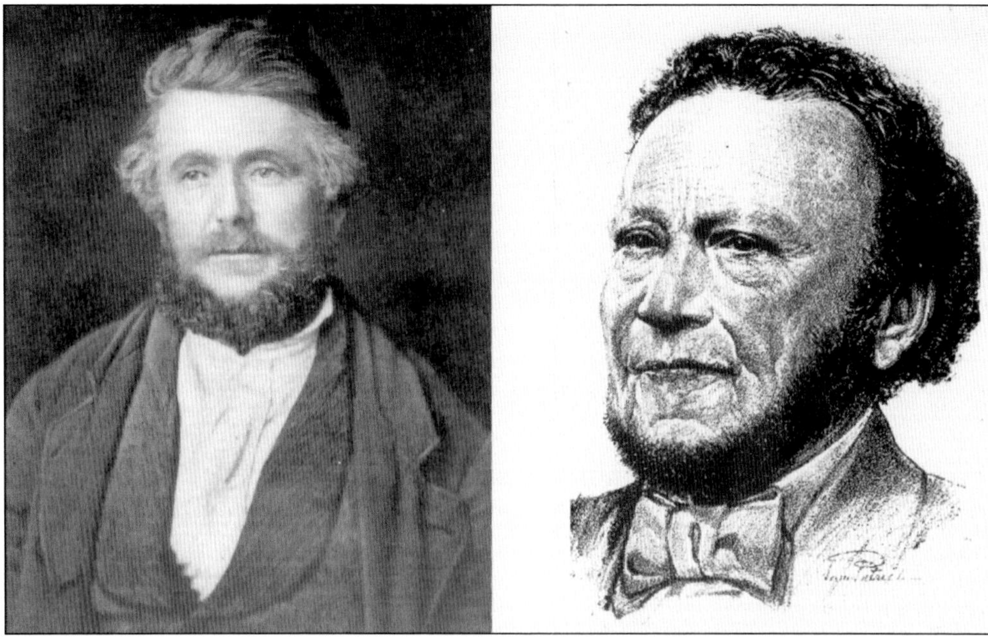

Christopher Columbus Simmons, the first white child born in Washington, entered the world in Washougal on April 14, 1845. His parents, Michael (left) and Elizabeth Simmons, journeyed overland with George Bush (right) and his wife, Isabella. George was of African/Irish descent, a Quaker, and a gifted farmer. The party settled first in Washougal, but land discrimination forced them to move farther north. (Courtesy Washington State Historical Society, Henderson House Museum.)

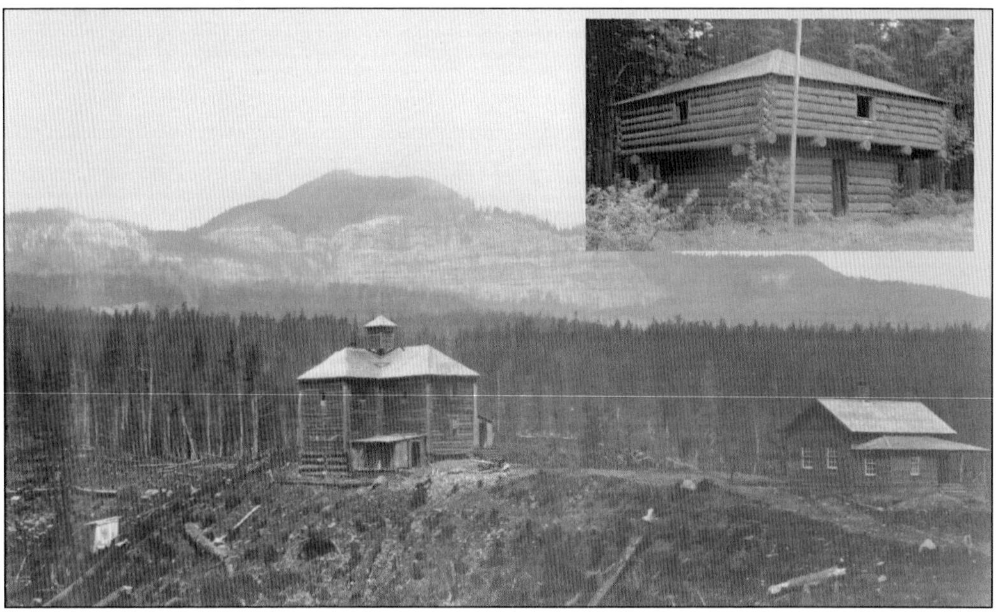

Relations between the incoming settlers and native tribes became increasingly strained. In 1856, near what is now the Bonneville Dam, Yakima chief Kamiakin attacked two steamboats and settlements along the river. At the upper cascades blockhouse, pictured here, six settlers were killed. At Fort Rains (insert), a young Lieutenant Sheridan is said to have distinguished himself in the fight. Nine Cascade Indians were hanged. (Courtesy Library of Congress.)

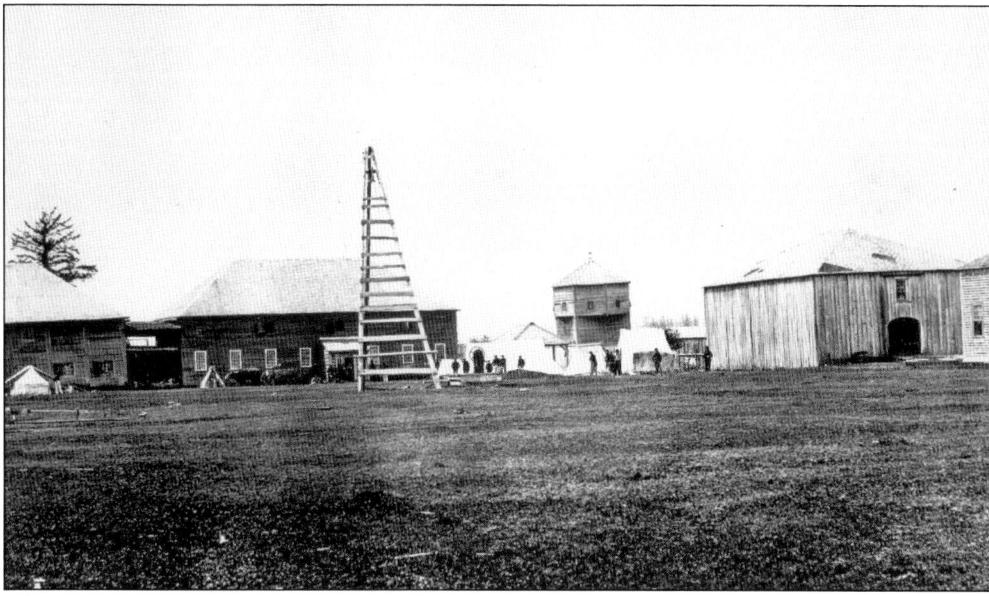

John McLoughlin built Fort Vancouver, headquarters for the fur-trading Hudson's Bay Company, in 1824. The British-held fort soon became a vital supply stop for American pioneers, and John McLoughlin emerged as an almost mythic figure of good sense and generosity. When the British retreated in 1846, America's new Oregon Territory stretched north to the Canadian border and "Clarke" County encompassed all of Washington State. (Courtesy Library of Congress.)

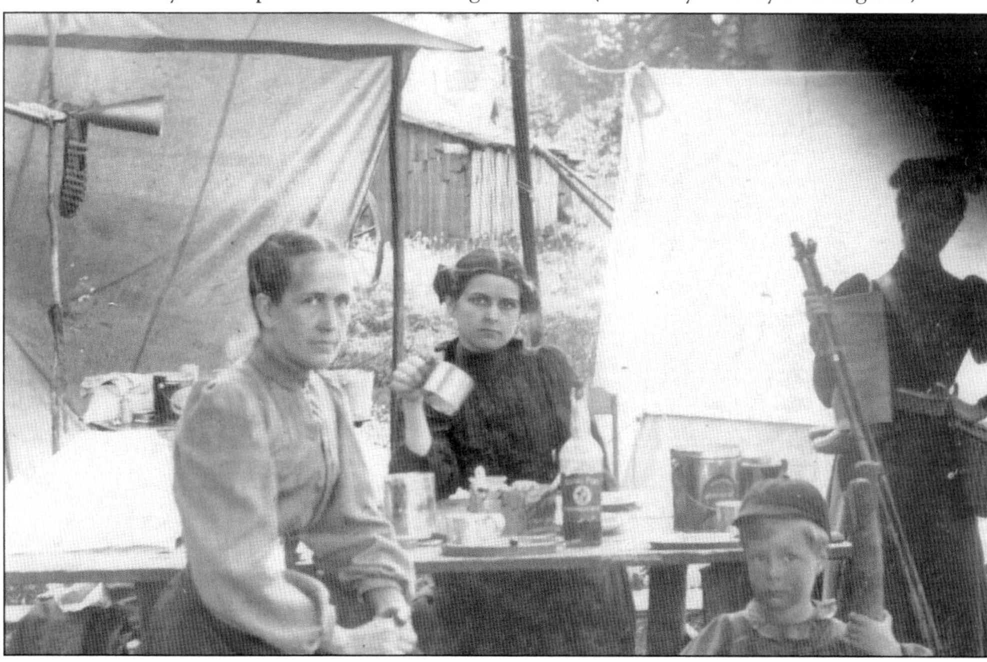

Born in Illinois to Swiss parents, Bertha Robinson Hughey (pictured but not identified) came west with her brother Jerome around 1897. Jerome's new claim at Marmot, Oregon, offered few amenities. Lumber had to be cut and split before houses, barns, or outhouses could be built. Bertha settled across the river and taught at the Prindle School. She married Edward Hughey of the Prindle School Board. (Photograph by Jerome Robinson; courtesy Curtis Hughey.)

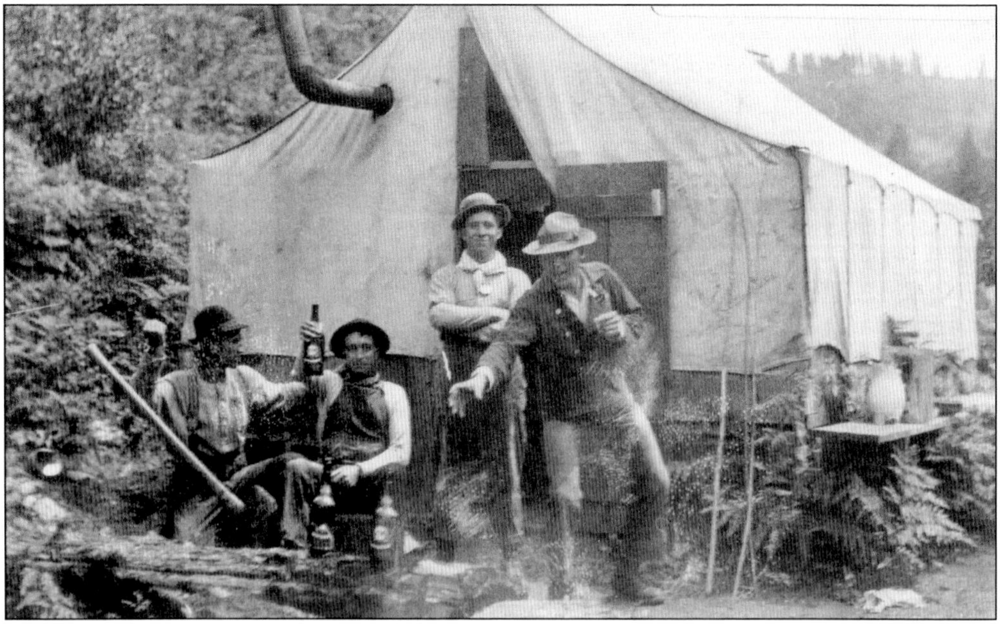

Settlers to Washougal entered a land of dense forests, volcanic boulders, and rushing waterways. In this 1903 photograph of settlers at Cougar Creek, a group of men pose with an axe, fishing poles, and bottles of drink. Temporary homes were built from planks, with sturdy canvas forming the sides and roof. The door kept raccoons and wolverines out. A chimney pipe protrudes from the canvas roof.

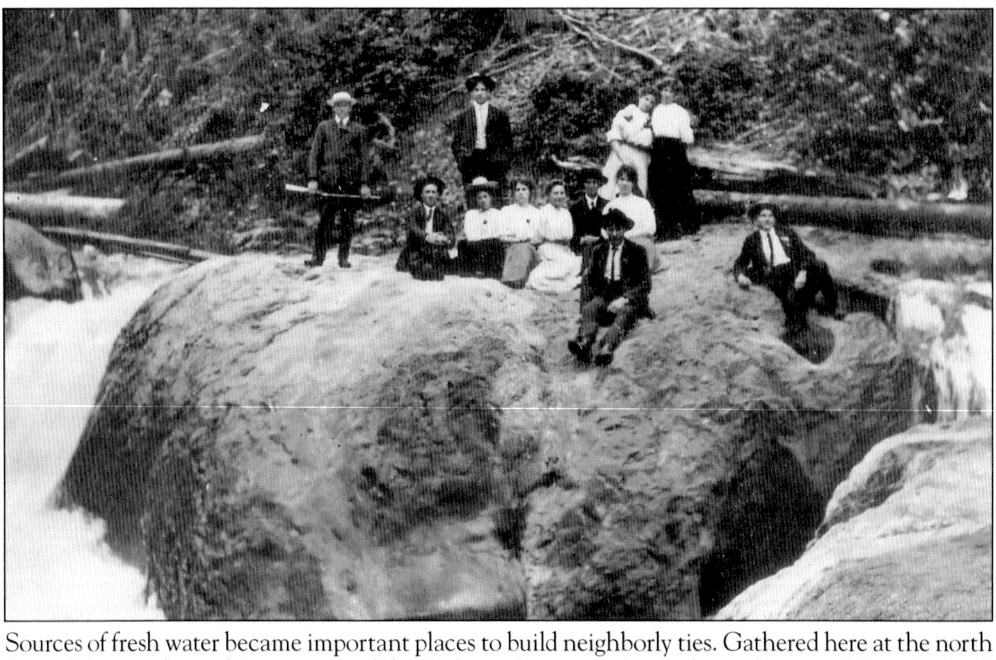

Sources of fresh water became important places to build neighborly ties. Gathered here at the north fork of the Washougal River, east of the Doherty homestead, are the Doherty, Pohl, and Shield families. Pictured, from left to right, are (first row) Emmit Shields and Albert Pohl; (second row) Peter Doherty, Marie Echtle, Nellie Shields, Lena Pohl, Floyd Hitchinson, and Anna Doherty; (third row) Gus Pohl, Maurice Shields, Kate Shields, and Margarite Doherty.

A number of immigrants to the Washougal area were of European origin, particularly Norwegian, German, or Swiss groups. This unidentified group of people stands together in 1897 on what looks like a homemade bridge. Local timber is perhaps being built into a house. During the early days, it was common for the girlfriends of loggers to come to work sites with picnic lunches. (Photograph by Bertha Robinson Hughey; courtesy Curtis Hughey.)

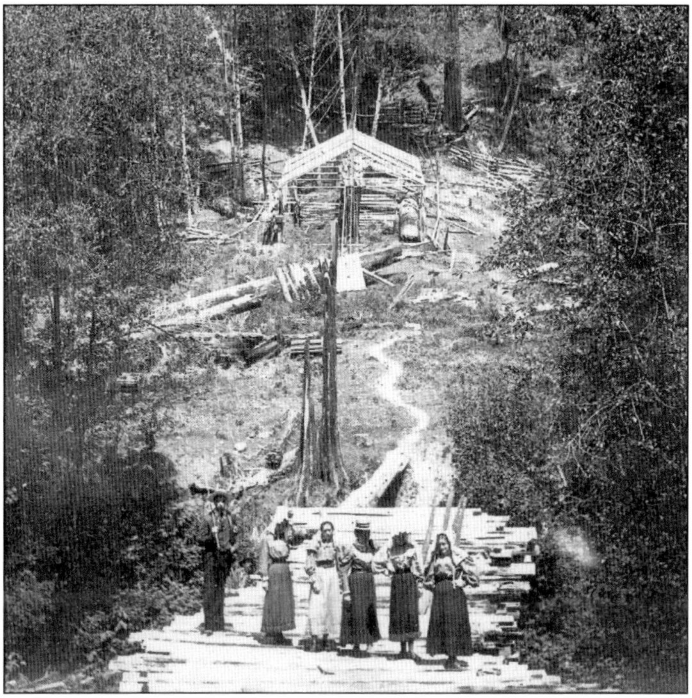

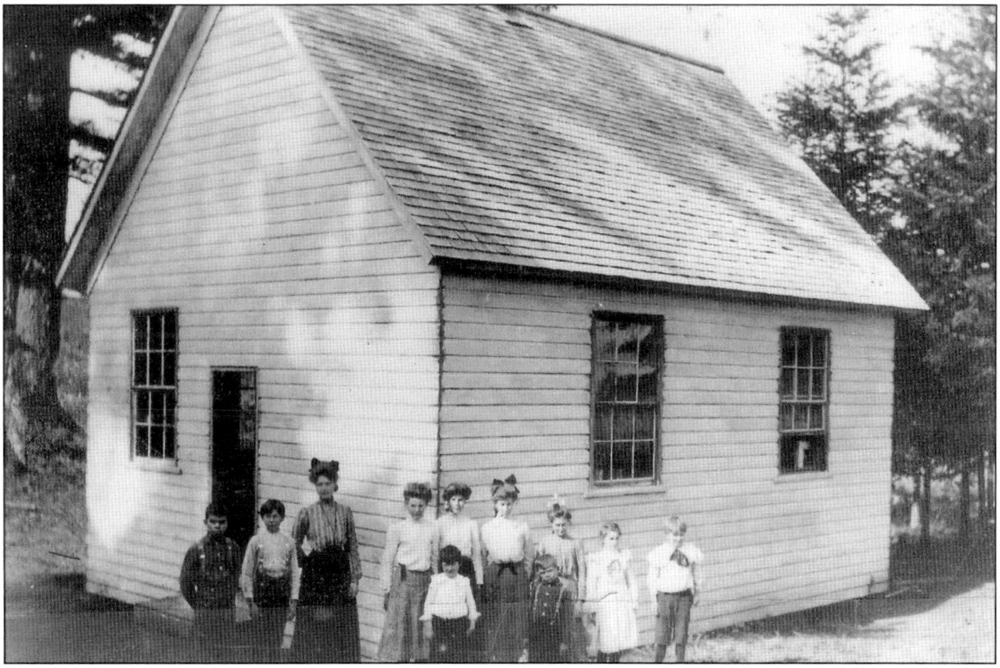

Built in 1884, Skye School was located on the Washougal River, just north of the Doherty homestead. Teacher Joanna "Jodie" Johnson probably stayed with a local family during the teaching term. These 1905 schoolchildren, pictured here from left to right, are (first row) George McDonald, and Otto Brauer; (second row) William Brauer, Joe Verbiski, Joanna "Jodie" Johnson, Josephine McDonald, Anna Verbiski, Margarite Doherty, Nellie McDonald, Agnes Verbiski, and Hubert McDonald.

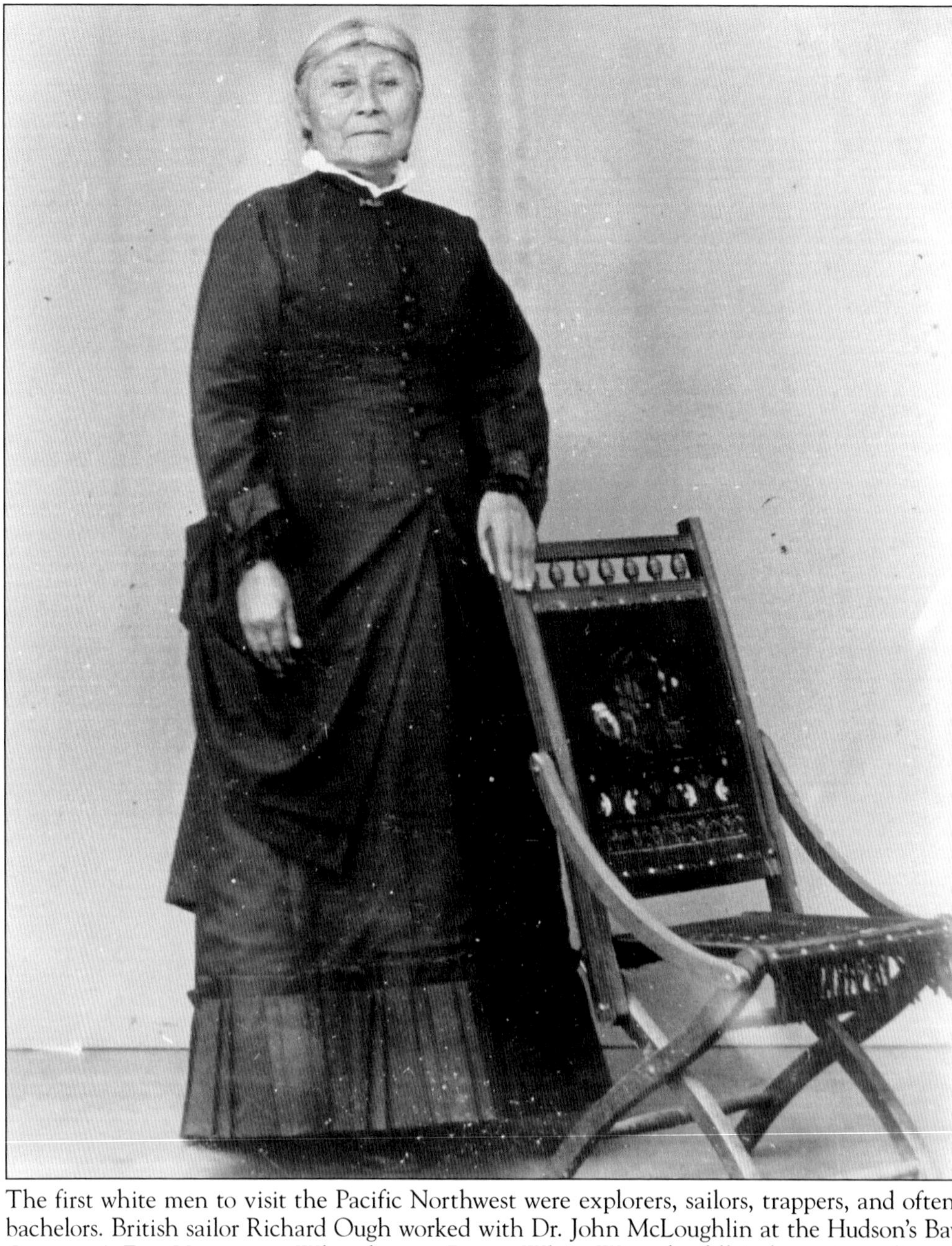

The first white men to visit the Pacific Northwest were explorers, sailors, trappers, and often, bachelors. British sailor Richard Ough worked with Dr. John McLoughlin at the Hudson's Bay Company's Fort Vancouver. When he met Betsey White Wing, he fell in love. According to the story, White Wing's father, Chief Slyhorse Schluyhus, agreed to the marriage as a political alliance, but he stipulated as a condition that Richard settle down. Richard agreed, and he and Betsey were married in 1838. They stayed at first at Fort Vancouver. Then, in the 1840s, Richard bought a large swath of land from a fellow settler. The land cost him $45, a horse, a saddle, and a few loaves of fresh-baked bread. In the 1850s, Richard registered his property as part of a donation land claim. Like the many settlers of Washougal, Richard and Betsey settled down and had children. In all, they had 10: Sarah, Grace, Richard, Benjamin, Elizabeth, Mary, Fredrick, Cecelia, Emma, and John Thomas.

Two

A Town Springs Up

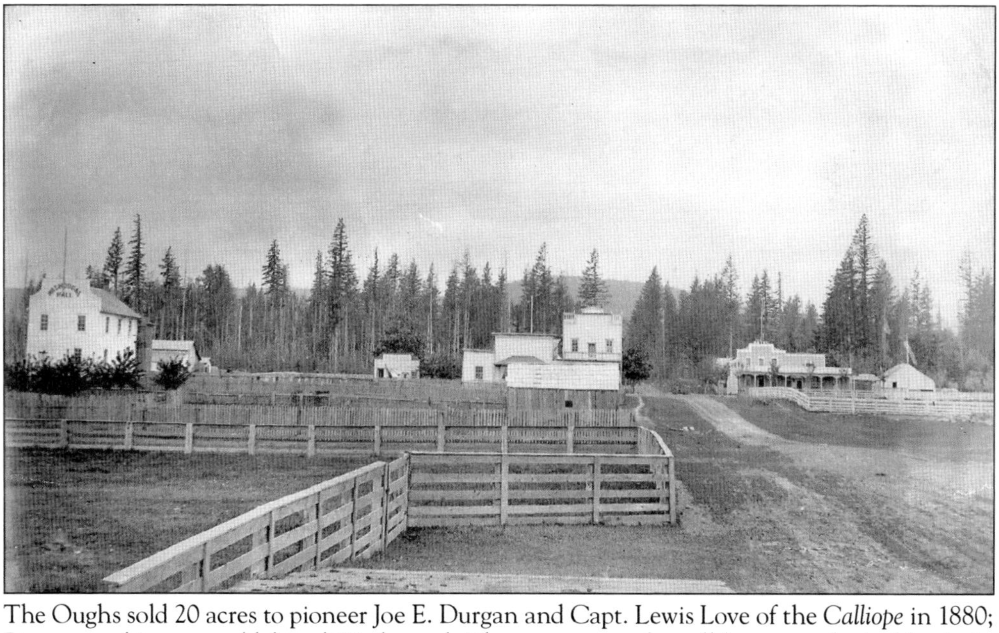

The Oughs sold 20 acres to pioneer Joe E. Durgan and Capt. Lewis Love of the *Calliope* in 1880; Durgan and Love would found Washougal. The town started small but never looked back. In 1887, B Street amounted to (left to right) Washougal Town Hall, Kersey's carpenter shop, Durgan's Store, Gary's Store (center), Fritz Braun's Park Hotel, Maple Grove and Barn (right), and a mud track to Steamboat Landing (center).

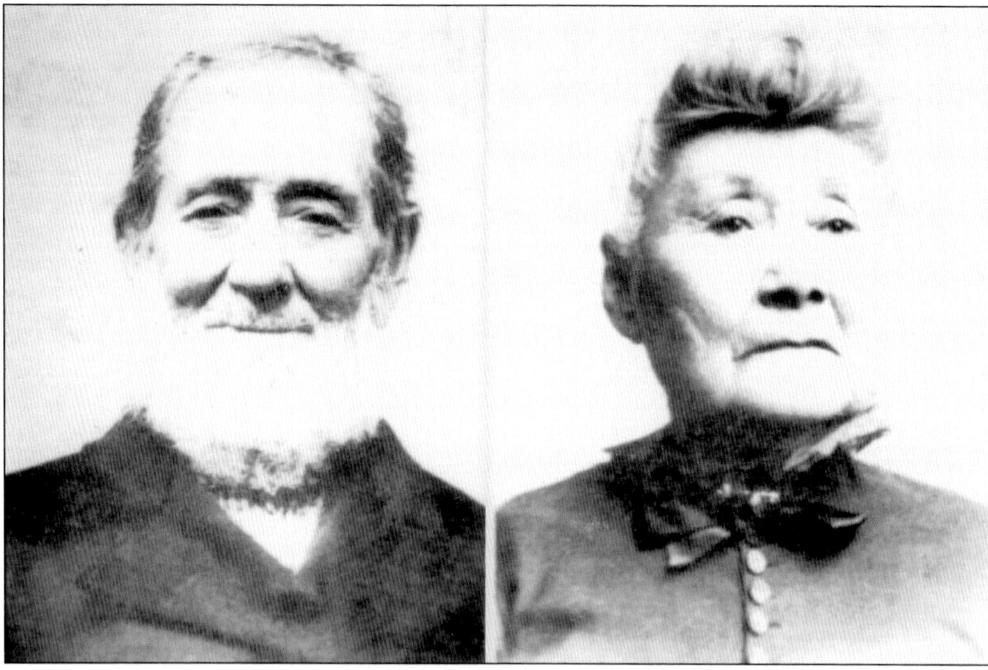

Washougal was founded on part of the original Ough land claim, and Richard (left) and Betsey (right) Ough were among Washougal's first and foremost citizens—upright and good-hearted. The Oughs were generous with food, money, and supplies for the many in need moving through the territory. Betsey, like other native women who became Western wives, managed to negotiate both worlds. Those who knew her affectionately called her "Aunt Betsey."

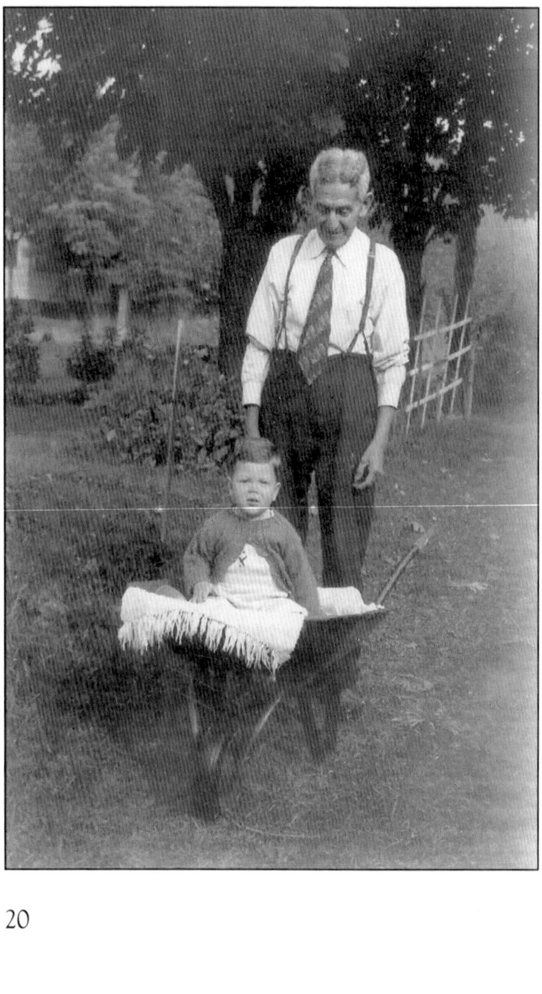

John Thomas Ough (standing), born in 1863, was Richard and Betsey's youngest child. Once grown, he captained the riverboat *Hattie Belle*, which he named for his wife. Later he worked on the family farm and at the paper mill in Camas. Thomas's son Thomas E. Ough also became a ship's captain. The baby in the wheelbarrow is yet another John Thomas Ough, named in honor of his grandfather.

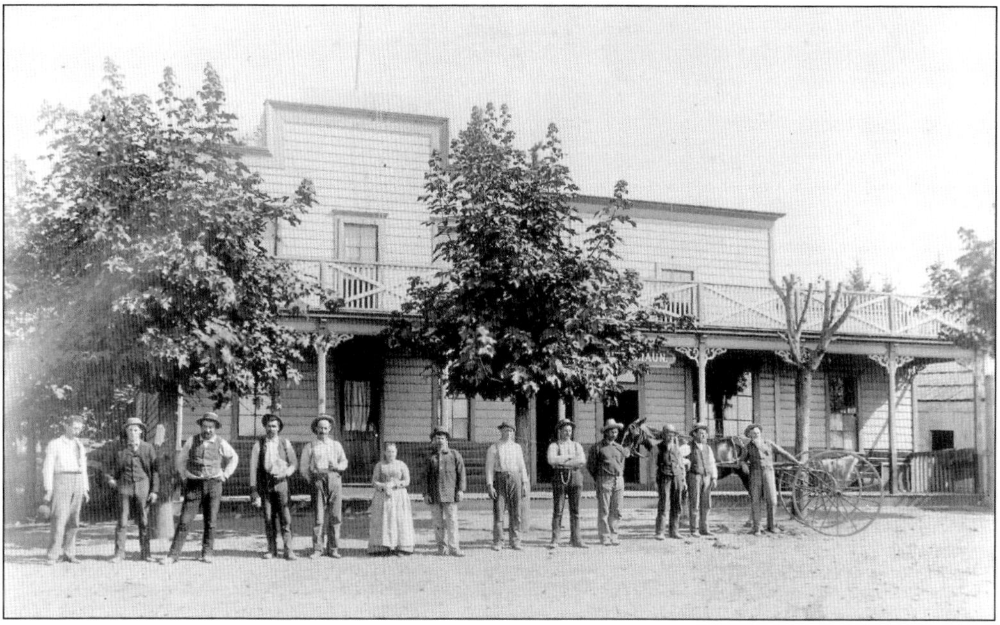

If there were ever a Wild West in Washougal, this was it. Those posing in front of the Park Hotel and Surber's Saloon in February 1888 represented many of the first families of Washougal. Pictured, from left to right, are David Gary, William Steenson, Richard Ough, William Dunn, Andrew Fletcher, Emilee Amelia Wachter Braun, William Strong, John Strong, unidentified, Bleutch Grinder, unidentified, Rudolph Surber, and Fritz Braun Sr.

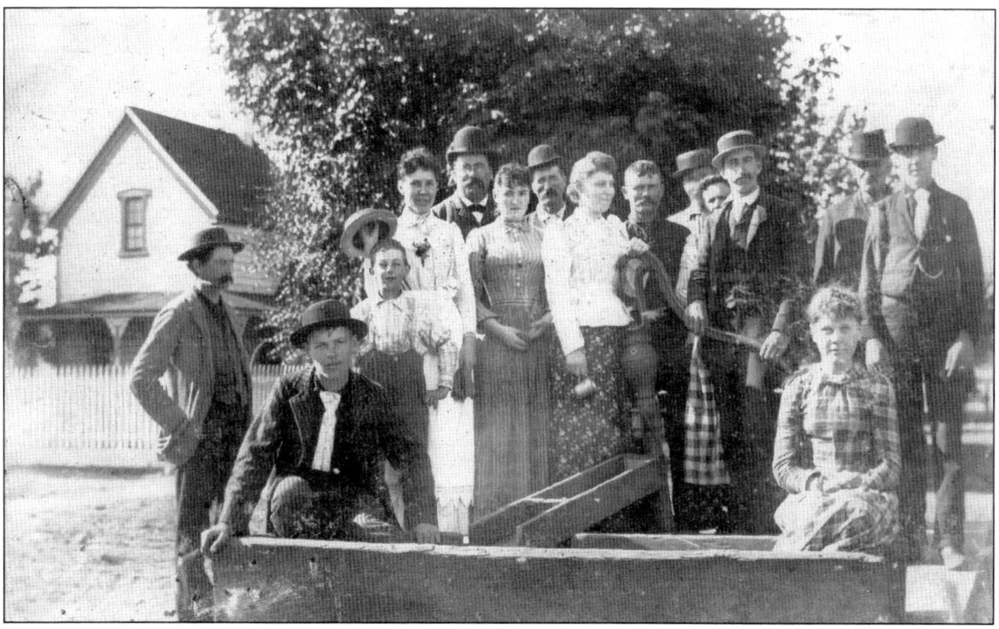

Washougal's town pump, dug in 1882, was located at the intersection of today's B and Seventeenth Streets. Town dwellers rejoiced at the time and energy it saved. The daily chore of hauling water became a pleasurable few moments with jostling, gossiping neighbors at the pump. So important was the pump as a symbol of progress and community that the town's founding family, the Durgans, posed for posterity around it once it was completed.

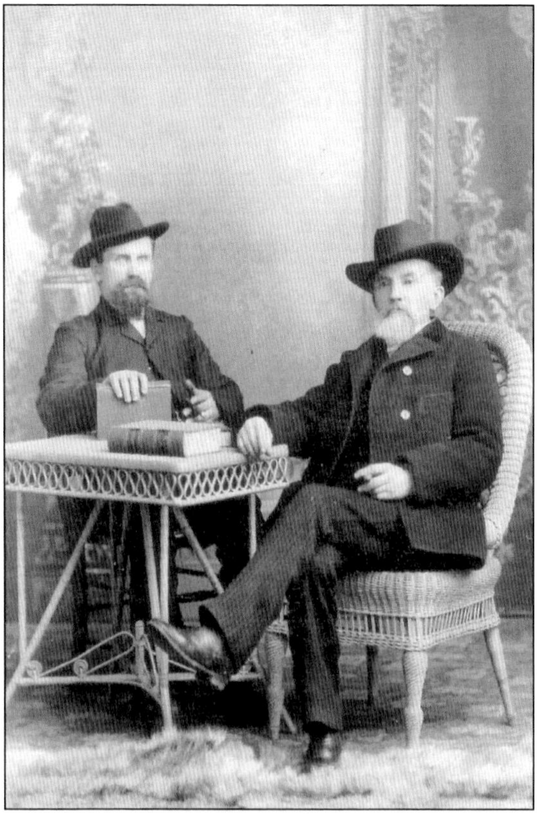

Franz Braun Sr. (left) and William Surber were Washougal founders and early businessmen. Braun owned the Park Hotel, built on the corner of today's B and Seventeenth Streets. Braun and his wife, Emilee, were German immigrants. They came first to Portland and then built a hotel in Parkersville. By 1880, they had moved the hotel from Parkersville to Washougal. Emilee worked at the hotel and also as a bartender.

The Braun's Park Hotel, pictured here around 1895, had a saloon, a barn, and a maple-grove park in back. William Surber was proprietor of the saloon, and a poster advertises "Star Hop-Cold Beer." The Park Hotel catered to townsfolk, loggers, miners, and merchants and was probably a good place for a game of cards. The maple grove was intended to attract tourists who came by steamboat along the Columbia River.

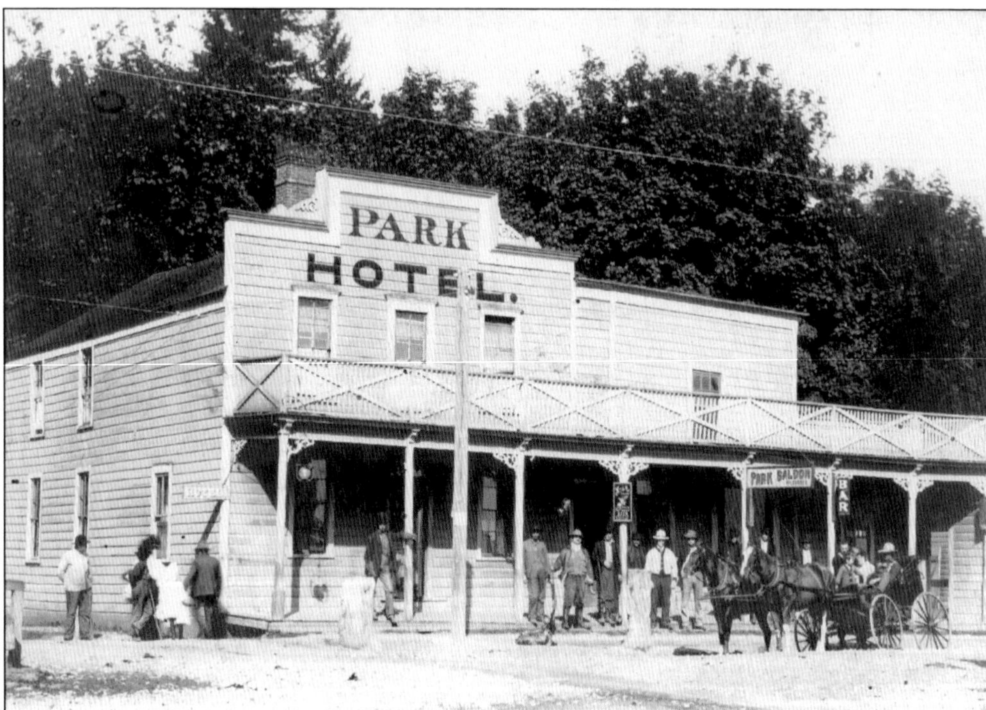

Frances "Frankie" Braun (right), born in 1881 and pictured here with her brother Fritz Braun Jr., was the first white child born in the city limits of Washougal. At the time, there were also many Native American children in Washougal. Frankie found among them fast friends and playmates. She married Sam Cheatham in 1899 and worked 30 years at the Pendleton Woolen Mill where she sewed army blankets during World War I.

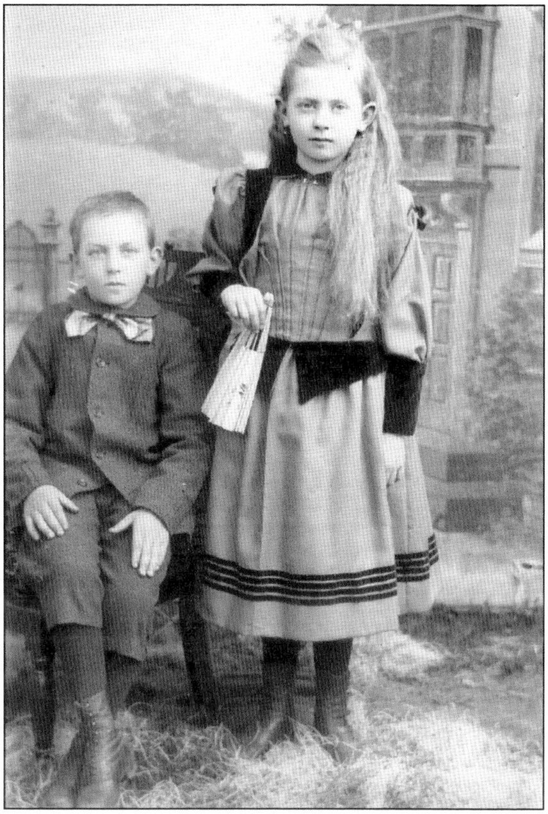

The Park Hotel dining hall was decorated with garlands and clusters of photographs on the walls. Condiments on the table include catsup and jam, with cake and beverages on the sideboard. Possibly a Victrola sits in the back corner. The man seated at center has a dog to his right. Restaurant fare around 1900 might include ham and eggs for 60¢, a sardine sandwich for 20¢, or, for 90¢, a New York steak.

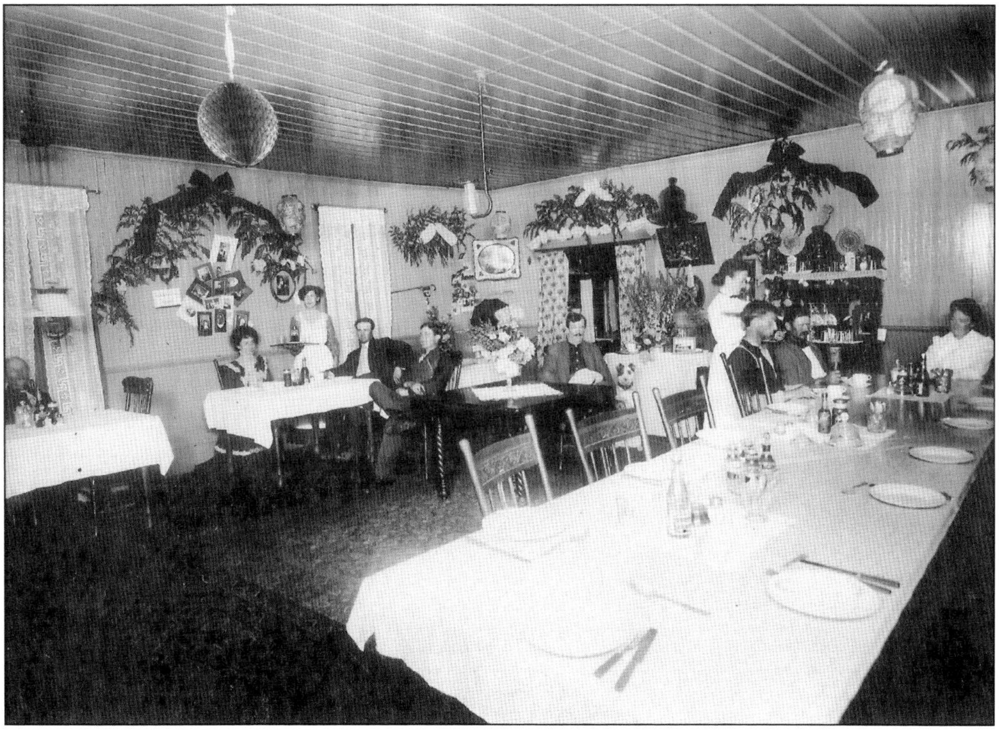

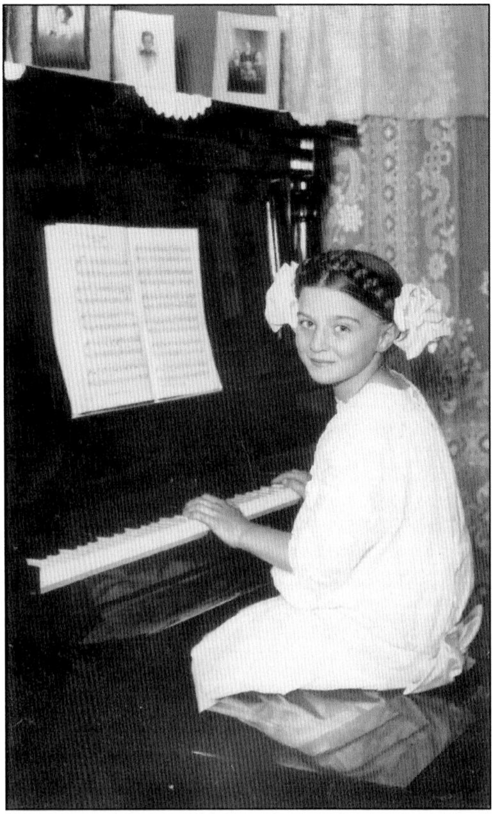

Frankie Braun married road-construction worker Sam Cheatham in 1899. Their daughter Thelma Amelia Cheatham, pictured here in 1914, took lessons at the piano like many other girls. Thelma had real aptitude. She played locally for the silent movies and then entered the music world. Her friends included many of the famous singers of her day—Jim Nabors, the Leland Brothers, and Liberace. Thelma would marry seven times.

Fritz Braun Jr., pictured here, owned a smoke shop in 1939 that included a liquor bar, dining area, and cards salon. Patrons could also buy ice-cream sodas or play pool. Items for sale at the cigar and candy bar included NoDoz, "To keep awake while driving," Probak Blades, Sen Sen, F&F cough lozenges, Lifesavers candy, Hershey bars, Walnettos, and fishing line and tackle.

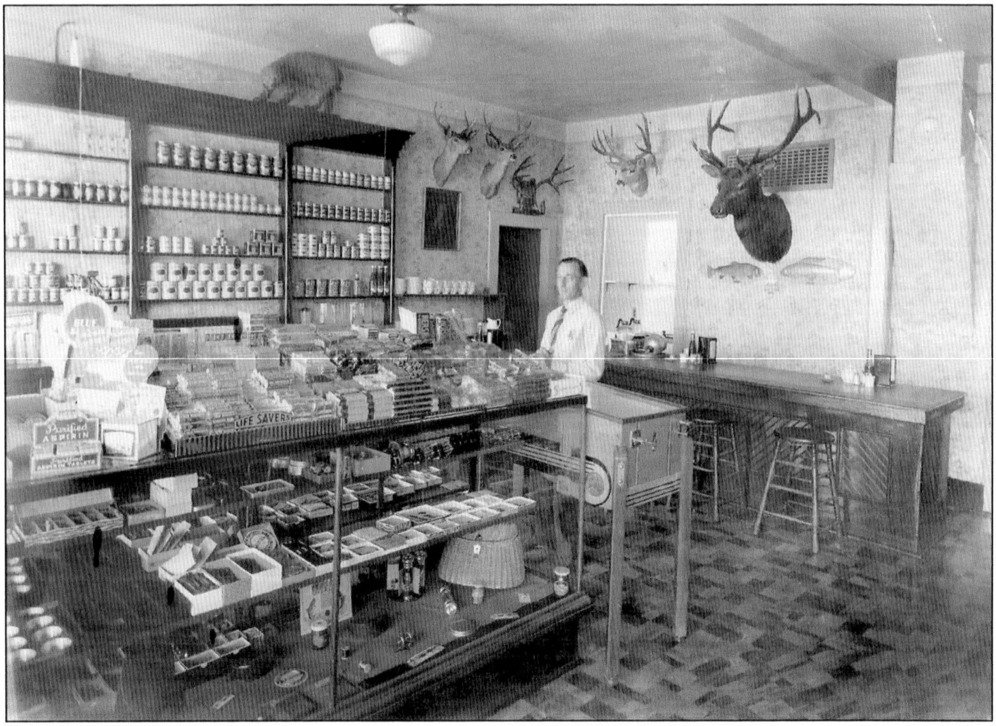

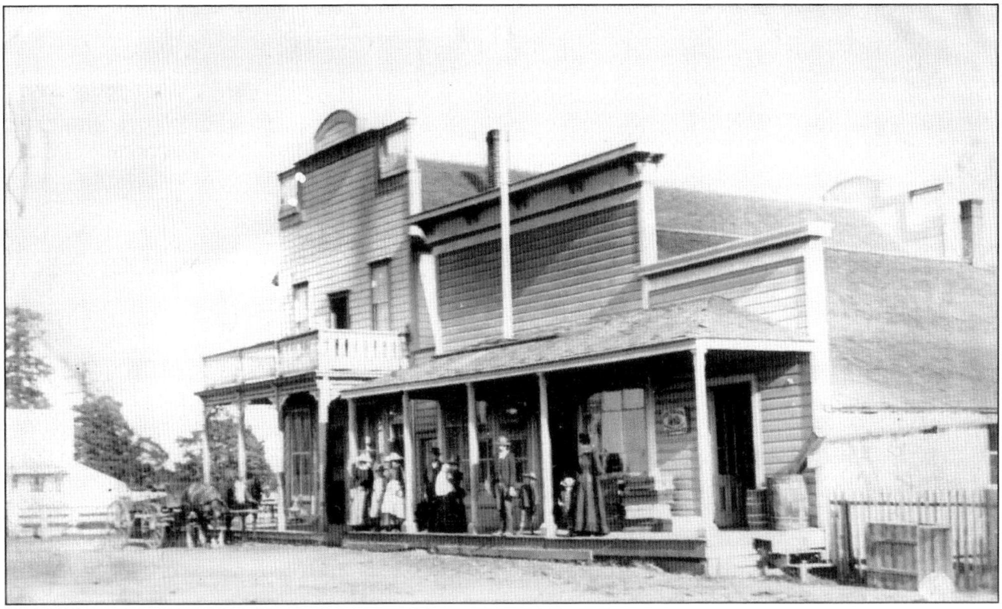

David H. Gary bought the J. C. Durgan store in Washougal in 1883. It was located on the northwest corner of today's B and Seventeenth Streets, with the Gary family home just behind it. Gary's Store, like Durgan's before it, sold just about anything anyone could ever want. Gary was also a dock agent and county commissioner in 1899.

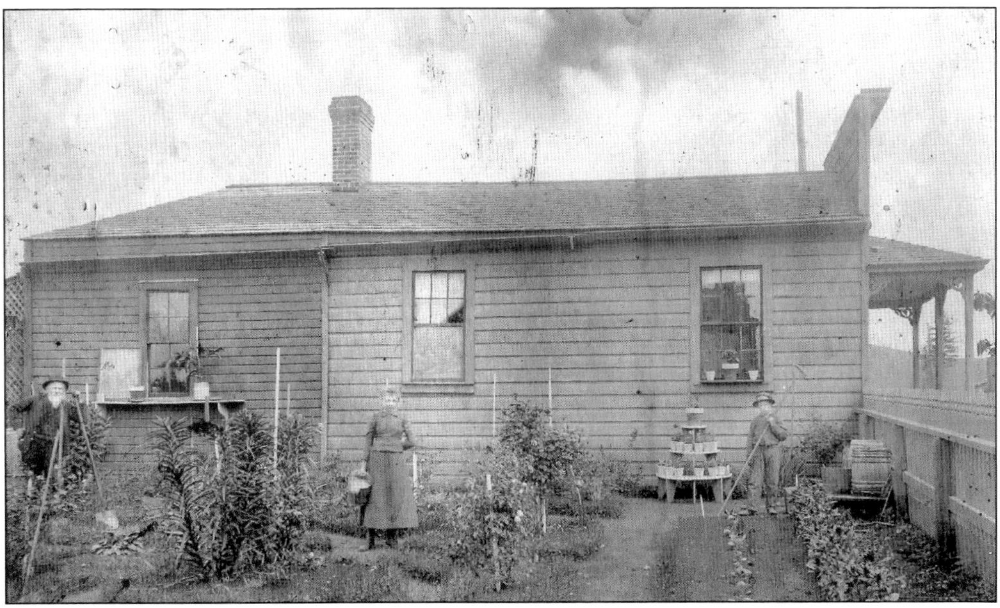

The old Gary family home is pictured on what used to be Second and Durgan Streets. Tending the home garden in 1893 are, from left to right, David Hampton Gary, Cynthia Julettia Gary, and one of their sons (unidentified). The Garys had three sons: Theodore Luther "Lou" ran the dock at Washougal, David Nelson "Nels" became a barber, and Harold Albert sold goat meat.

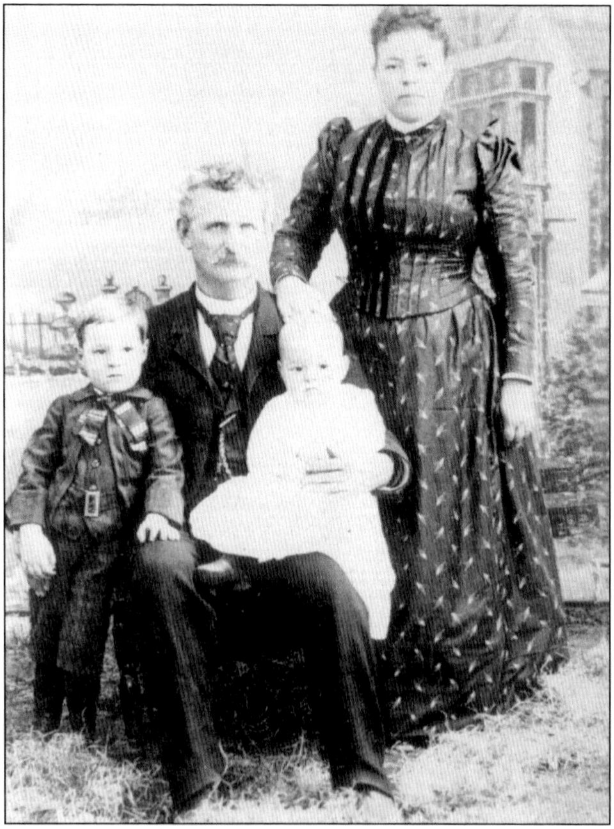

Shop owner Henry H. Carpenter (seated, center) was known to drive a surrey, wear a black silk top hat, and carry a small brown satchel. He earned a reputation for dependability and went regularly to Portland by steamboat, transacting business for himself and on behalf of others. In 1886, Henry married Phoebe Carleton (standing). Their two oldest sons were Henry Carleton (left) and Benjamin Franklin (right).

Henry H. Carpenter built this store in Parkersville in 1877, later moving it to B Street in Washougal. On the pole in front, a poster advertises Star Beer in bold letters. This popular beer came in barrels, and perhaps the gentleman at far left is sitting on a delivery. Another poster announces a "Grand Ball" to be held at a new hall in Washougal on June 4, 1904.

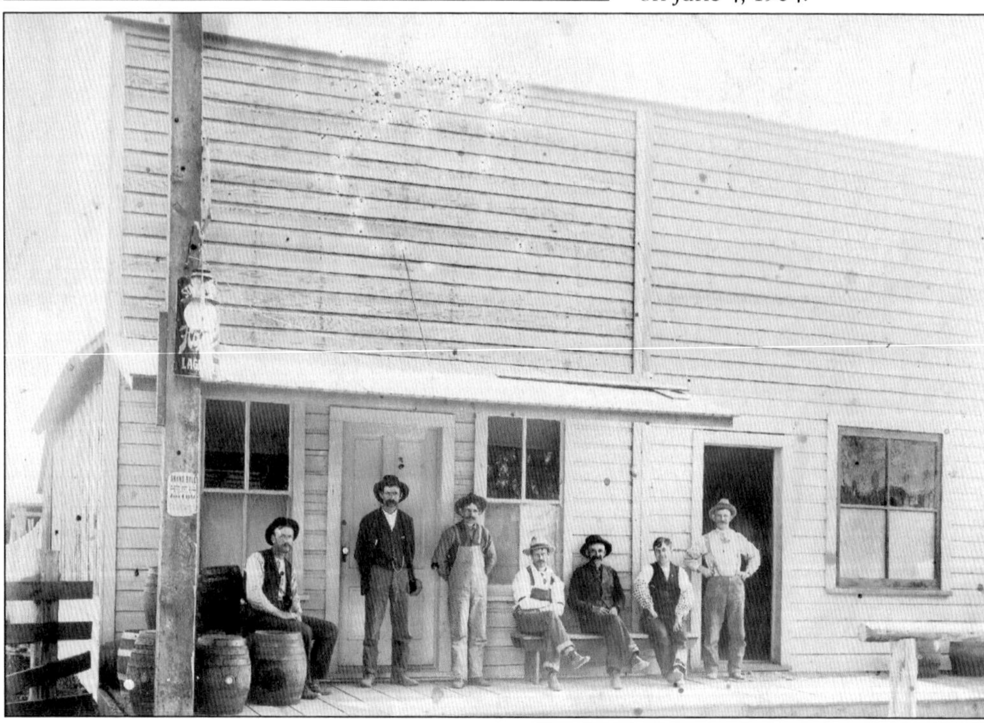

Henry and Phoebe had three children, Henry Carleton "Carl," Benjamin Franklin, and George Cook. The family lived adjacent to their store in a home that smelled tauntingly of Phoebe's homemade doughnuts. As a boy, Ben would sometimes accompany his father to Portland, literally holding onto his father's coattails as Henry hurried with his business in town.

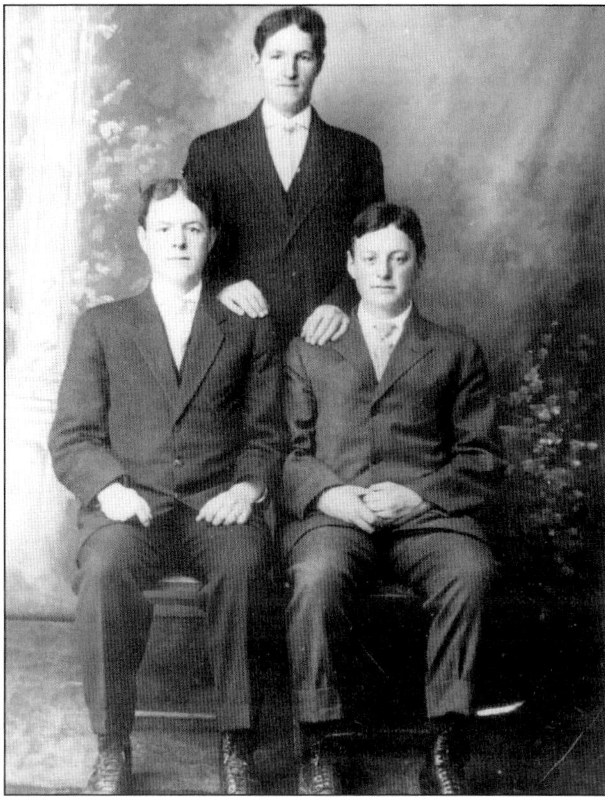

Henry and Ben Carpenter ran the Carpenter Brothers General Merchandise and Twentieth Century Grocery until 1926. They sold all manner of groceries and dry goods, shoes, furniture, fabrics, notions, and McCall patterns. After 1926, the building was leased to other grocers and then became a variety store. It was used as a post office through some portion of the 1930s and 1940s and eventually became part of Bolger's Pharmacy.

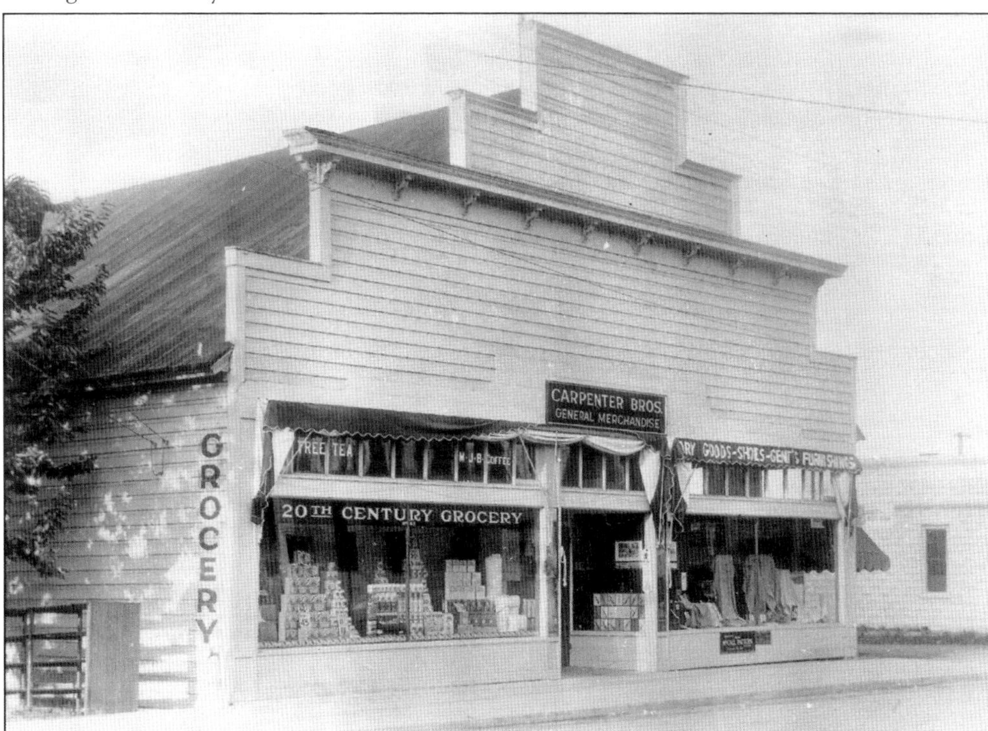

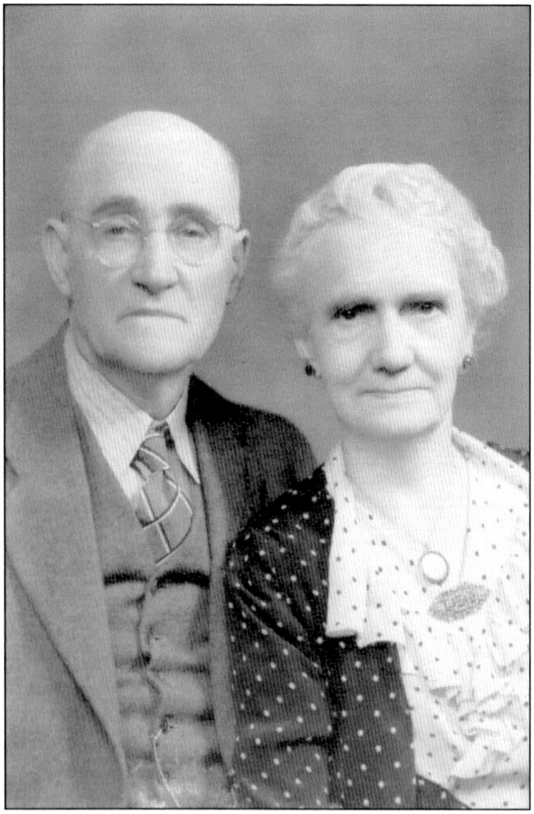

Can-do citizens Charles Warner and Elizabeth Freseden Cottrell, pictured here in 1930, came to Washougal in 1888 with four young children. They spent two years in Mount Pleasant, where Charles opened a post office, blacksmith shop, and sawmill, and edited the *Mount Pleasant Breeze*. The Cottrells then moved to Washougal where Charles ran the Grange store and Washougal Post Office until 1897. In 1910, Charles would bring electricity to Washougal.

Charles Cottrell built this three-story, 25-barrel-rolling gristmill and sawmill on the Washougal River in 1897. A dam provided the necessary power, and farmers brought sacks of grain from as far away as Amboy and Eureka for grinding. The sacks were emptied, carefully refilled with flour, weighed, labeled, and sewn closed. In 1915, both mills closed, and the building became a machine and repair shop.

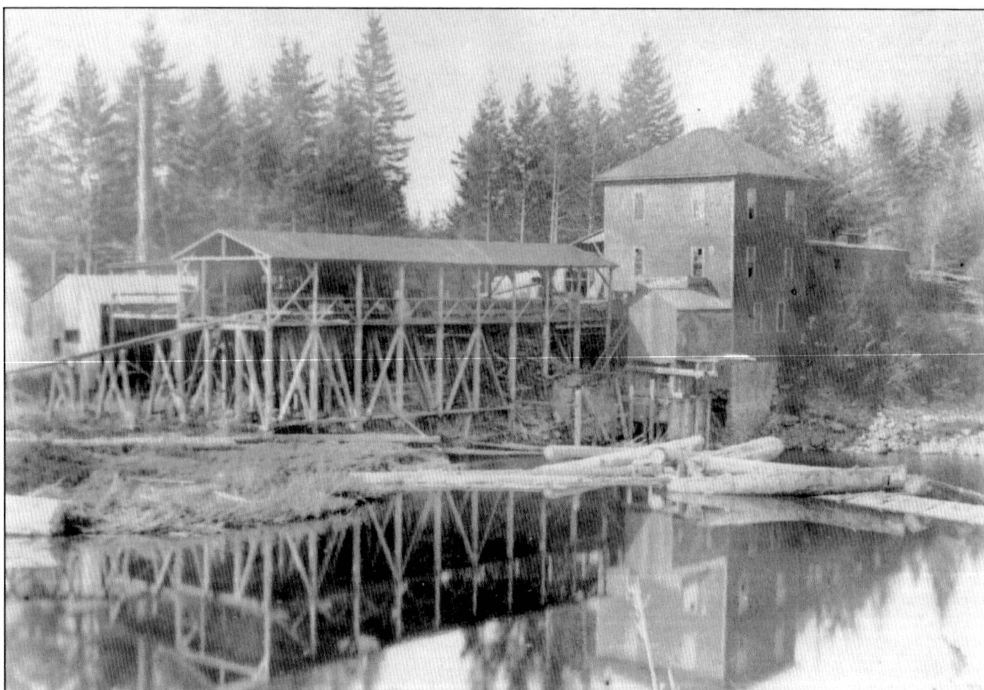

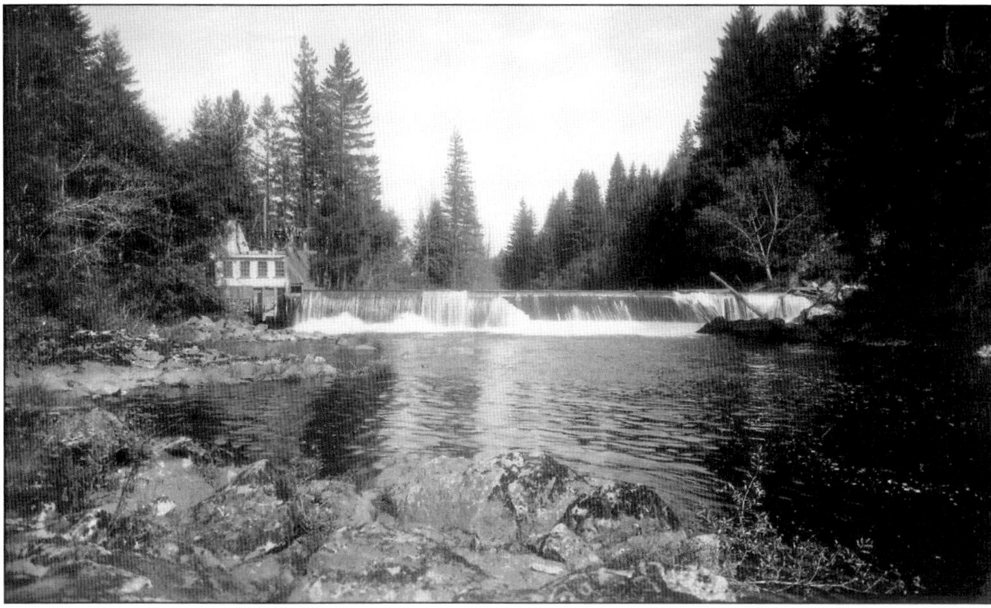

In 1910, Charles began his biggest venture. With his son Glenn, now an electrical engineer, Charles built dams on the Washougal River and established the Western Light and Power Company. Waterwheels, and later four diesel engines running day and night, generated electricity and supplied power to Camas and Washougal. Parts of the lower dam, pictured here, can still be seen today.

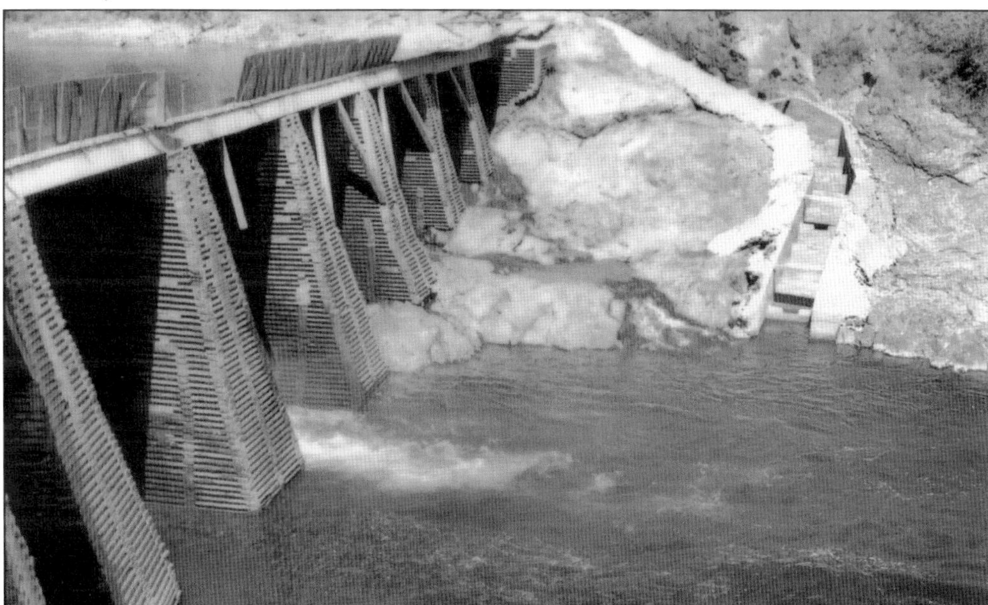

The Cottrells built three dams. The upper dam, pictured here, included a fish ladder. The lower dam, which had originally supplied power to the gristmill and sawmill in 1897, now generated power for rate-paying customers. The middle dam, near Cougar Creek, was destroyed by vandals before it could be put into use. Charles worked well past retirement with a goal of uninterrupted service and low rates.

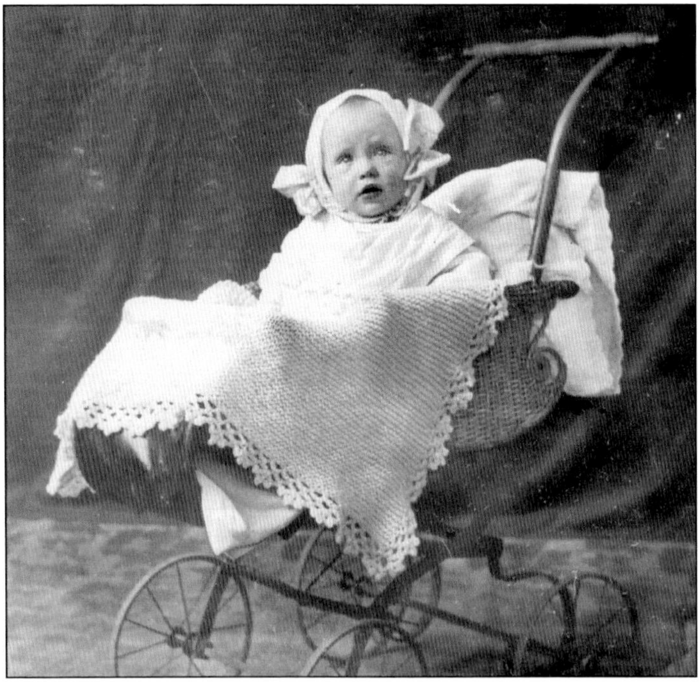

Born in 1910, Dolphe Seba Perry (pictured) was Charles and Elizabeth Cottrell's granddaughter. She worked for her grandfather at the Western Light pay station in Camas typing out bills and repairing appliances. In 1933, Dolphe married Nick Mueller. Nick earned $1 a day at the Crown Zellerbach Paper Company, but it was enough then to build a house. In 1960, Nick died in a mill accident. Dolphe was remarried in 1968 to Millard Gilbreath.

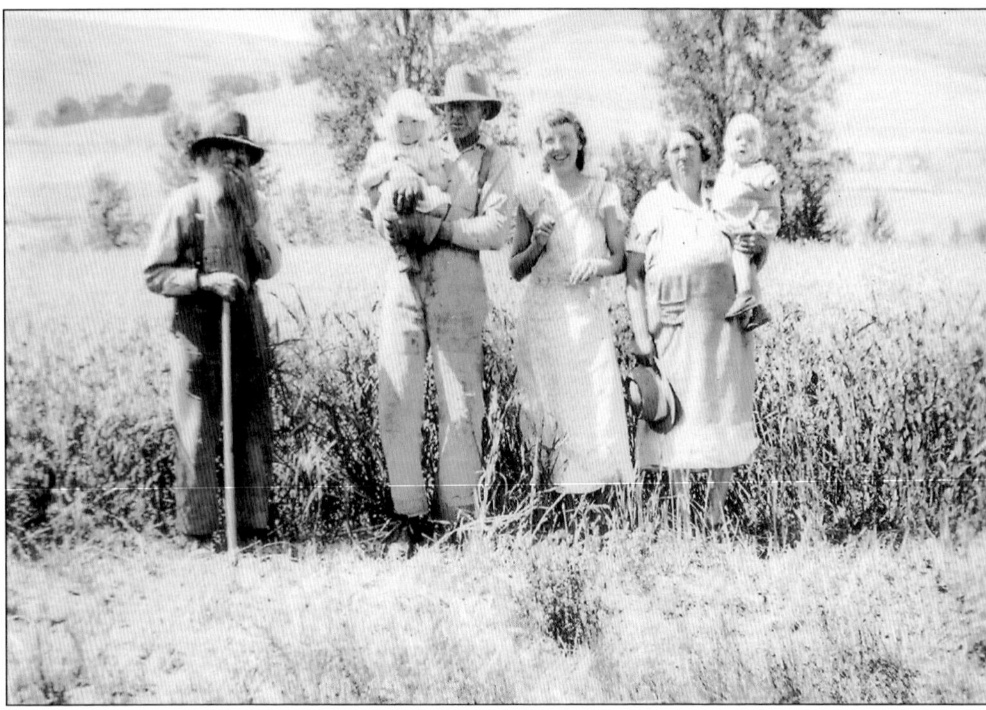

Charles and Elizabeth Cottrell's daughter Zella Blanche married Oliver Perry in 1909. The Perrys had a homestead east of Washougal. Zella's daughter Dolphe Seba became a gem cutter and lecturer and recorded much of her family's history for future generations. Pictured in 1936, from left to right, are Horace Dwight Perry, Edith Marie Mueller, Oliver Ensign Perry, Dolphe Seba Perry Mueller Gilbreath, Minnie Buttler, and Bernice Mueller Rosel.

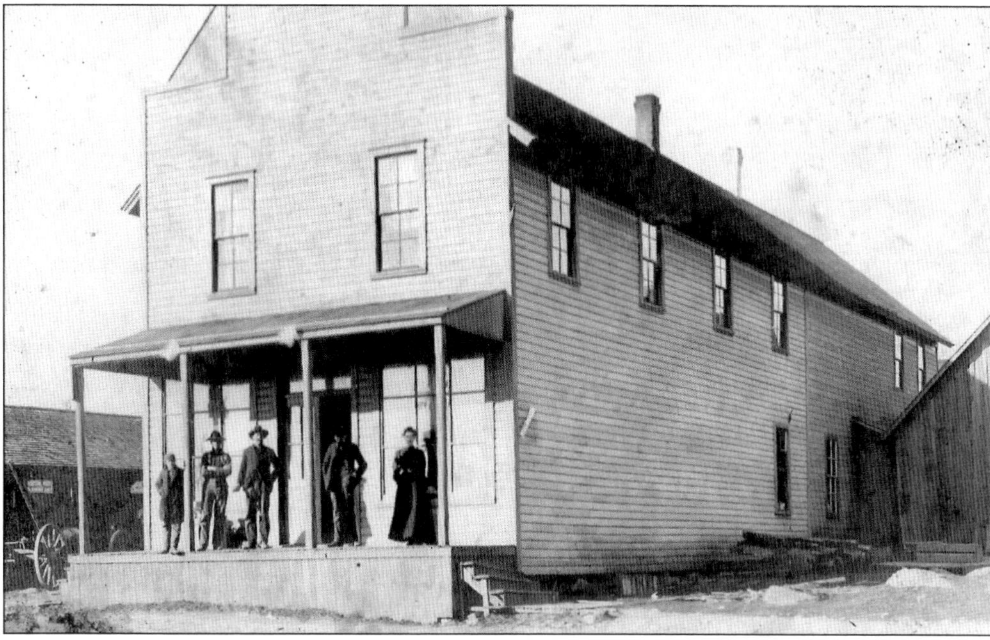

Jorgan and Henrik Henriksen's store and grange hall was smack dab in the middle of Washougal. Those living east of the store were in "east Washougal," and those to the west in "west Washougal," thus all the gossip, east and west, could be had at Henriksen's. The Henriksen's store also housed the first Camas-Washougal telephone company. In this 1907 photograph, Henrik "Henry" stands fourth from the left.

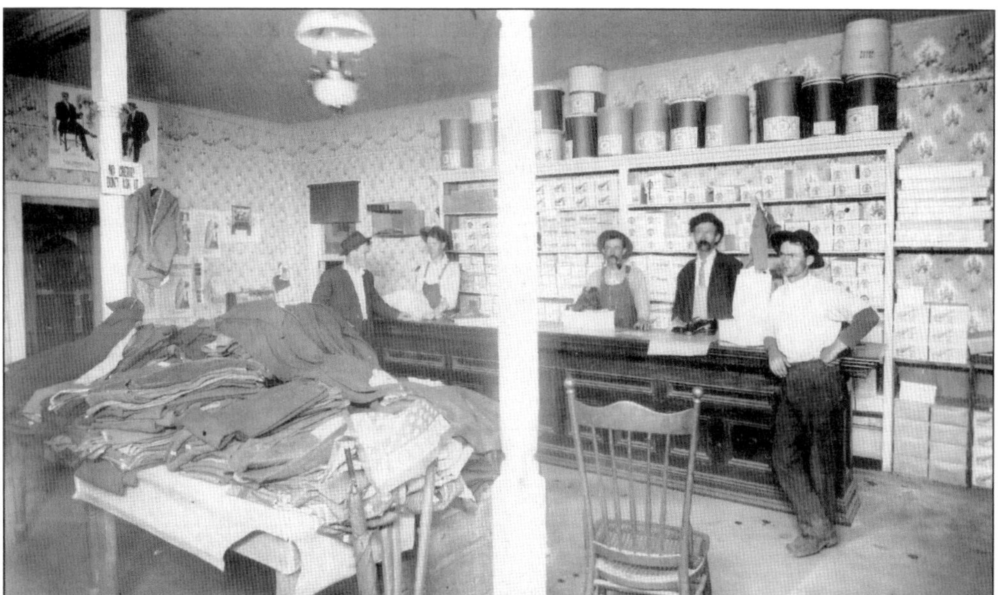

The proprietor of this men's clothing shop in 1912 is unidentified. Flyers on the wall advertise "clothes that satisfy" from Carl Joseph and Company. Shoe boxes behind the counter are labeled "red star," "hickory," and "$3.00 a pair." Items for sale include suits, handkerchiefs, and umbrellas, and the boxes lining the top cabinet probably contain men's hats. Jess Mathew had a men's store on B Street in the 1920s.

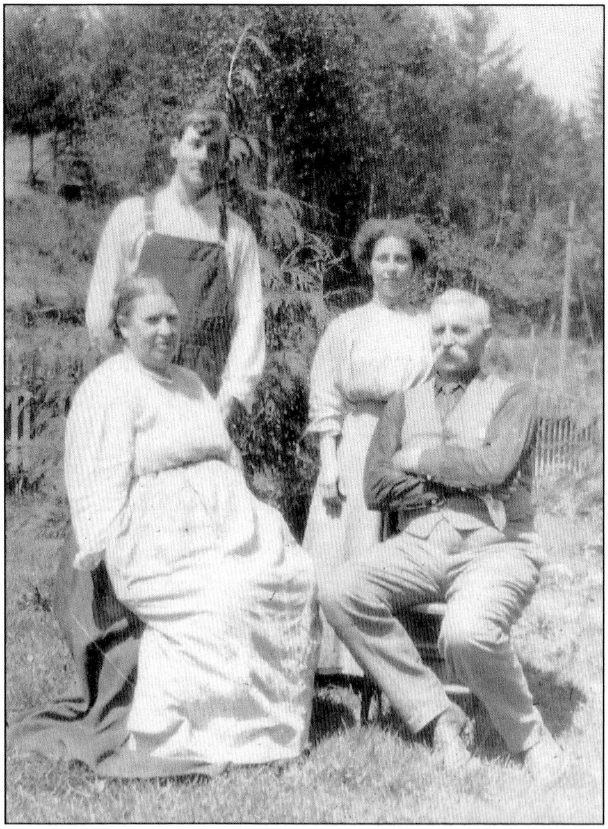

Peter Olson and Mary Erickson Aune emigrated from Norway, settling in the Mount Norway District of Washougal in 1887. Mary was a midwife, and Peter farmed but was primarily a carpenter. He was active in the Independent Organization of Odd Fellows and with the Washougal Grange. The Aune family, pictured here from left to right, include Mary Erickson, Albert Victor, Amy Obida, and Peter Olson.

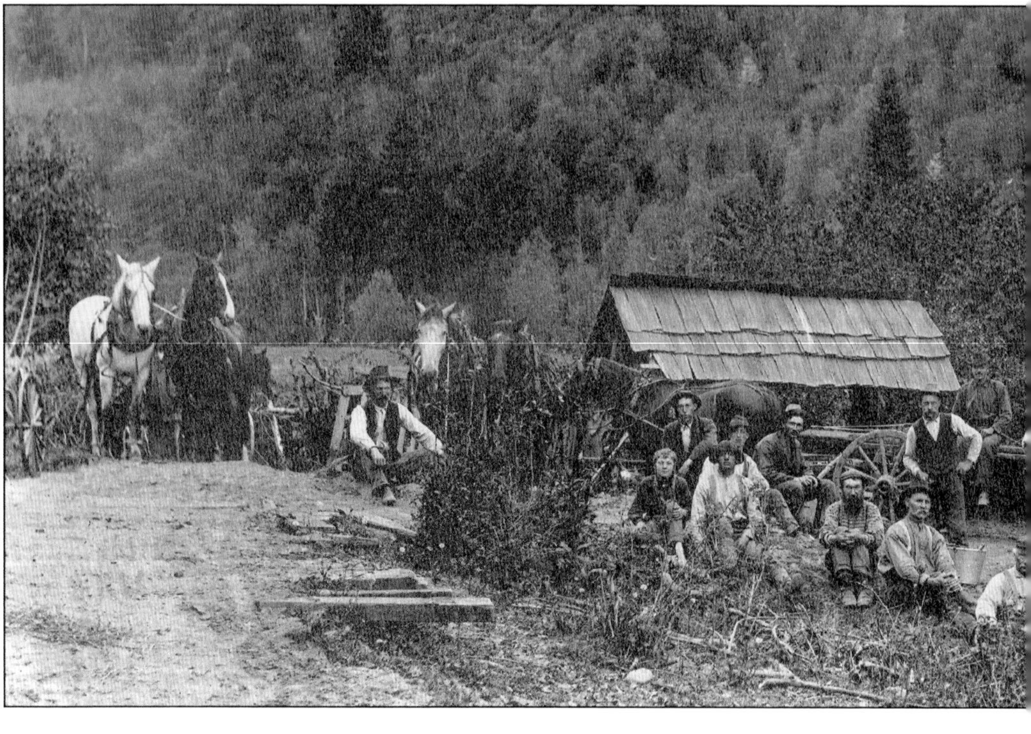

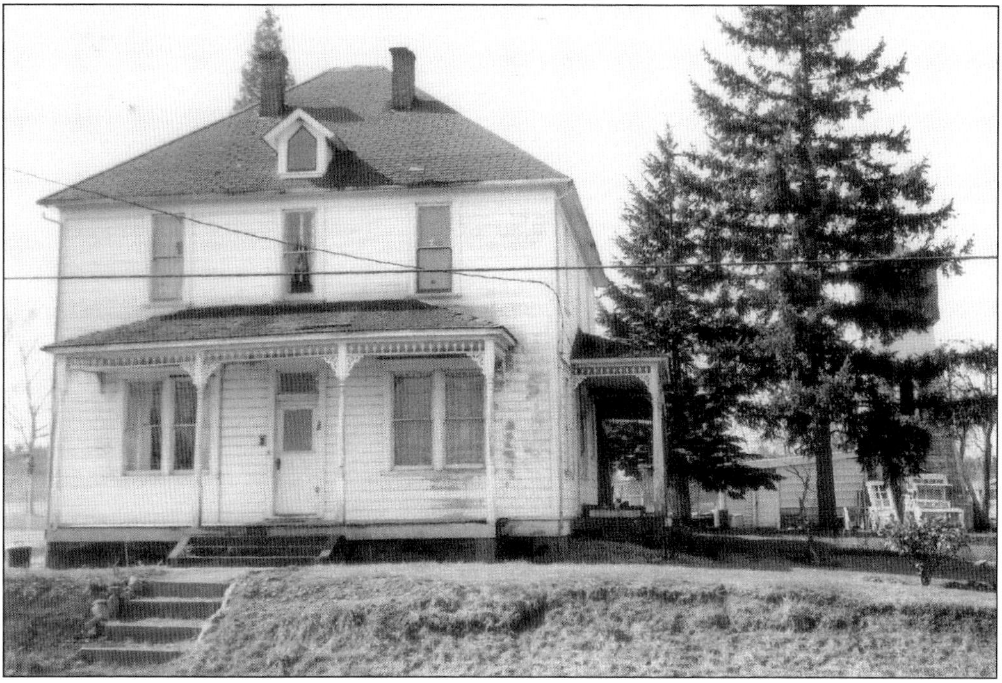

Early travel was by wagon or on foot, and men were known to walk from Vancouver to Cape Horn carrying 100-pound sacks. The stagecoach was another option. This house, located near the Washougal Golf Course, was a stage stop where travelers could receive food and lodging. The stage itself was a three-passenger buggy drawn by a two-horse team. A round-trip from Washougal to Vancouver took 14 hours.

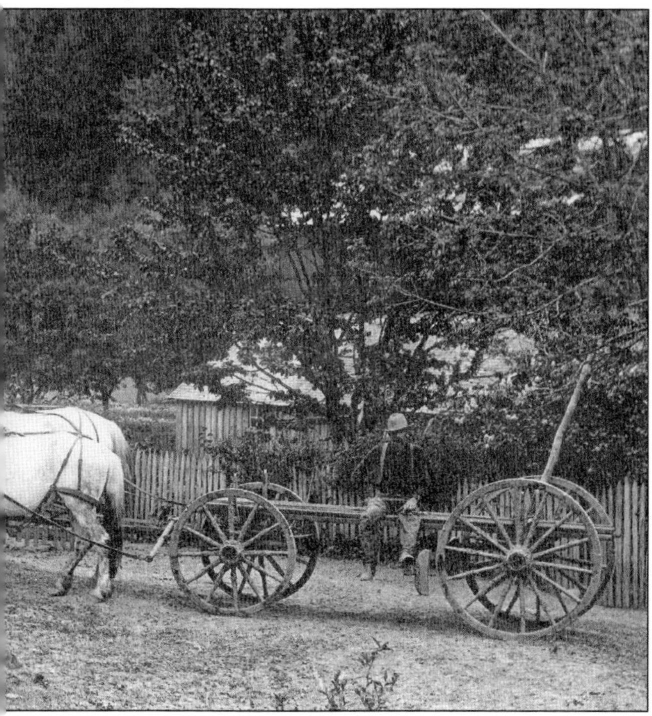

In 1889, road building required specialized, horse-drawn grading tools that had to be dragged across the ground over and over again. Weary horses or teams of oxen carted heavy loads of gravel in 50- or 100-pound sacks. Everything was done by hand. Rocks had to be dug out and trees felled to be split and hauled away. Tree stumps and roots had to be pulled and the soil tamped hard. Even so, the roads turned to slick, impassible mud after a good rain. Only the strongest horse teams were able to get through. This road crew worked near the Aune place on Mount Norway and included Emil Krohn, Gustav Kloninger, Peter Aune, Fred Ammeter, Roy Carleton, C. C. Anderson (far left), Albert Aune (small boy), and Sam Berger (on wagon).

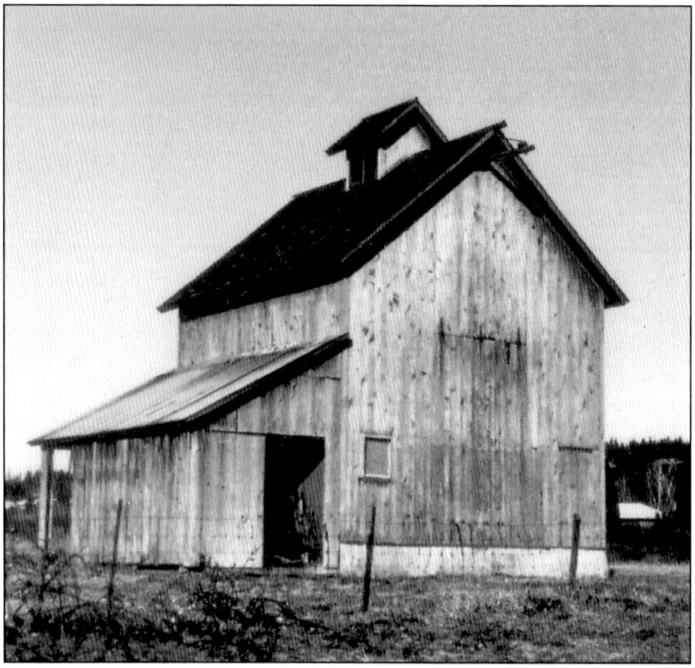

The Goot-Husby Barn is for many an iconic image of Washougal. Goot's Barn, almost all that is left of the old dairy farm located at Third and C Streets, finally collapsed in 2006. The Goots were well known and respected and were sought out for help and advice by neighbors and newcomers alike. Morris Webber, Washougal's first mayor in 1908, first rented land from Albert Goot.

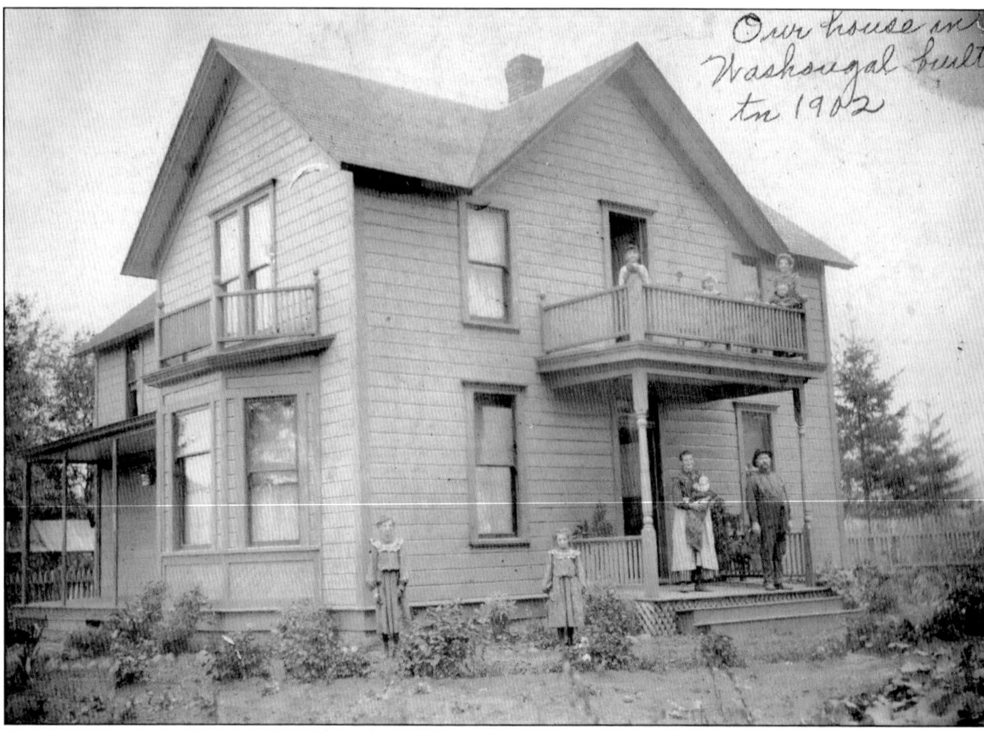

Swiss immigrants Morris Webber (at right on porch) and Bertha Burkhart (at left on porch) married in Portland before moving to Washougal. In 1902, Webber built this eight-bedroom house for their growing family. The Webbers would have 10 children: Bertha, Albert, Flora, Frances, Lizetta, Theodore, Emily, Nelle, Morris Jr., and Anne. By 1910, Webber was a successful businessman and owned a 600-acre dairy farm on Lady's Island.

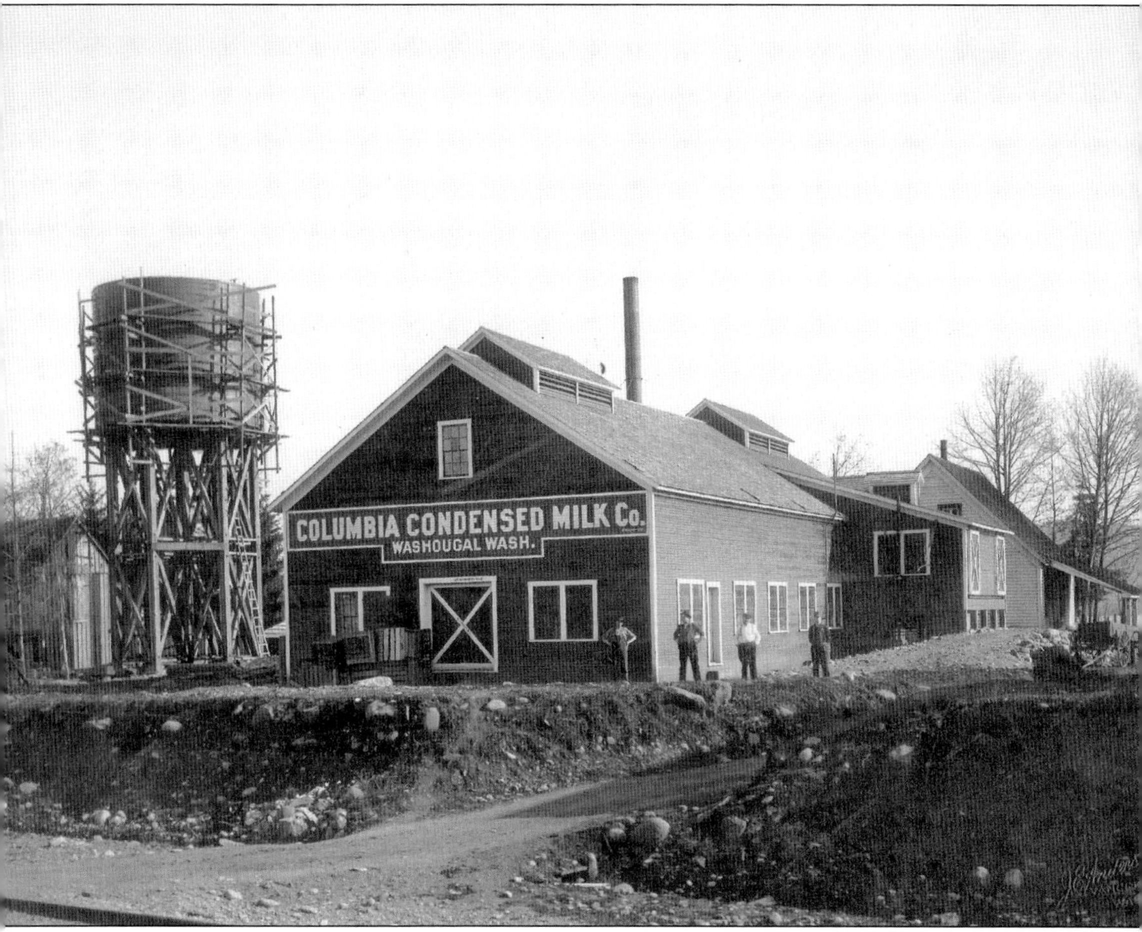

Morris Webber and Albert Goot opened the Columbia Condensed Milk Company sometime after 1902. There were likely other investors as well, and shareholders probably included the Hendriksens, Ackers, Campens, Pierces, and others. The milk company bought cream from local farmers in five-gallon quantities, taking note of the butterfat content. Morris dug a well deep enough to use as a water-storage tank. The vats of milk were set into the water to keep cool. Churning was done by steam-powered engines, and steam was also used for sterilization. The churned butter was pressed into pans and placed in the creamery basement to cool overnight. Very early in the morning, the butter had to be cut and wrapped by hand and placed in boxes that held 50 butter rolls each. The boxes were packed and ready every morning in time for transportation by steamship to the Portland market. The steamship departed at 7:00 a.m. In addition to butter, the creamery also made sweetened condensed milk. Buttermilk was a by-product, and farmers could take it home and feed it to their hogs free of charge.

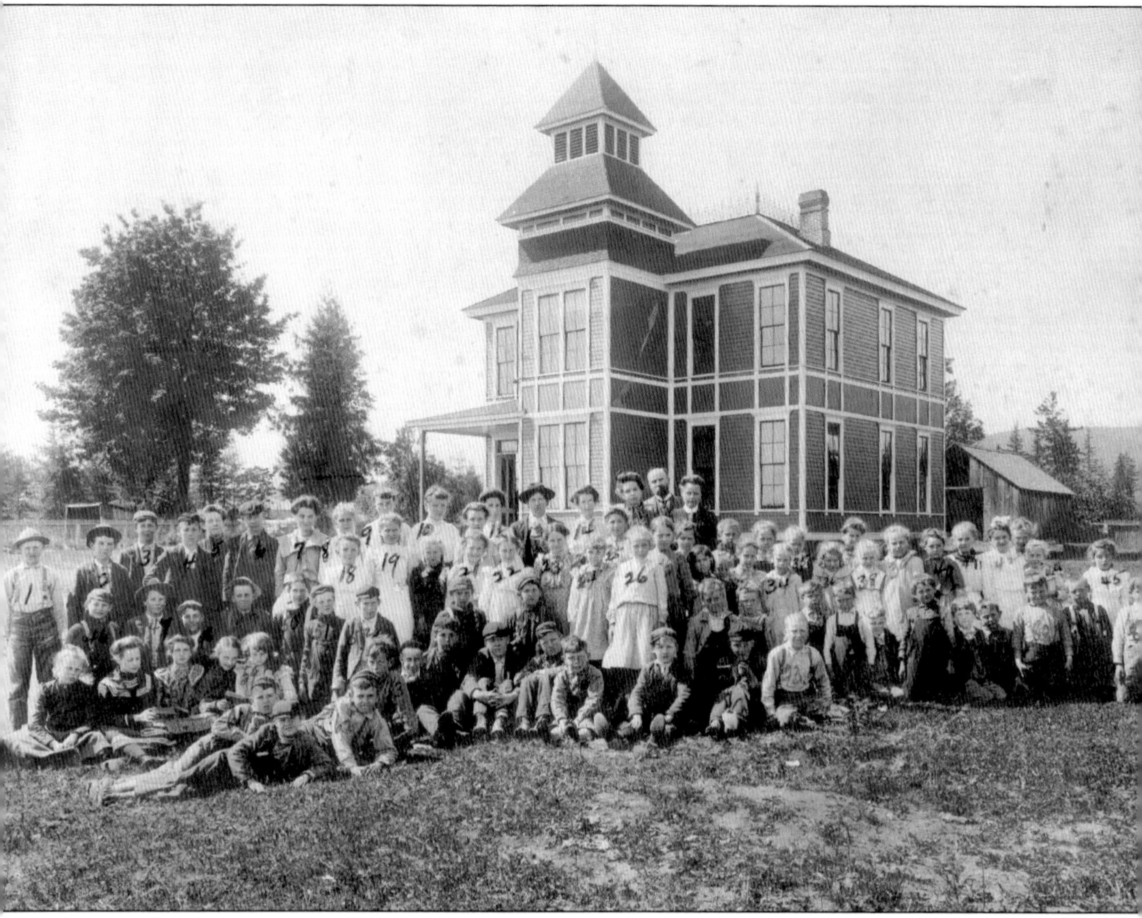

Washougal was a town of big families and many children. In 1904, Washougal's old four-room school boasted at least 82 students and many sets of siblings. Pictured, from left to right, are (first row, seated) Josie Kramer, Tillie Chilberg, Emily Webber (Bright), Katie Klein, Mamie Schlotterback, George Bailey, Stevie Wright, Frank Knowles, Chester Powell, Carl Herzig, Oscar Kern, Ben Carpenter, Ernie Wright, George Powell, Otto Acker, Roy Knowles, Arthur Buslach, Vance Roley, Morris Webber, Carl Goot, George Carpenter, and Ed Reinseith; (second row) Emily Goot (McLeod), Mary Pieritz, Ida Herzig, Nellie Webber (Schwartz), Dottie Slaughterback, Pauline Gresy Johnson, Josie Kramet, Frances Long (Roth), Freda Acker, Barbara Gregg, Flora Camper, Ella Peterson, Lois Hathaway, Viola Workman, Grace Buslach, Jessie Cooley, Carl Campen, Ruben Kayer, Ernest Workman, Ethel Bailey, August Campen, Carroll Wright, Frank Gibbons, and Ernie Campen; (third row) Mason Buslach, Albert Goot, Alfred Kern, Albert Aune, Julia Chilberg, Earl Morgan, Maud Workman, Hattie Pieritz, Julia Olson, Martha Kloninger (Ford), ? Steevenson, Martha Goot (Wright), Henry "Carl" Carpenter, Bertha Webber (Nagel), Leona Jacob (Lavanture), and teachers Mr. Jacob and Mrs. Jacob.

Three

At Work in a River Town

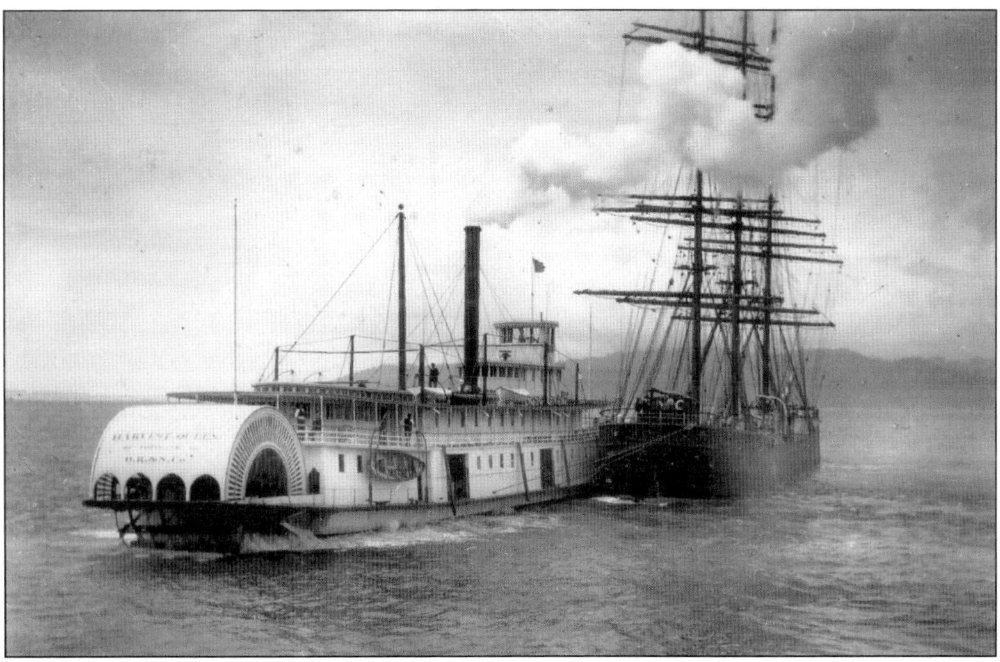

Stern-wheelers were huge riverboats. They used wood-fed steam engines to power paddle wheels located at the stern of the ship. These paddle wheels pushed the ship through the water. The *Harvest Queen* stern-wheeler, launched in 1896, was 846 tons and 200 feet long but sank shortly after. It was raised and put back into service before being replaced by the *Harvest Queen II*, which in 1924 was the first stern-wheeler on the Columbia River to have a radio.

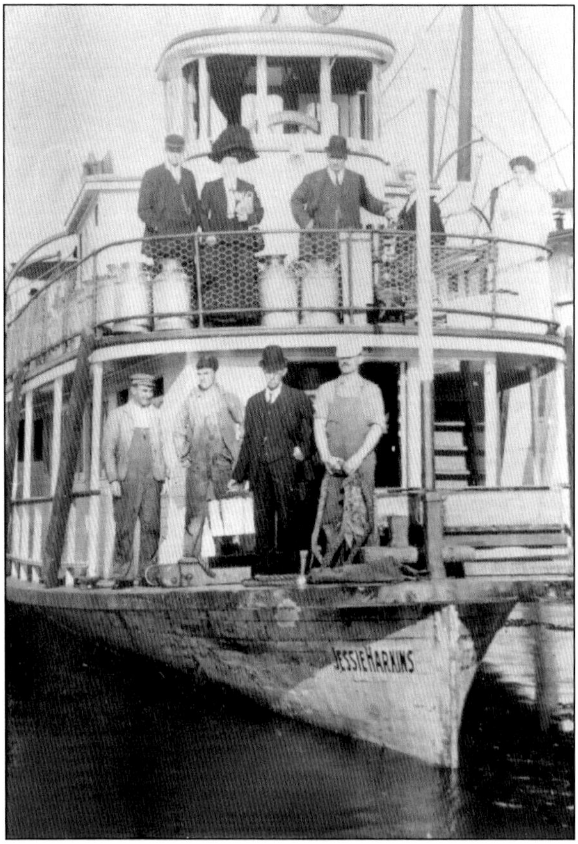

The *Jessie Harkins* made a regular round-trip from Portland to Washougal. It came in at 7:00 a.m., picked up passengers, supplies, and goods from the mills, and fruit, nuts, milk, or cream from the local farmers, and headed to Portland. It left Portland at 2:00 p.m. and returned to Washougal by 6:00 p.m. Washougal residents had approximately three hours in Portland for pleasure or business. The trip cost 25¢.

Portdock was one of several Washougal docks. River landings connected people with commerce and travel. On the journey upriver, the traveler would pass one landing after another—Fisher Landing, Remmington Landing, Gentry's Landing, the three fisher's quarry docks, Parkers Landing, Steamboat Landing, Pendleton Mill Dock, Cape Horn Landing—on and on up through Cascade Locks and into Stevenson.

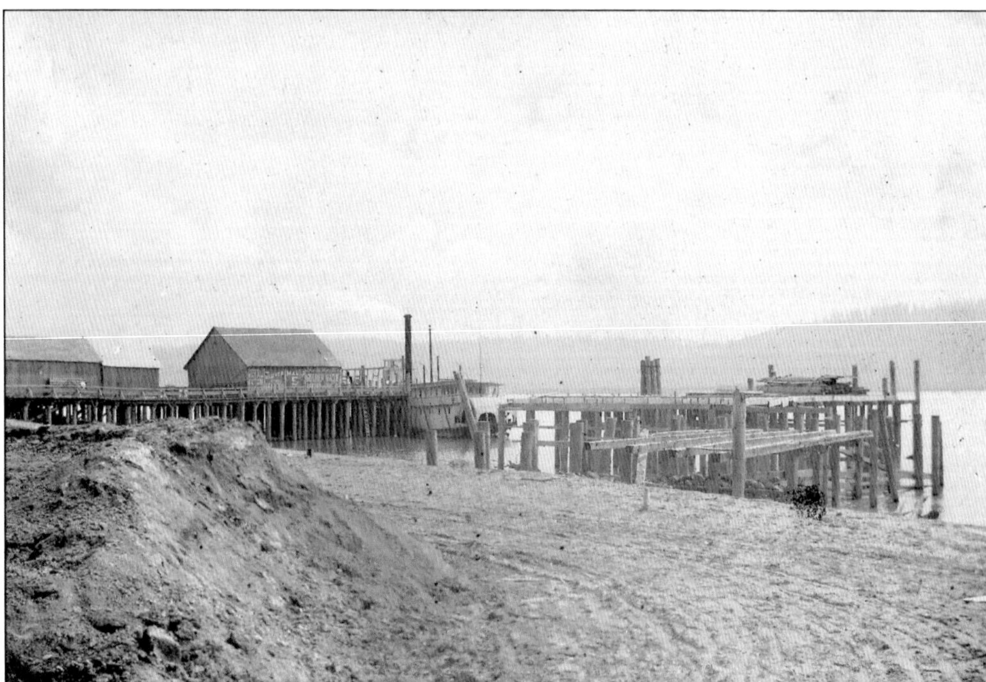

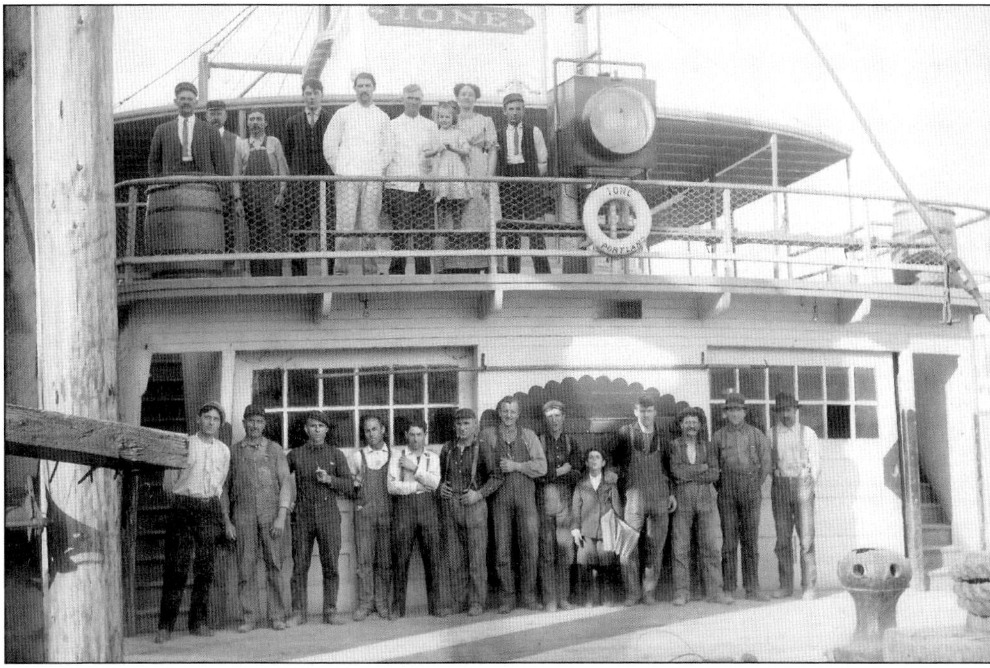

The stern-wheeler *Ione* was 148 feet long and weighed 389 tons. Built in Vancouver in 1911, it cost $50,000 and could carry 500 passengers. It was designed to haul any sort of cargo, from lumber and farming products to industrial products, dry goods, and other kinds of merchandise. The *Ione* sunk more than once, lastly in 1937 when a collision tore the planking from its starboard hull.

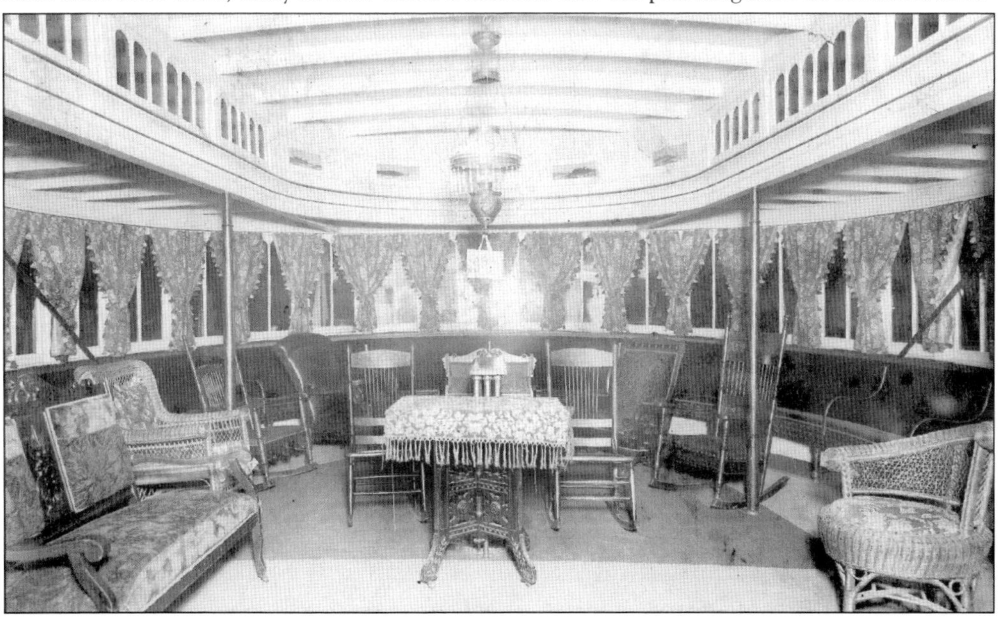

This passenger parlor in the riverboat, the *Regulator,* shows the typical accommodations for passengers. Period décor favored fringe and brocade, and tables were set out so that passengers could play cards. But the captain of the ship set the tone for the voyage, and some were quite strict. In one such story, a puppy smuggled aboard ship by a little girl was summarily seized and thrown overboard by an irate captain. (Courtesy Thomas Gentry.)

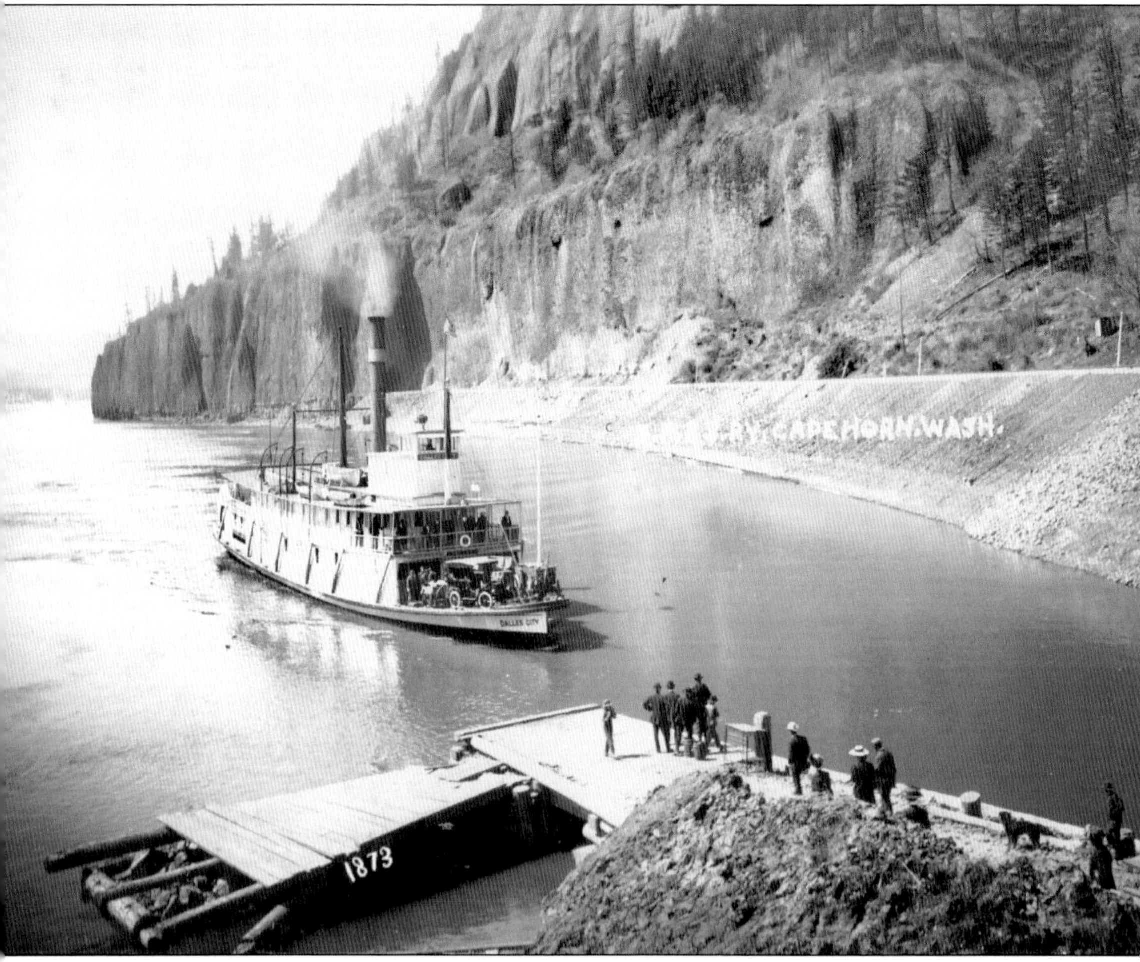

The *Dalles City* comes into Cape Horn Landing around 1913. The ship will exchange passengers and pick up fuel. Stern-wheelers required huge amounts of fuel to feed the steam-powered engines, and farmers would cut, split, and haul four-foot lengths of firewood and stack them ready to sell to any needy captain. Captains often had favorite ports of call. Captain Short of the *Dalles City* stopped regularly at Remmington Landing, just south of Washougal, because he was smitten with a local girl. While the crew supervised the loading at the dock, Short would seek out his sweetheart and beg for a kiss or a slice of pie. Capt. Lewis Love of the boat *Calliope* was known for his dependability. He regularly took eggs from a Cape Horn farmer's wife to the Portland market. When one day she was one egg short of a dozen, she asked Love if he would wait until one of her hens laid another egg. This he graciously did. Soon enough, there was a full dozen, and Love was on his way again.

Sportfishing was as popular then as it is today. So plentiful were Washougal waters that an hour's work might net a person an entire tubful of fish. Pearl Bethea of Mount Pleasant remembered a sturgeon so big that to get it to the cannery it had to be loaded into a truck. Even so, its tail stuck out the back. (Courtesy University of Washington Libraries, UW22036.)

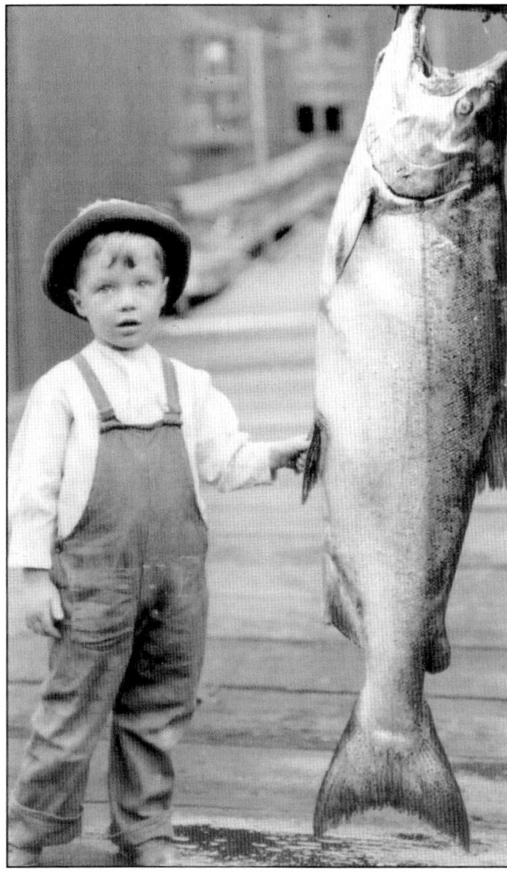

The big stern-wheelers were by no means the only passage over or along the river. Boys challenged each other to swim across—a badge of manhood for those who made it. Some people had their own fishing boats, rowboats, or even rafts. There were also small ferryboats to take passengers across the river or to or from an island, such as used by this party around 1900 at Portdock.

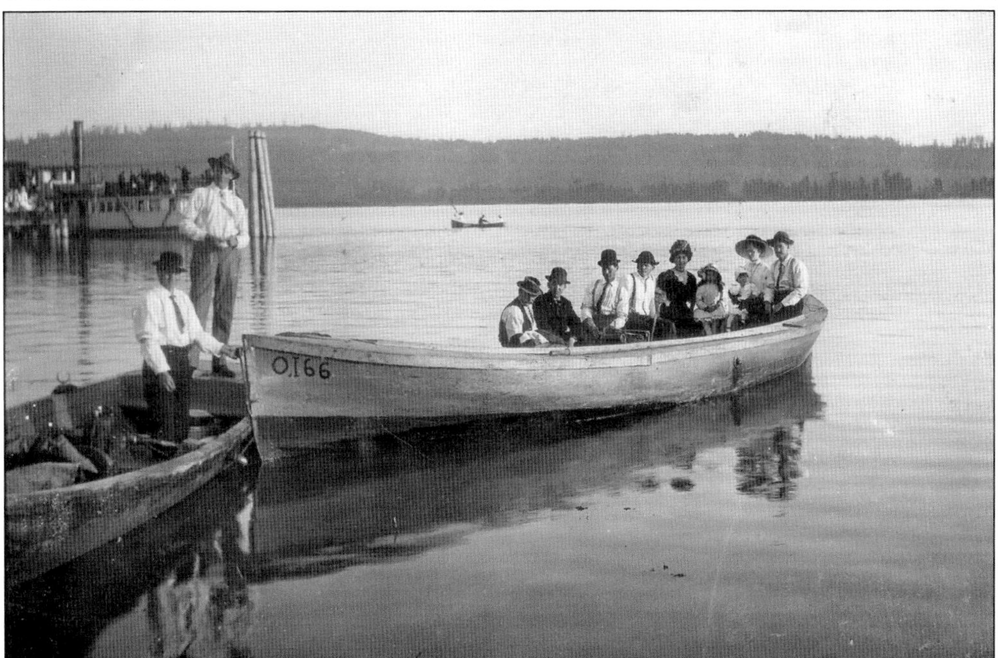

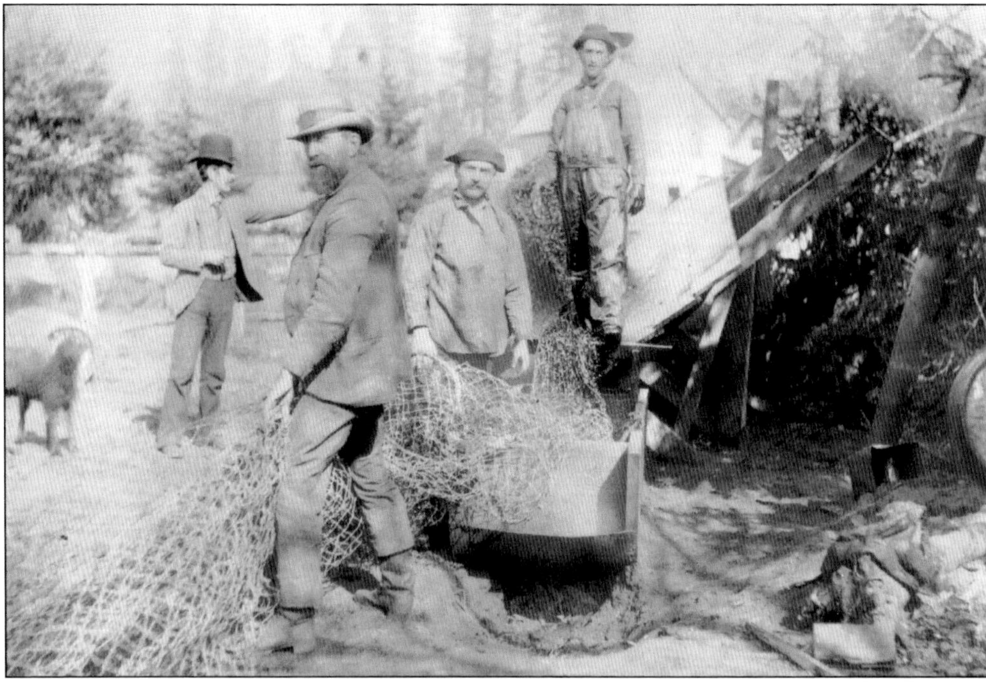

Fishermen's boats were a common sight, and fish caught near Washougal were probably processed at Ellsworth Cannery, built *c.* 1860. These unidentified Columbia River fishermen dip nets in tar to improve their durability. In addition to line, hooks, and waterproof netting, virtually every fisherman's boat had a Primus stove for good, hot coffee. (Courtesy University of Washington Libraries, Tollman and Canaris Collection, UW12690.)

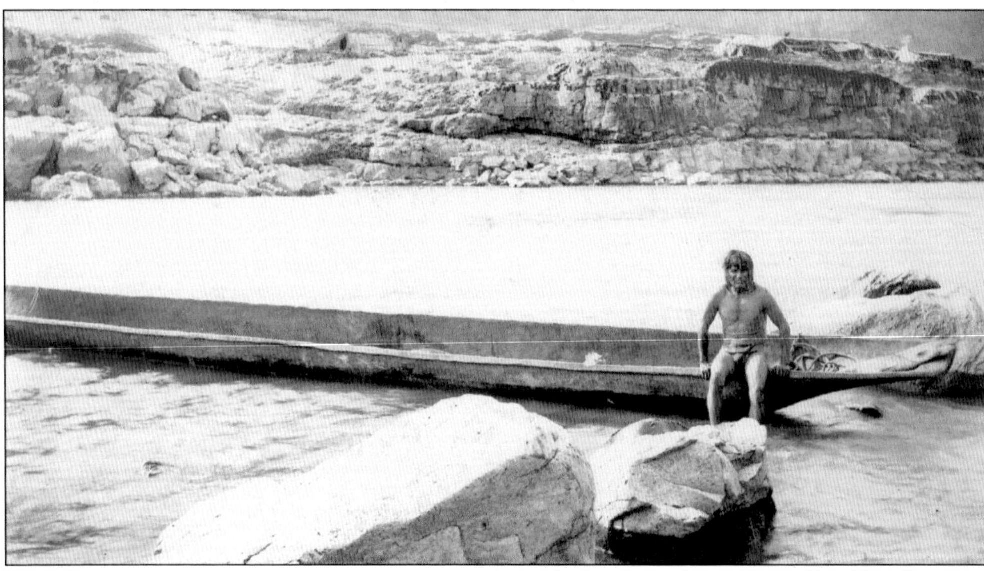

A man, probably of the Wasco people, rests on a canoe at Celilo in 1987. The Dalles Dam in 1956 swamped Celilo Falls, an ancestral fishing ground vital to native Indian tribes, which was an economic, social, and spiritual catastrophe for the Cascade and Chinook people. Native fishing techniques at Celilo consisted primarily of using dip-nets and spears to harvest salmon. (Photograph by Benjamin W. Gifford; courtesy Library of Congress.)

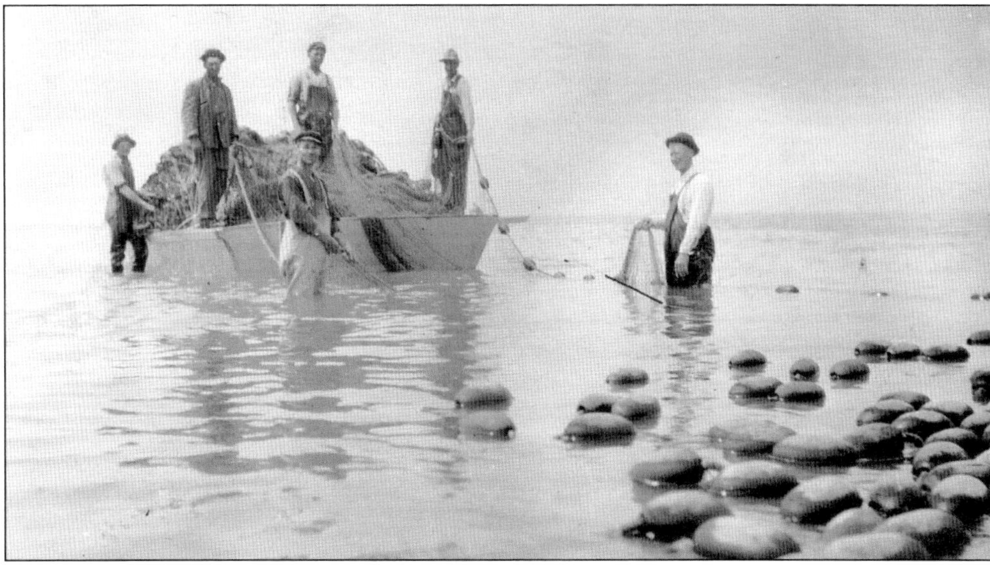

These fishermen fish using the method of beach seining. A net is placed between the shore and a boat in the water. The boat then pulls the net in a steady semicircle from the beach, first out into the river and then back to the beach again like a big scoop. Fish could be held in the net and sorted for harvesting. Horses were also used to move the net when seining.

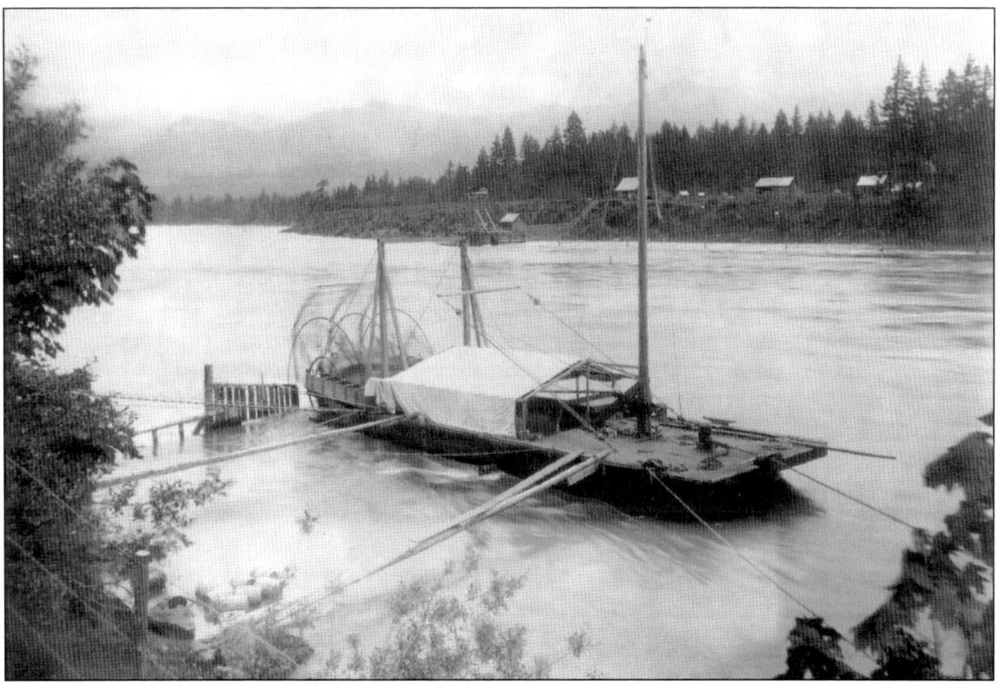

Thorton William patented the fish wheel in 1881. That same year, William McCord improved it, constructing the first two-dip fish wheel near today's Bonneville Dam. Fish wheels, like this one on the Columbia River in 1897, were turned by the river current. Fish were drawn into the rotating baskets, lifted out, up, and around, and then deposited into an inner-netted pool where they awaited harvesting. (Courtesy University of Washington Libraries, Tollman and Canaris Collection, UW12669.)

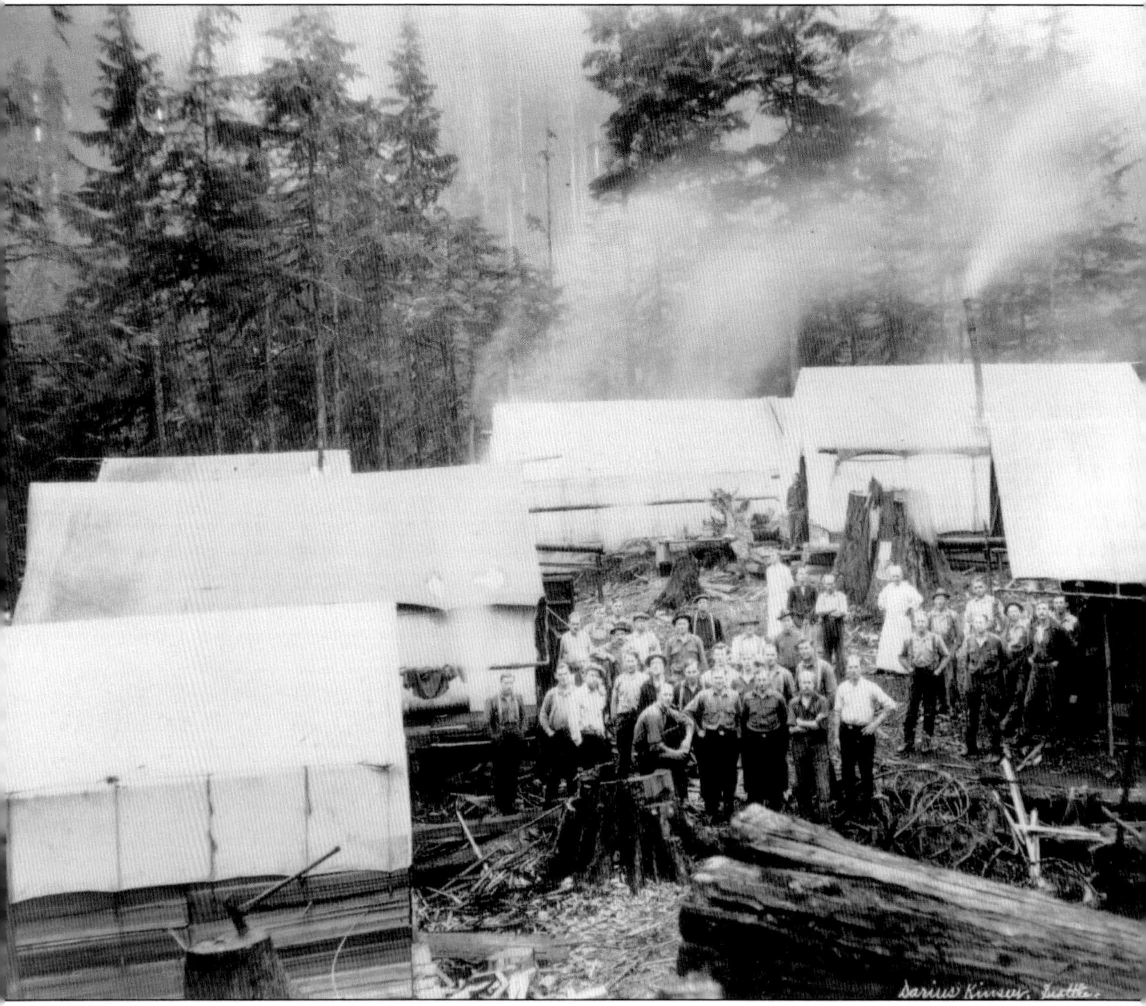

Fur traders sailing the Northwest Coast were among the first to recognize the economic potential of Washington's dense forests. Fur trader John McLoughlin built the first sawmill on Washington soil at Fort Vancouver in 1828. In 1850, gold-crazed cities, such as San Francisco, developed an insatiable appetite for lumber. Waterways such as the Washougal River and Trout Creek were ideal conduits for timber. Splash dams allowed loggers to float logs downriver to mills at Cascade Locks or along the Columbia River for export. Steamships took the lumber south. By 1900, annual timber harvests in Washington had reached two billion board feet, and for a lucky few, fortunes were made. By all accounts, logging camps were wet, miserable places with inadequate bedding, heating, and food, and to make it worse, the pay was poor. It was only after loggers organized in 1917 that they gained better conditions and the eight-hour workday. (Photograph by Darius Kinsey; courtesy University of Washington Libraries.)

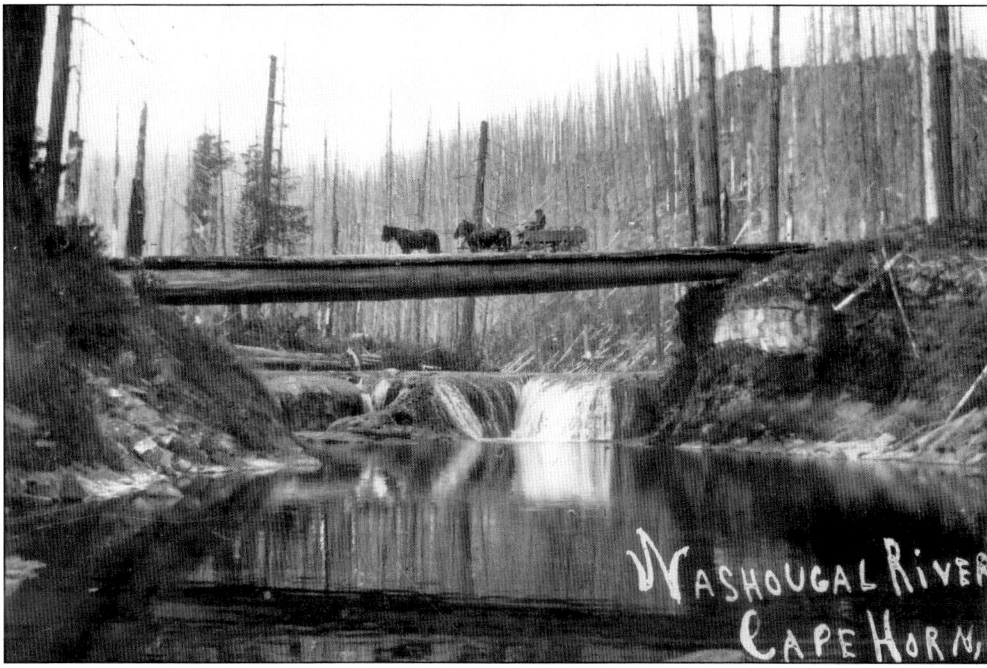

Two men and a four-horse team cart barrels across the Washougal River at Cape Horn. Behind them is a charred landscape. Early on, forests burned with little to stop them. The largest fire ever in Washington was the Yacolt blaze, which scorched 239,920 acres near Washougal in 1902. It burned so hot it charred livestock where they stood. Those who witnessed it called it an apocalypse. (Photograph by Charles Meredith.)

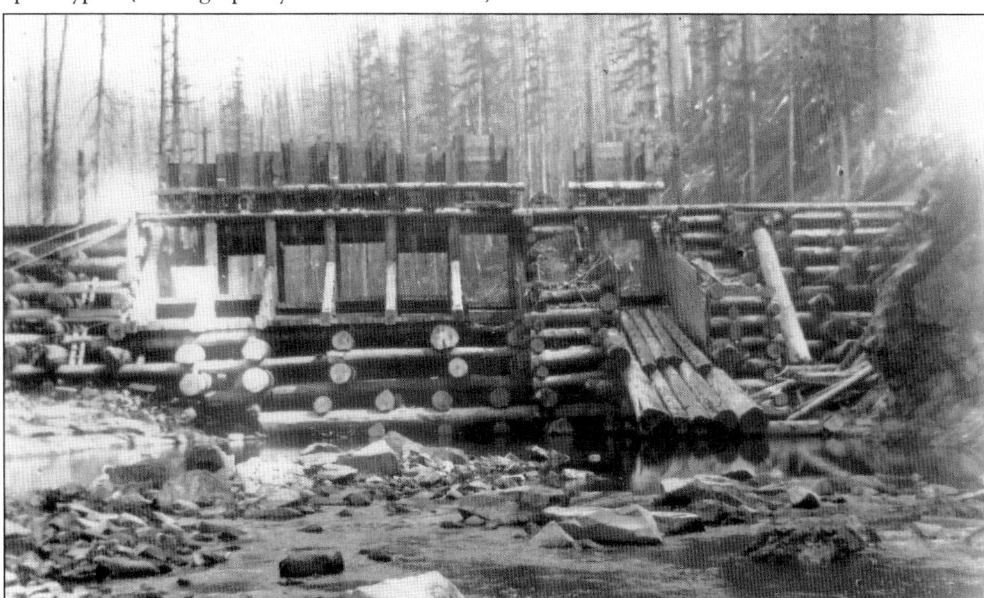

Logging companies built dams to facilitate log transport. Franck Dam, built on the Washougal River at Cape Horn, created a small lake to float the timber. When the gates of the dam opened, water poured out, flushing or sluicing the logs downstream. This dam was later destroyed to restore fish habitat. (Photograph by Charles Meredith.)

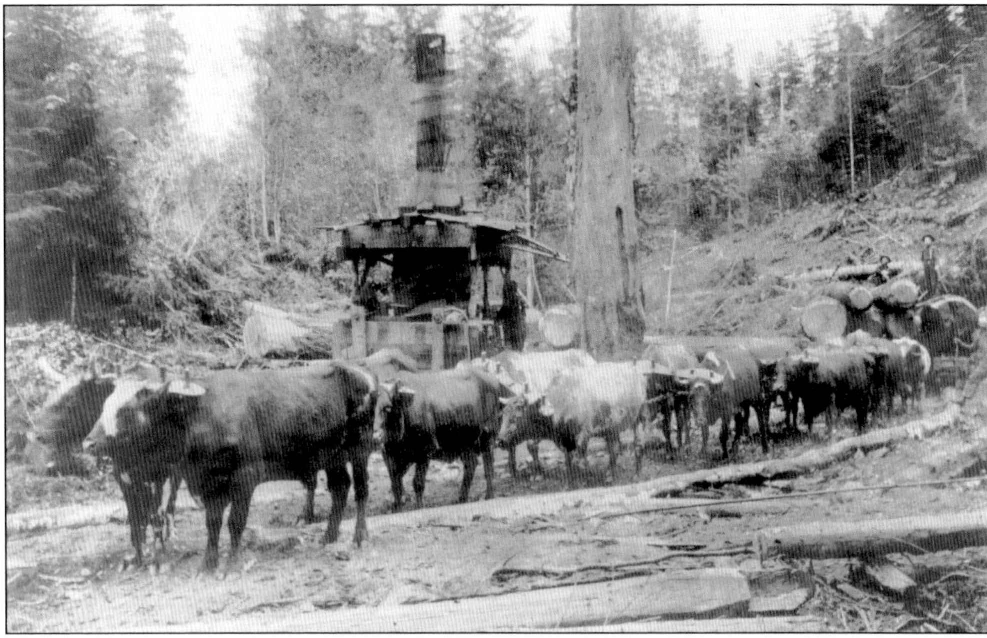

The steam-powered Donkey engine, invented by John Dolbeer in 1881, industrialized logging. Previously, loggers used horses and oxen for heavy hauling. In this undated Washington-area photograph, oxen, in a bull team, haul logs along a skid road while a Donkey sits idle in the background. Stronger and more efficient, the Donkey largely replaced the ox—perhaps except when the machinery was not working. (Courtesy University of Washington Libraries.)

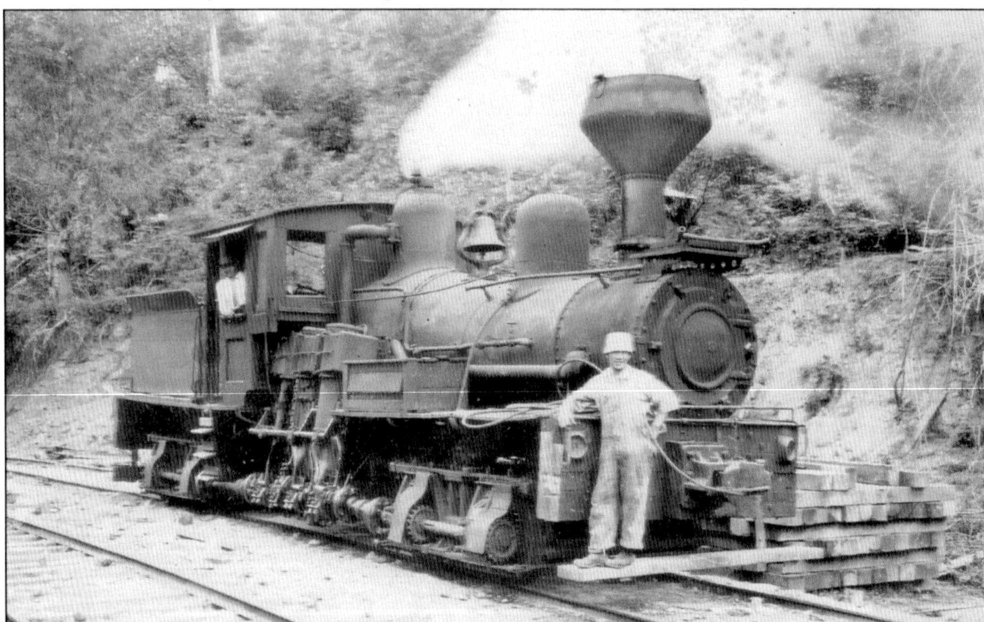

Ephraim Shay patented the Shay locomotive in 1881. A geared train, the Shay could push heavy loads uphill and around corners. Trestle roads and bridges accommodated the Shay, and large numbers of logs could be transported over land. The Shay was a boon to all industries that required heavy hauling. This particular engine was used at Fisher Quarry. (Courtesy Thomas Gentry.)

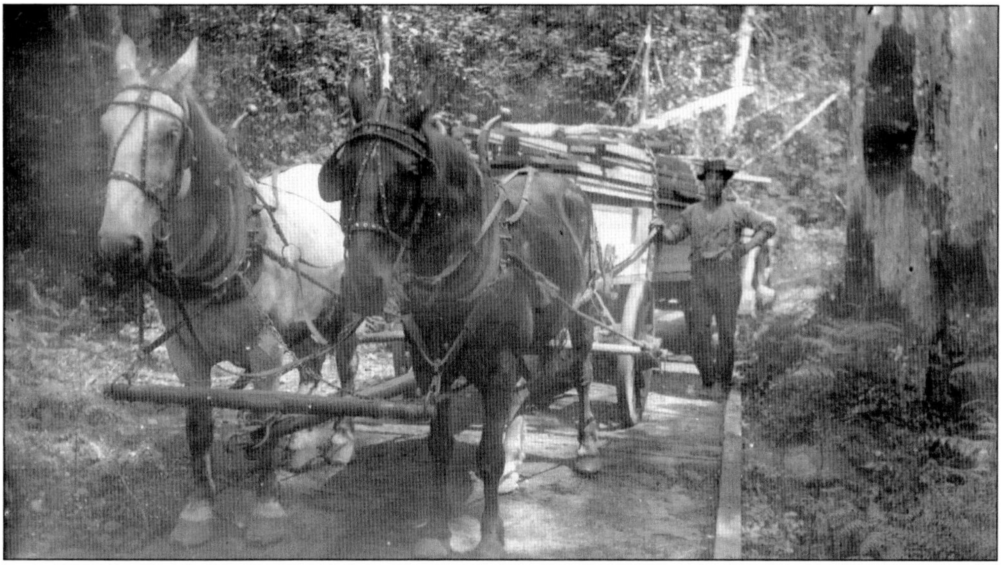

While logging camps dotted forests along inland rivers, many sawmills were built close to growing settlements. Lumber was needed locally to build homes, shops, boats, and businesses. Quite a few local families owned sawmills, such as Jorgen Hendricksen in Sunnyside. Lumber from these little mills was transported by horse and cart along dirt roads for sale or trade to a neighbor or to market.

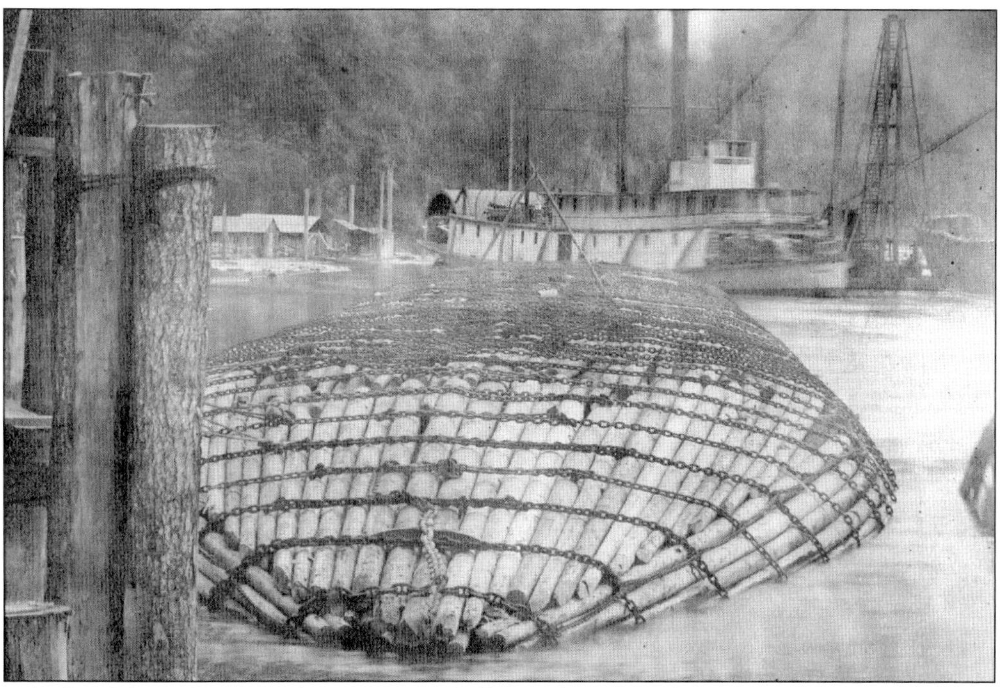

Whether delivered by water, locomotive, or bull team, logs arrived at rivers such as the Columbia, ready for sale or export. Local sawmills purchased some logs, and the rest were floated downriver into channels where men used derricks to assemble them into heavily chained cigar rafts. The rafts were tugged or pushed out to sea by steamers, such as the *Hercules*. (Photograph by J. F. Ford, c. 1904.)

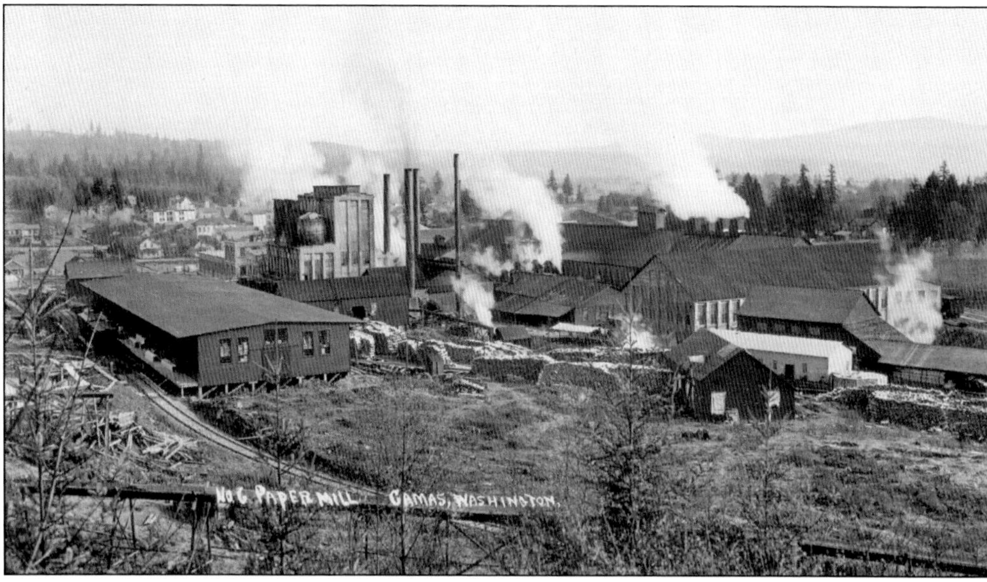

Henry Pittock established the Lacamas Colony Company on 2,600 acres of land in 1883, investing with J. K. Gill and William Lewthwaite to form the Columbia River Paper Company in 1884. Pittock, founder of the *Oregonian* in Portland, needed newsprint and he got it. By the late 1880s, the mill, seen here in an undated photograph, produced over three tons of newsprint every day.

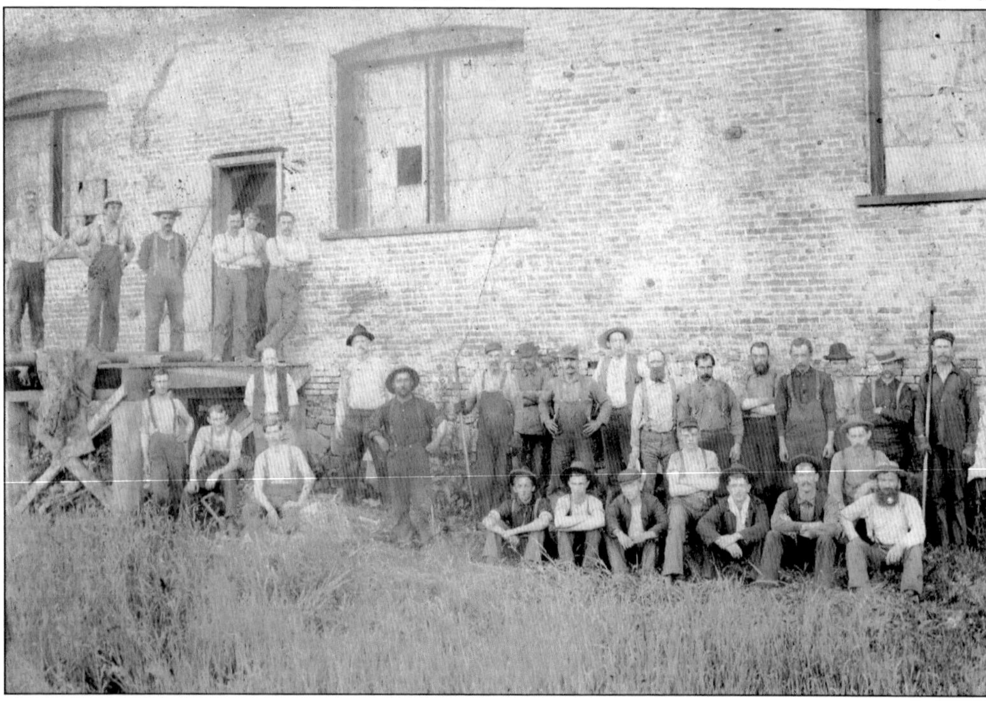

The Chinese, whose hard labor contributed greatly to the building of the mill, established a camp with laundry and cookhouse facilities. Soon enough, the mill attracted more permanent workers, and the Chinese were squeezed out. The first school in Camas opened in 1884. By 1892, mill workers (unidentified) were well on their way to forming the town of Camas. Camas was incorporated in 1906.

Labor issues everywhere grew in importance by 1915. Complaints at the then Crown Willamette Paper Company included poor wages, child workers, long hours, and dangerous working conditions. The men pictured here in 1916 include Ernie Cox, ? Edmunds, Joe Ast, John Zugler, and Joe Leeson. They would see wages increase in 1917, but an attempt to unionize that same year failed; mill workers waited until 1934 for local union representation.

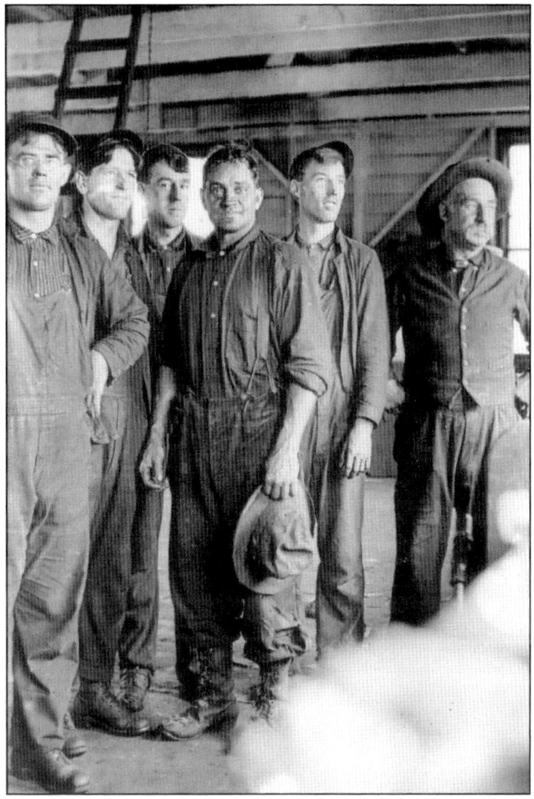

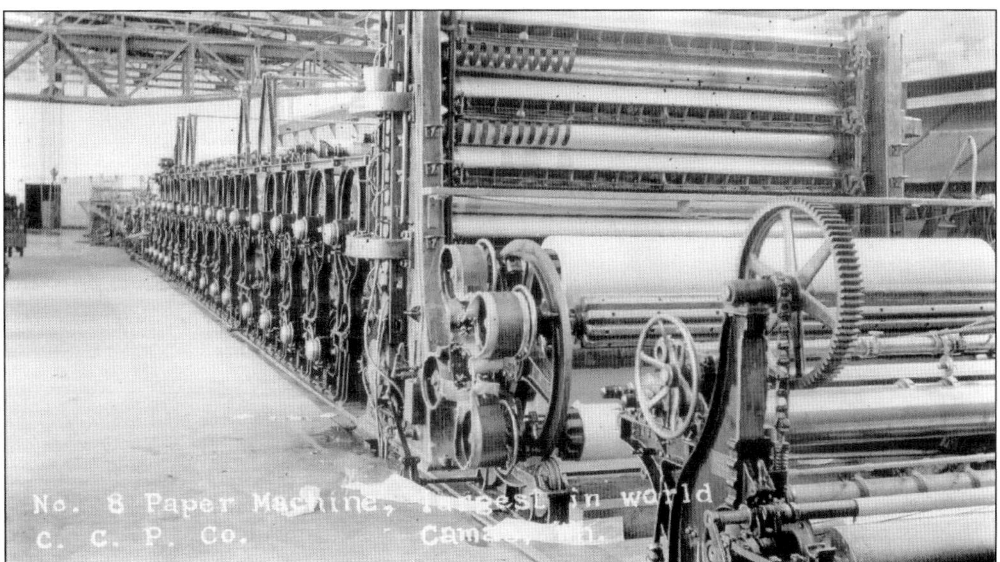

A state-of-the-art factory, the Columbia River Paper Company changed names but rarely changed hands. Mergers came in 1905, 1914, and 1928, but quality remained high. This paper machine in 1916 was then the largest in the world. The 1980s brought a $425 million modernization and sale of the mill to the James River Corporation. Another merger followed in 1997. In 2000, the mill was sold to Georgia Pacific.

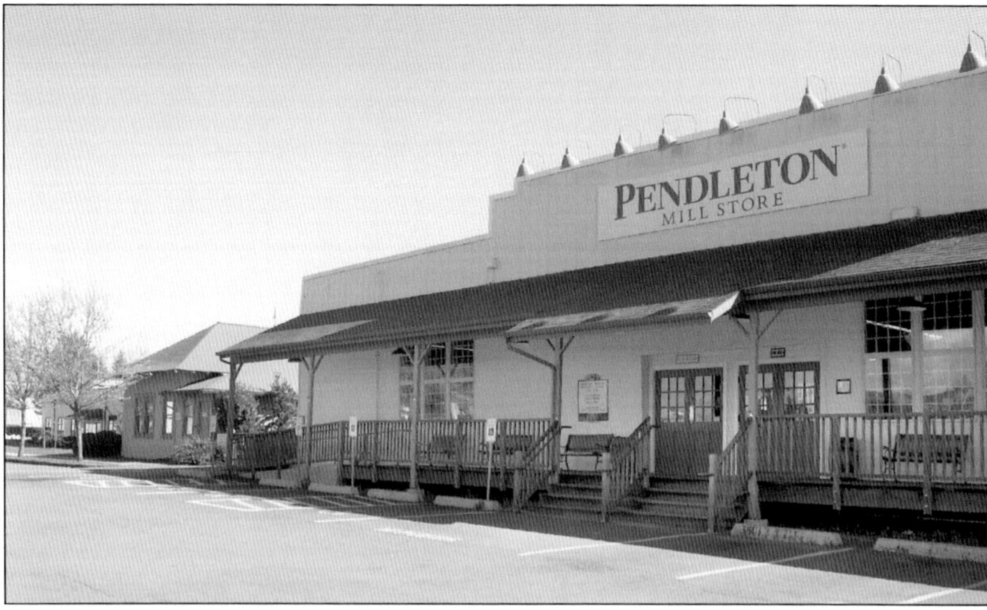

Pendleton Woolen Mills has been part of the Washougal community since 1912. As it was 100 years ago, the mill today is a contemporary textile-manufacturing facility still owned and operated by the Bishop family. Regular tours allow visitors to see the facility and learn its history. The Pendleton Mill Store, located on the mill campus along State Route 14, is a favorite with locals and visitors alike.

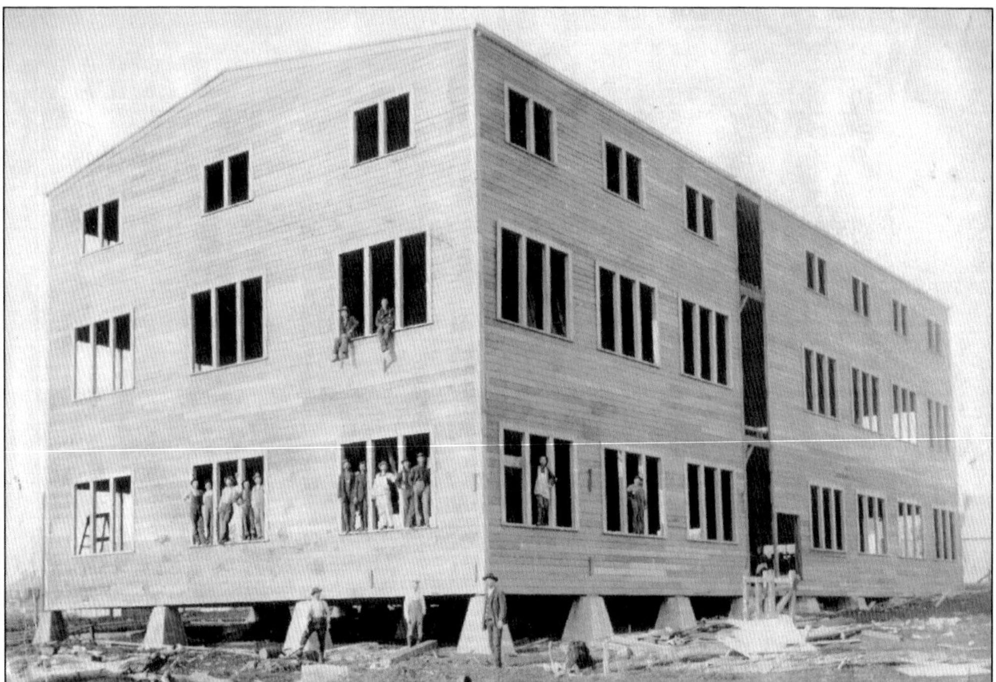

The original owner of the mill at Washougal was J. F. Bailey, a physician from Portland, Oregon. Bailey built the Union Mill in 1910. He chose an ideal location for his mill, placing it between the Columbia River and the lines of the North Bank Railroad. Bailey may have contracted Thomas Jenny Sr. to construct this first three-story mill building.

The local community undertook construction of the Union Mill in 1910 with enthusiasm. Early trucks brought support beams, boilers, and other materials from the dock and along B Street. Prior to construction, the area had been farmland and subject to floods. Ben Campen, who cut hay on that land in the late 1890s, remembered that the oats planted there grew as tall as his head. (Photographs by Goff's Studio.)

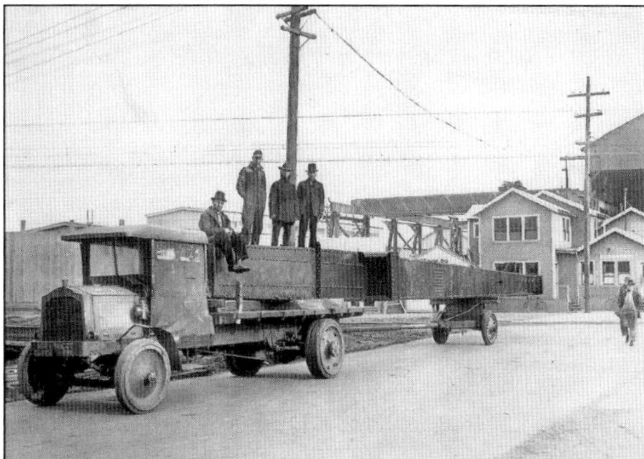

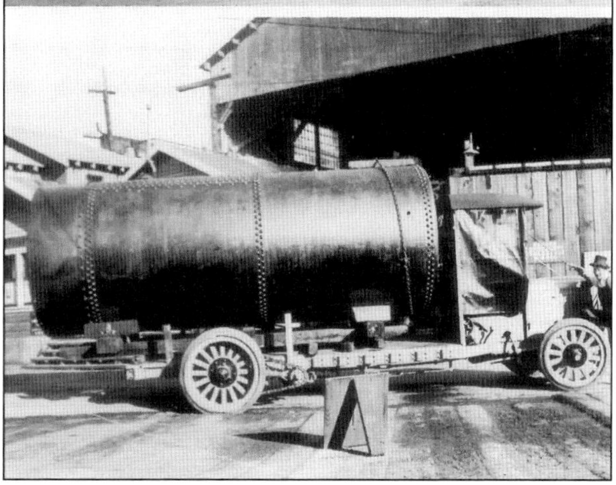

These Union Mill employees went to work in 1910 in a brand new building with reportedly 12 new machines. J. F. Bailey employed women as well as men. Usually the men ran the machines and the women sewed. It was generally the women's job to fix any broken threads by sewing them back into the finished fabric. Unfortunately the Union Mill failed. Bailey's mill went into receivership in 1912.

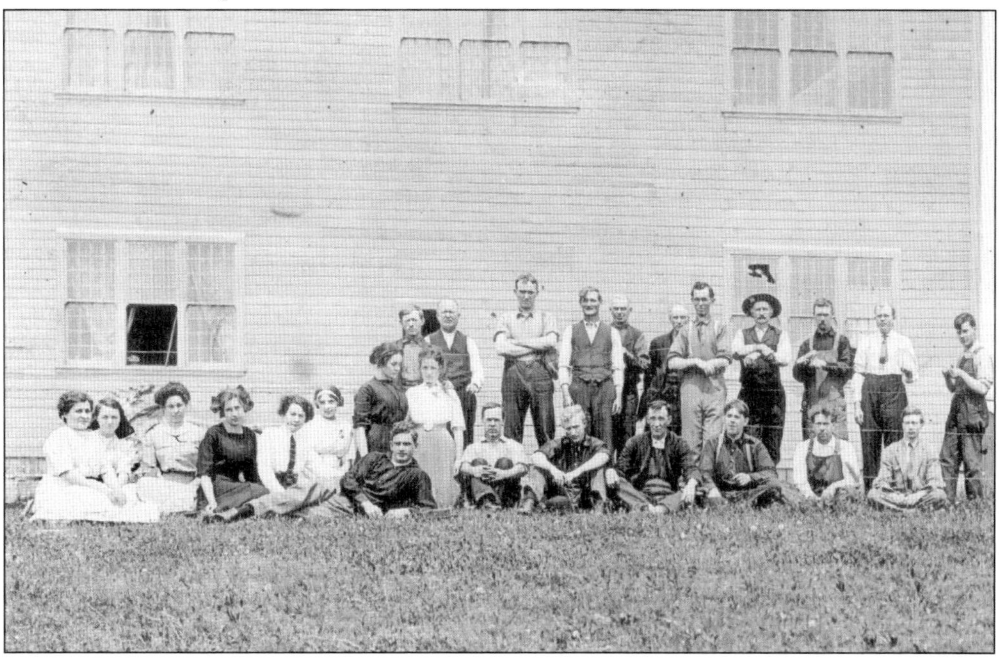

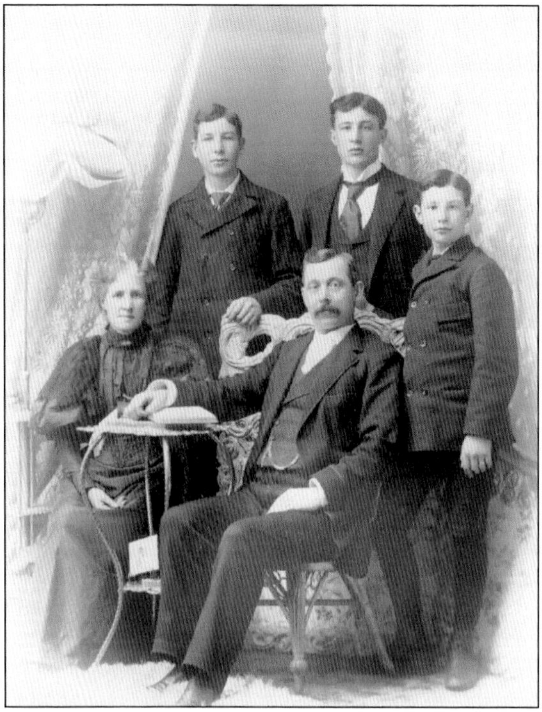

The Bishop family purchased the bankrupt Union Mill in 1912. They were a family with know-how. Thomas Kay, his daughter Fannie, and her husband, C. P. Bishop, built the successful Pendleton Woolen Mill in Oregon in 1893. The Bishops, pictured here from left to right in 1896, are (first row, seated) Fannie Kay Bishop and C. P. Bishop; and sons (second row, standing) Royal Thomas, Clarence Morton, and Robert Chauncey. (Courtesy Pendleton Woolen Mills.)

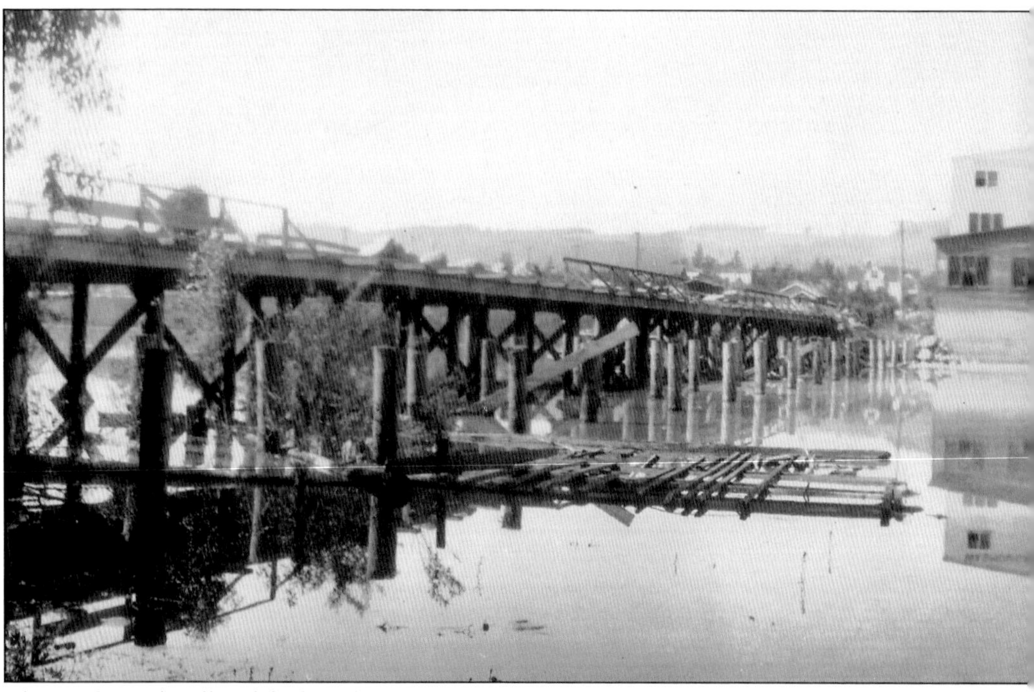

The Washougal Mill and dock underwent extensive renovations in 1915. Machines were brought from Marysville and production tripled. In 1919, Clarence M. Bishop moved to a new Pendleton headquarters in Portland where he married Harriet Broughton in 1922. Clarence kept a room at Washougal's Commercial Hotel, however, and was on hand in 1936 when Washougal had the chance to assist a discomfited Washington governor. Gov. Clarence Martin, who was visiting the

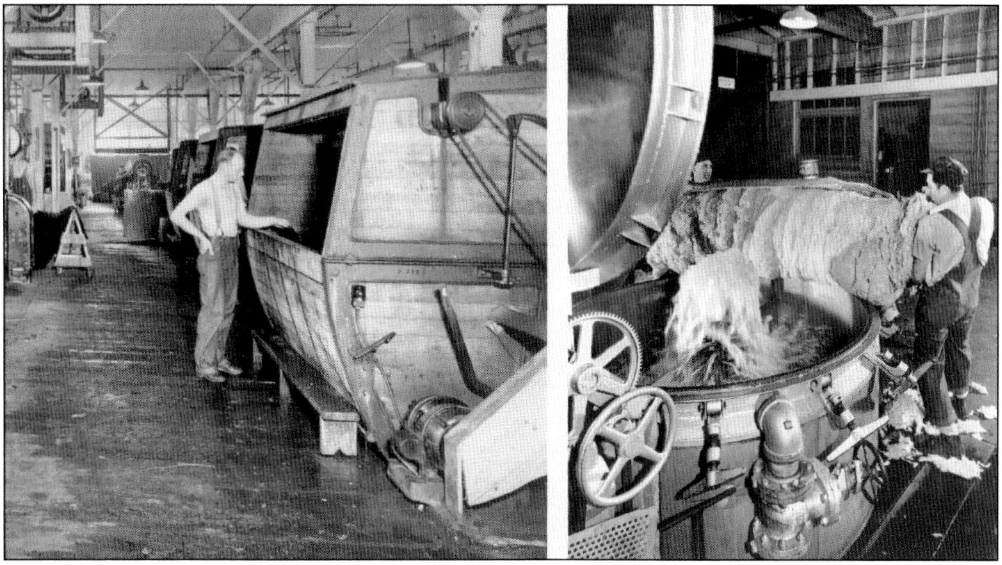

Fulling (left) is a felting process applied to fabrics after weaving is complete. Pendleton's process, pictured here in 1940, is unique and results in a fuller, warmer fabric that is still soft and tactile. Dyeing (right) was also a specialty process. The clear water of the Pacific Northwest facilitates the vibrant colors Pendleton blankets are known for. The sign in back reminded workers to "keep this place clean." (Courtesy Pendleton Woolen Mills.)

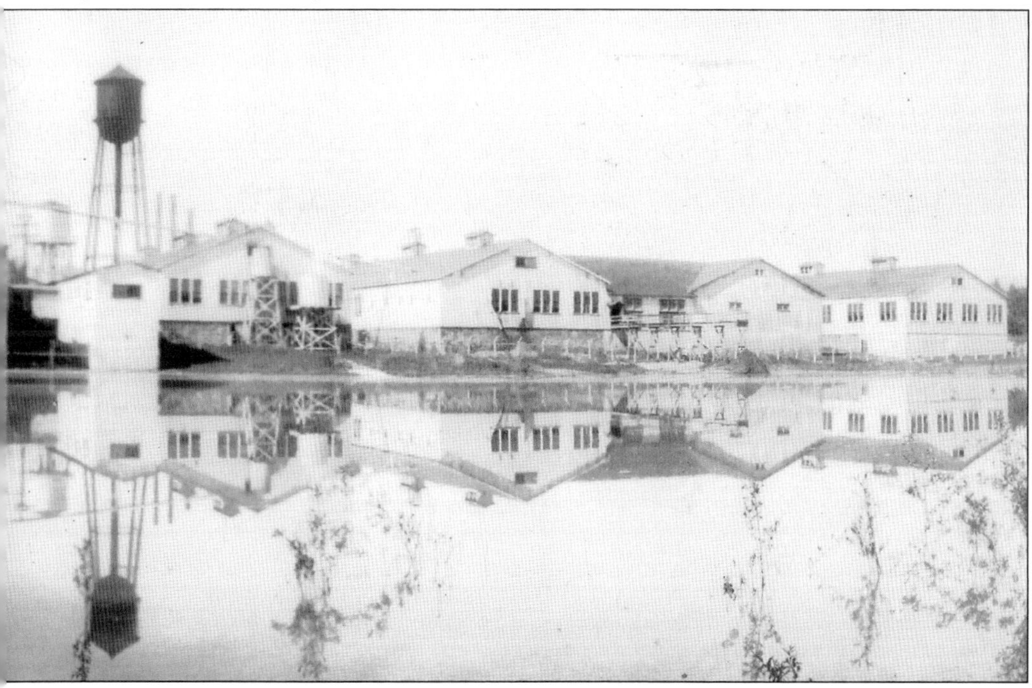

local manufacturing mills, caught his pant leg on the door of his new Chrysler, ripping a gash in the fabric. A machinist from the paper mill in Camas brought a file to smooth the door, but Washougal did one better as Clarence M. Bishop presented the governor with a new suit-length segment of the coveted "Washougal cloth," a specialty "Bishop Cassimere" compliments of the Washougal Mill.

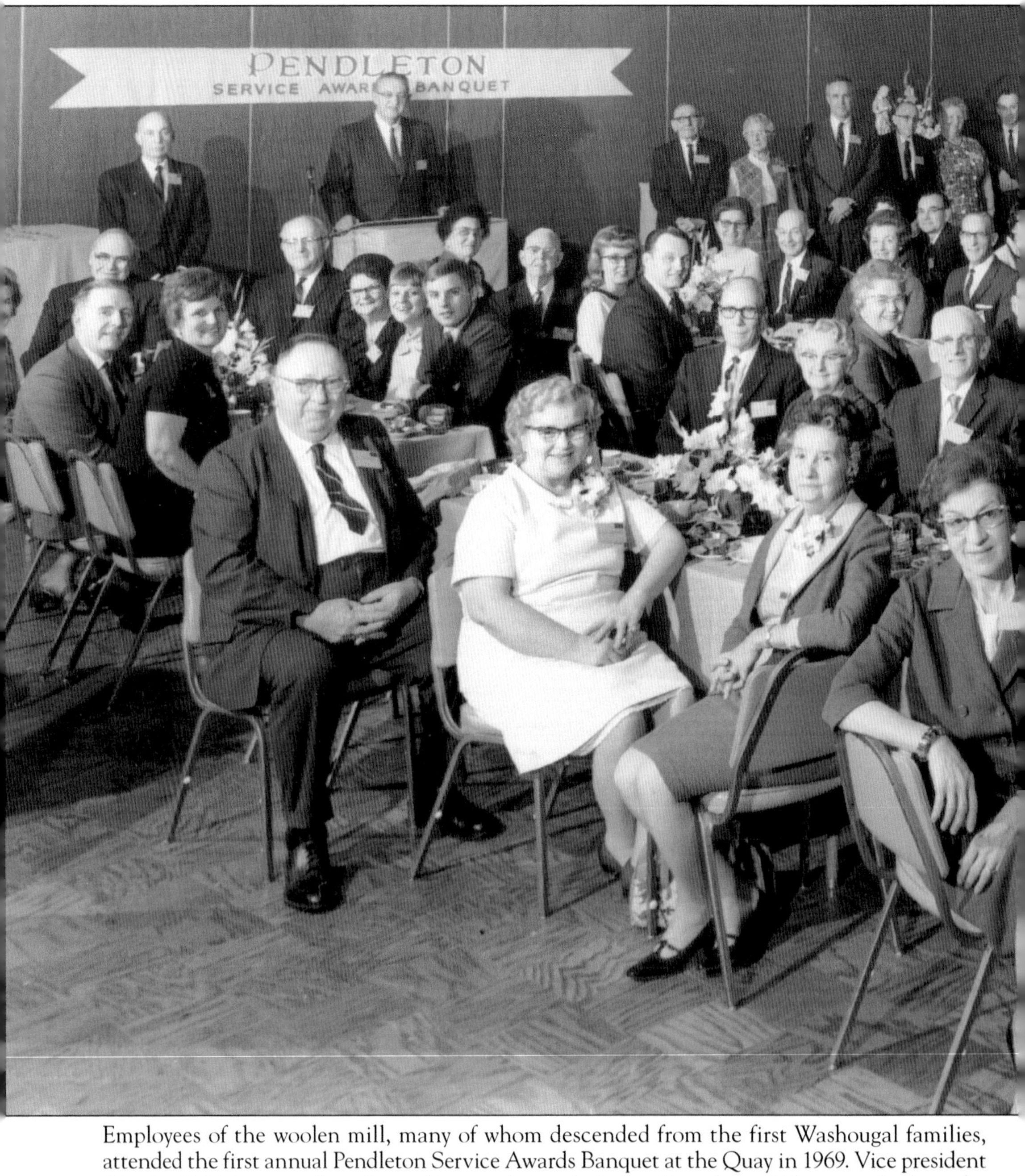

Employees of the woolen mill, many of whom descended from the first Washougal families, attended the first annual Pendleton Service Awards Banquet at the Quay in 1969. Vice president Charles K. Bishop stands at the podium, and vice chairman Broughton Bishop stands along the far back wall, fifth from the left. Also pictured are Mr. and Mrs. R. J. K. Thompson, Mathilda Michels, Martha Fah, Mr. and Mrs. Carl Sadewasser, Mr. and Mrs. Alvin Baldwin, Mr. and Mrs. C. M. Bishop Jr., James Hoffman, J. C. Aitchison, Mr. and Mrs. Leo Martin, Mr. and Mrs. Gary Benson, Mr. and Mrs. Ulf Kahn, Dr. Dorothy Johnstone, Hervey Barton, Mr. and Mrs. Homer Lackey, Mr. and Mrs. George Richardson, Mr. and Mrs. Reo Mack, Lester Kiser, Mr. and Mrs. William Brown, Albert Defoer, Mr. and Mrs. Jacob Hahn, Peter Crofts, Verna Wallace, Mr. and Mrs. Anton Zaletel, Mr. and Mrs. Ernest Stelter, Mr. and Mrs. Robert Marshall, Sam Rasmussen,

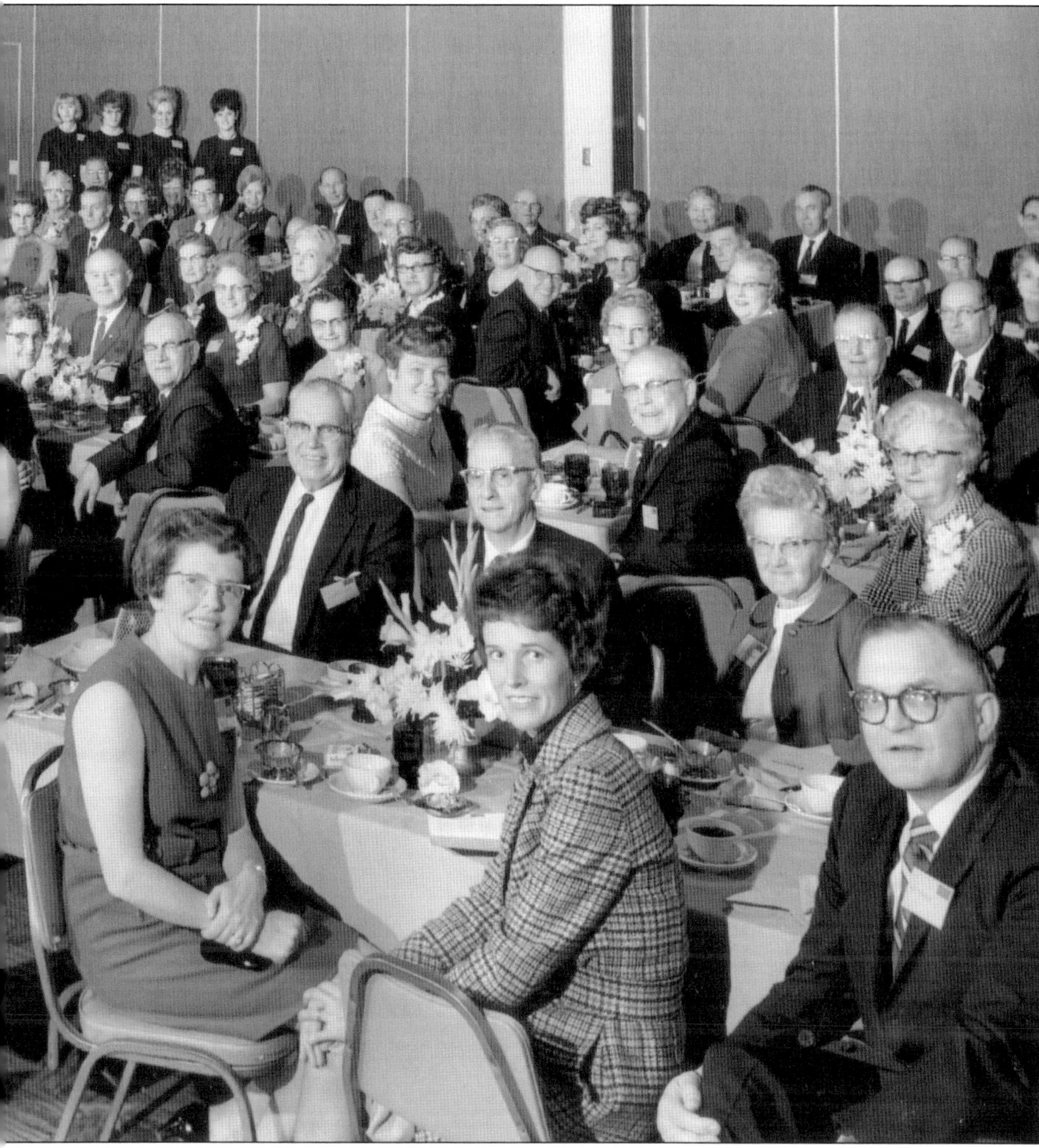

Mr. and Mrs. Carl Guenther, Mr. and Mrs. Melvin Sampson, Mr. and Mrs. E. F. Clark, Mr. and Mrs. Robert Smith, Mr. and Mrs. Stanley Durgan, Edna Berreman, Mr. and Mrs. Mark Sault, Mr. and Mrs. M. E. Potter, Mr. and Mrs. Edward Farrell, Mr. and Mrs. Keith White, Mr. and Mrs. Chris Restorff, Edith Ruettgers, Lois Ketter, Mrs. C. M. Bishop, Max Sampson, Emil Jarmann, Mr. and Mrs. Charles Haglund, Mr. and Mrs. John Michels, Helma Stevens, Mr. and Mrs. Gudell Mack, Mr. and Mrs. Wesley Wilson, Louella White, Mr. and Mrs. E. W. Haggerty, Gloria Gimarelli, Gwen Smith, Sandra Rutledge, Marjorie Broersma, Mildred Hays, Mr. and Mrs. Louis Schelling, Mr. and Mrs. Earl Rogness, Clarence Kiser, Mr. and Mrs. William Bergman, Mr. and Mrs. Clifford Jensen, Mr. and Mrs. Sim Nystrom, Mr. and Mrs. Deemer Fryberger, Elton Nystrom, and Howard Martin. (Photograph by Photo Art Commercial Studios; courtesy Pendleton Woolen Mills.)

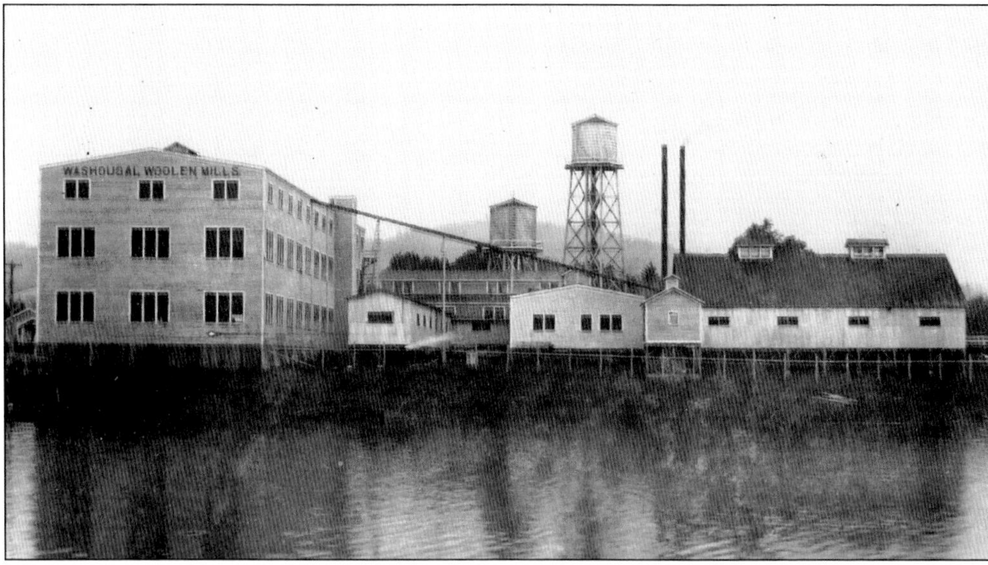

The Bishops owned several mills, running each separately. The mill in Washougal, pictured here after 1915, was known as Washougal Woolen Mills. In August 1953, the Bishops consolidated their holdings and the mill was reincorporated and renamed Pendleton Woolen Mills. George Sault was the first superintendent at Washougal, and Jacob Zanker was boss weaver. Lester Kiser was boss weaver after Zanker retired. (Courtesy Pendleton Woolen Mills.)

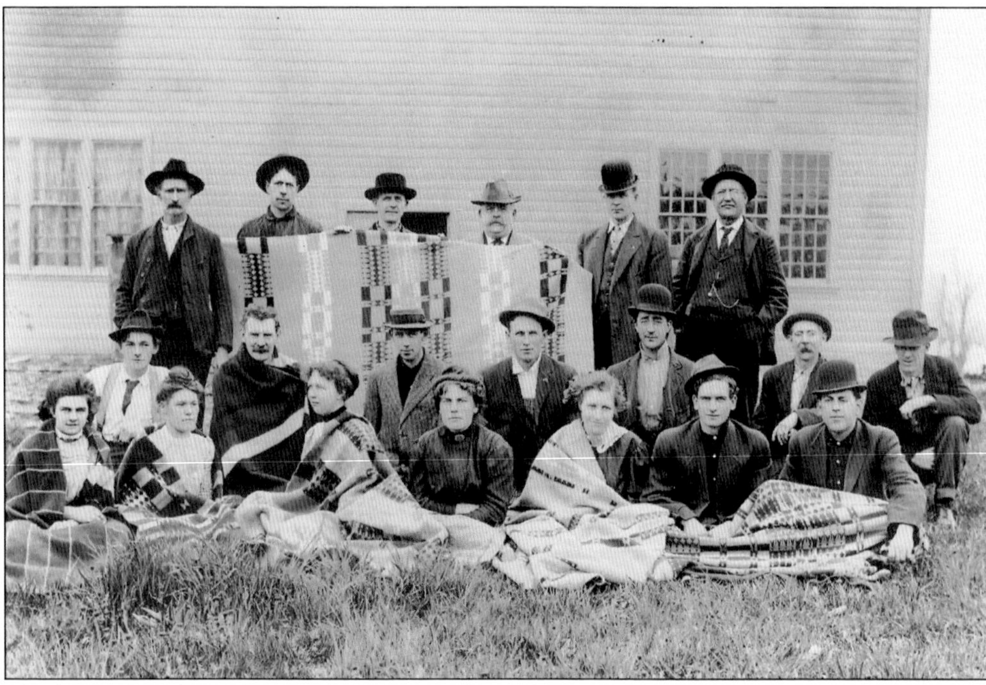

Blanket making has a long tradition in Washougal. During World War I, the mill ran day and night to supply blankets to the army. These mill workers, c. 1912, wrap themselves in the colorful and Native American-themed blankets Pendleton became famous for producing. Among those who sewed the bindings in the 1920s were Martha Roley Fah, Esther Munch, and Washougal's first daughter, Frankie Braun Cheatham. (Courtesy Pendleton Woolen Mills.)

Four

Life in Town and Country

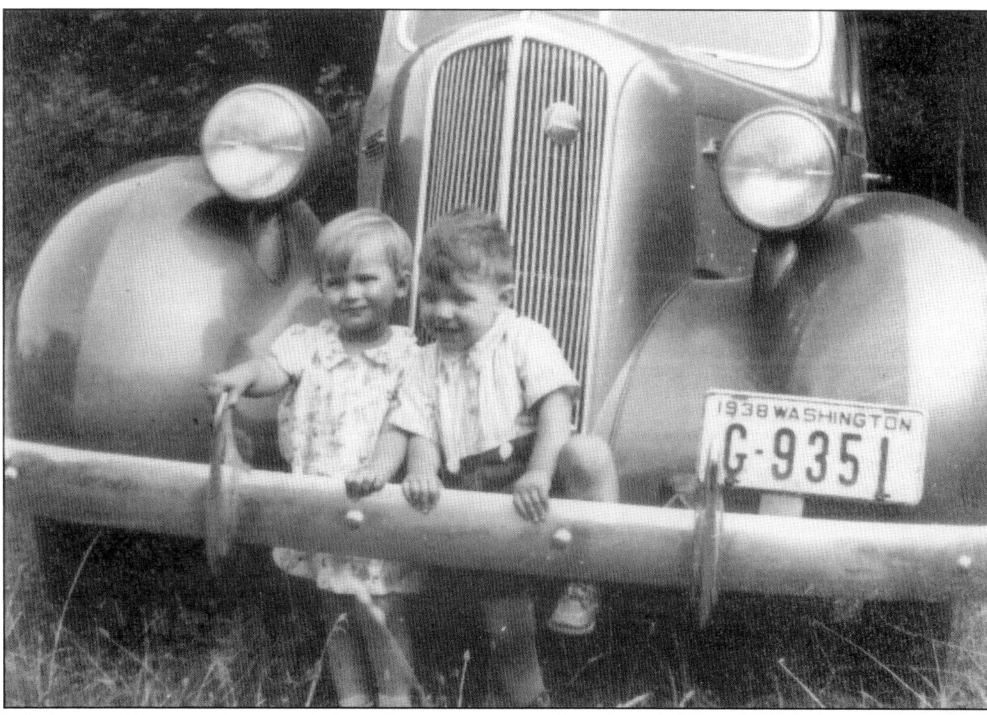

Washougal blossomed in the 1930s. The community that forged through the turn of the century had survived fire and flood, World War I, and the Depression. Wages were up, businesses lined its streets, dairy and farm production were good, and just about every family had a car—though toddlers Myrna Austin and Harvey Erickson, tucked here behind the bumper of a 1937 Studebaker, were just a bit too young to drive.

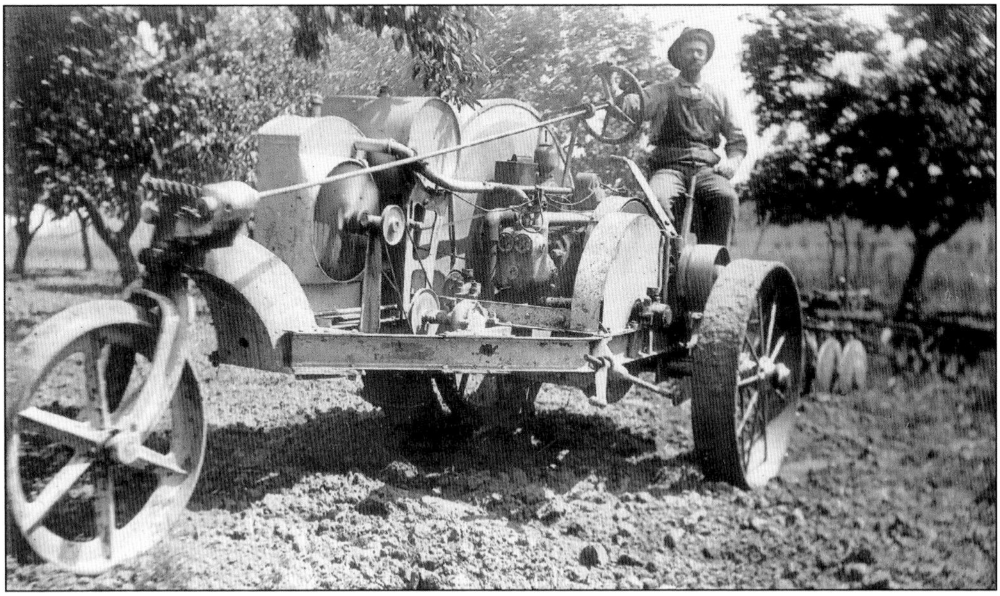

The first farm tractors were explosive, steam-powered, miniature locomotives weighing upward of five tons. The first gasoline tractors were available by the 1920s. Ira Roland poses with an early gas-powered, front Russell tractor. The engine shows the radiator in front, an elevated, gravity-fed center gas tank, and likely a large pulley, in lieu of a transmission, behind. Russell tractors made few gasoline tractors, closing shop in 1927.

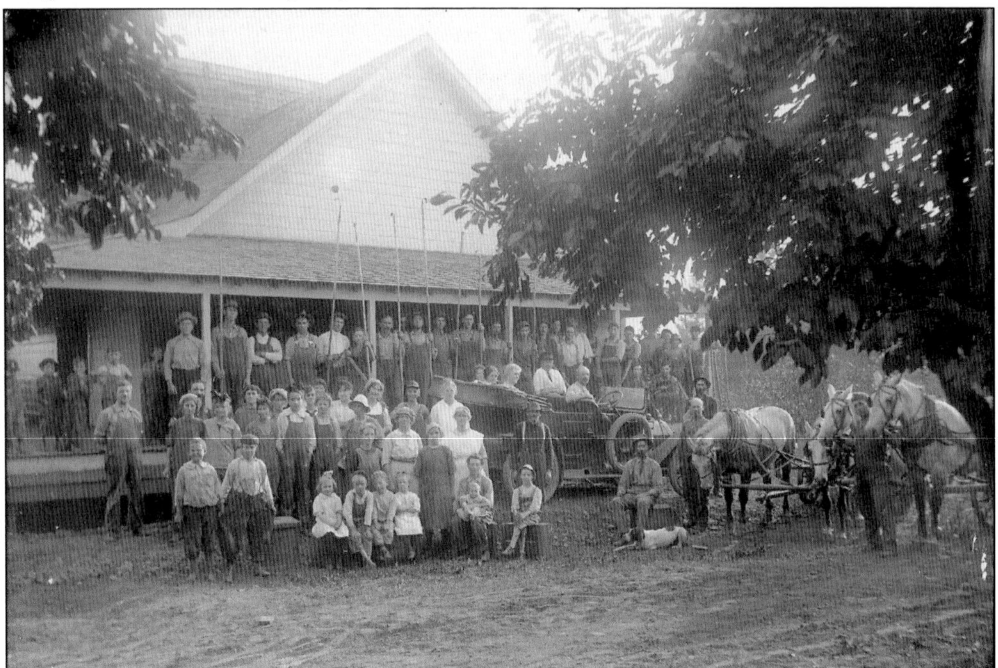

Prunes were a major crop until the 1940s. Plums were harvested in the fall and dried and shipped out by rail. Picking crews included shakers who wielded long poles to jar the fruit from the trees. Women and children, many barefoot, put the fruit into boxes. These families, pictured in 1912, worked together on William Brown's prune farm. In 1914, pickers were paid 7¢ a box.

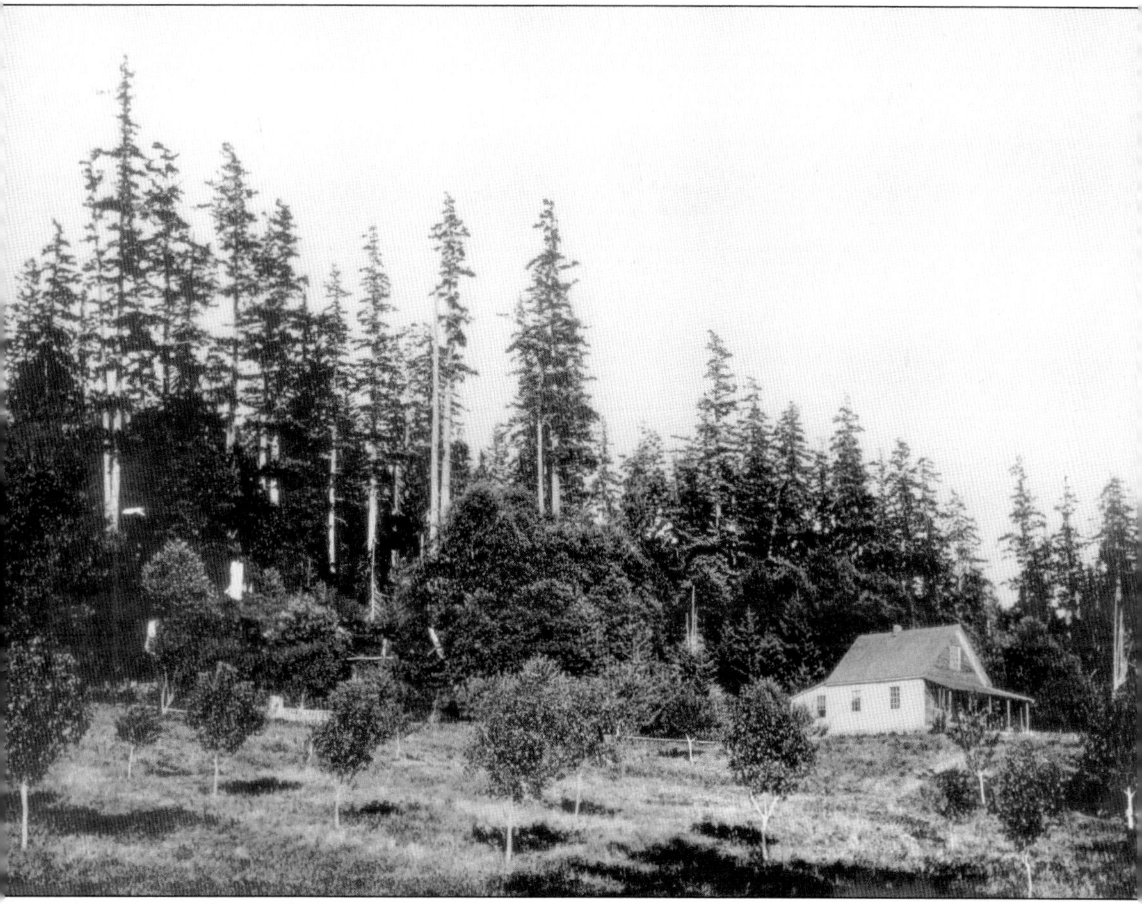

In the rainy Pacific Northwest, corn and wheat were tricky to grow and turkeys were hard to raise, but dairy cows loved the plump oats and green grass and fruit trees blossomed. John McLoughlin was probably the first to grow apple seedlings, but by the 1920s Clark County was the prune capital of the world. This photograph of a Pacific Northwest prune orchard was probably typical of the first of its kind in the Washougal area. Before fruit trees could be planted, long-standing cedar forests had to be removed using handheld axes and whip saws. In the late 1800s, tree stumps were removed with a stump puller, a tool that consisted of gears, chain cables, and four sturdy horses. Balthaser Acker, who purchased the Peter Stice homestead on Mount Norway in 1870, was among the first farmers to invest in the new fruit industry. In addition to dairy farming, Acker planted 11 acres of Italian prunes. Farmers in 1900 earned 5¢ for every box of fruit. (Courtesy University of Washington Libraries, UW14516.)

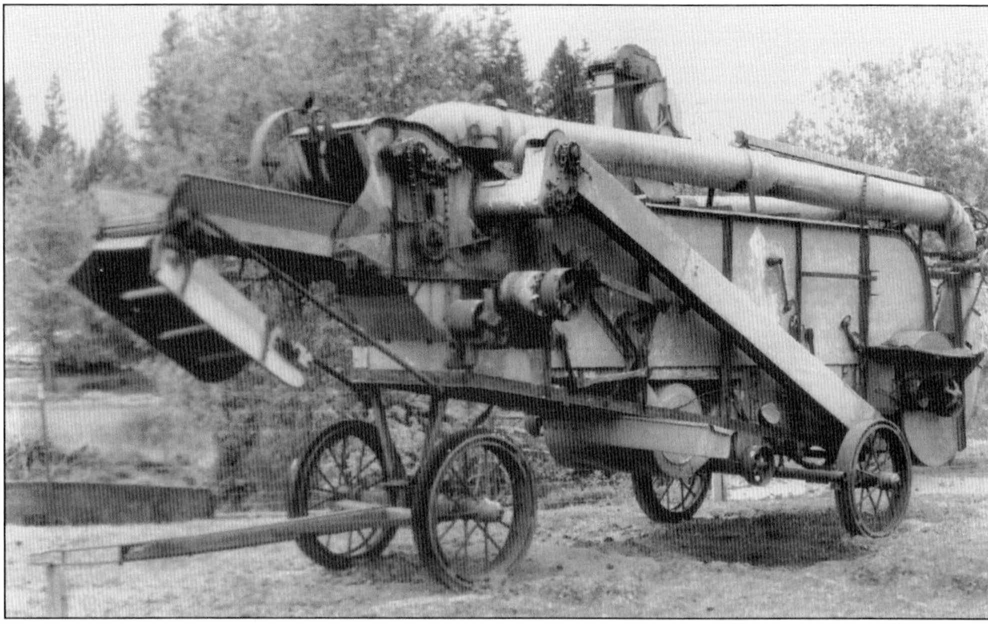

This mechanical threshing machine harvested grain by separating the kernel, chaff, and straw. Threshers were time savers but pricey. And the horses needed to cart them through the field were expensive to keep and feed. Cooperative crews moved from farm to farm so costs were shared among neighbors. This Allis-Chalmers threshing machine, owned by Dorris Robb, did one better than the rest as it blew the straw directly into the barn.

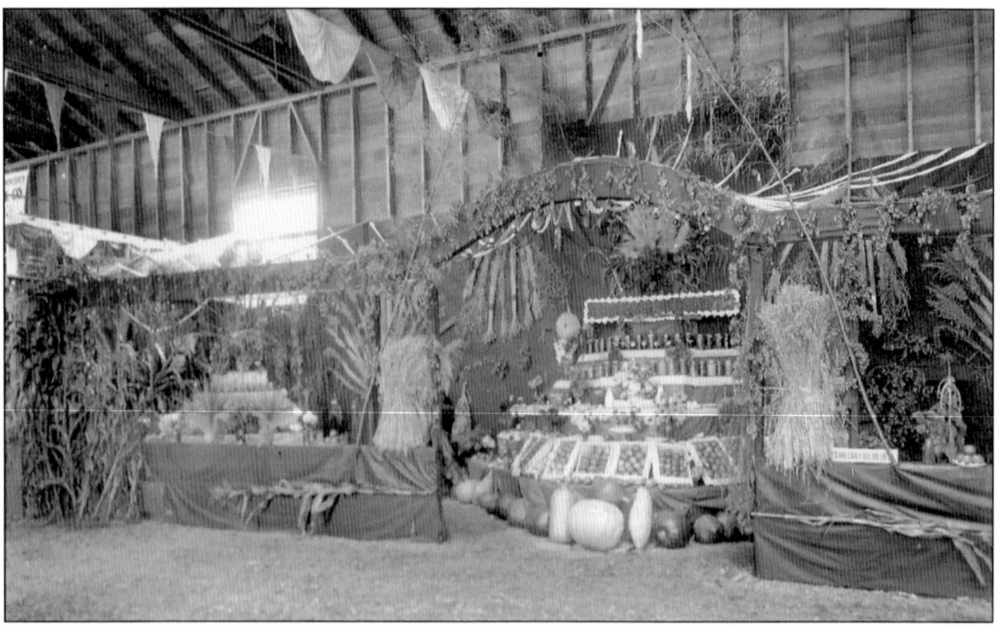

The Grange was an important social and political network for farming families. Sunnyside homesteader Anna Kloninger oversaw this Washougal Grange produce display at the Clark County Fair around 1895. The Washington State Grange was established by eight local granges at the Camas Odd Fellows Hall in 1889. The "grangers," in an attempt to thwart big eastern business interests, supported populist issues, including women's rights, direct voting, and public utilities.

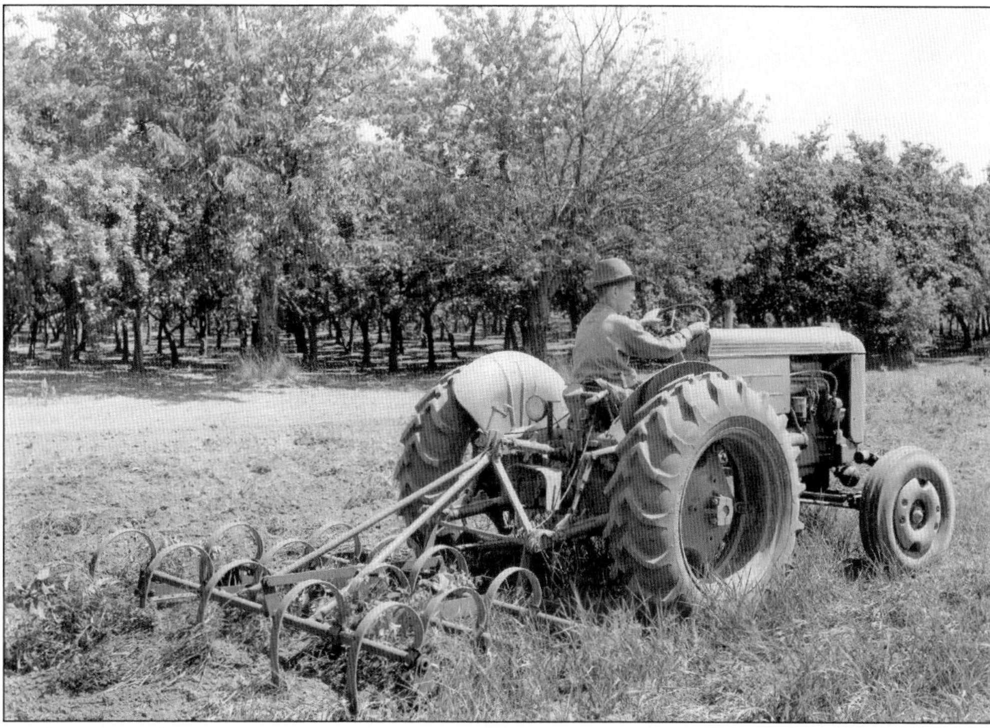

Twelve-year-old Danny Holderman operates a Case tractor on Fritz Braun Jr.'s hazelnut orchard, at Thirty-fourth and A Streets in 1950. In the 1940s, due to the combination of World War II, embargoes, and insect damage, the prune business ceased to be profitable. Many orchardists diversified by planting nut-bearing trees such as the hazelnut.

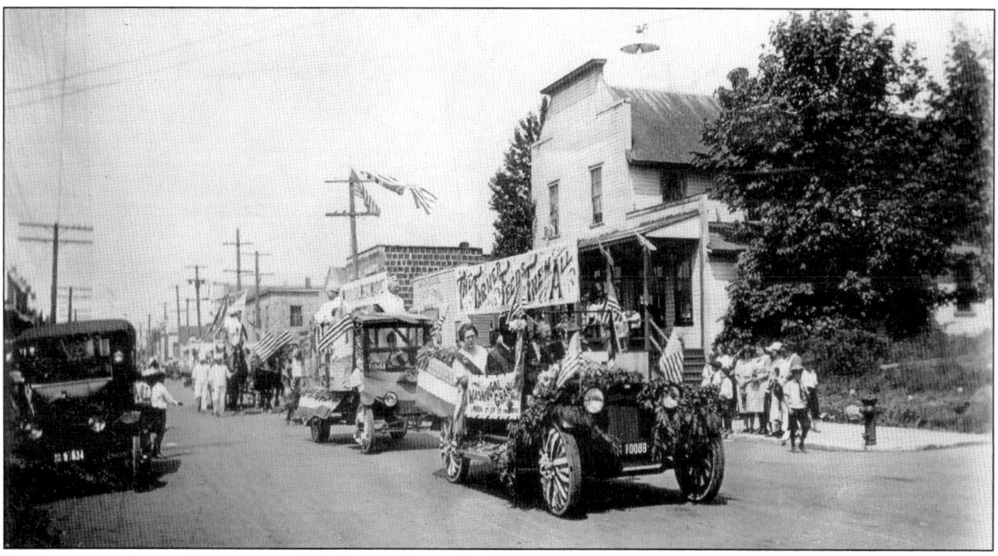

In this parade in downtown Washougal in the 1920s, the car in front belongs to the Washougal Grange and is strewn with flowers, ribbons, and flags. The banner on the truck following reads "Washougal Meat Market." Both vehicles are in front of the grange building where a banner reads "The Farmer Feeds Them All." The Washougal Harness and Saddlery Shop is to the left of the grange.

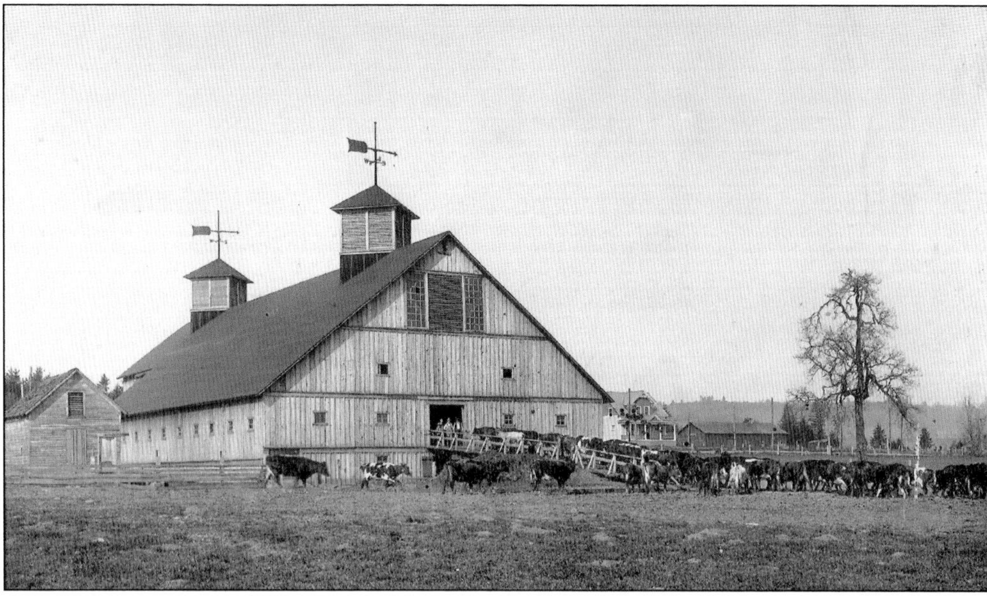

Many Washougal-area dairies were prosperous, including the Steigerwald Dairy pictured here. Washougal land was perfect for dairying, and the Portland market was bottomless. Dairy farmers worked long days the entire week and were protective of, and proud of, their herds. James Knox Polk Jones ran a small dairy farm. Some of the names he gave his calves included Come Along, Bumblebee, Wait a Minute, and I Will.

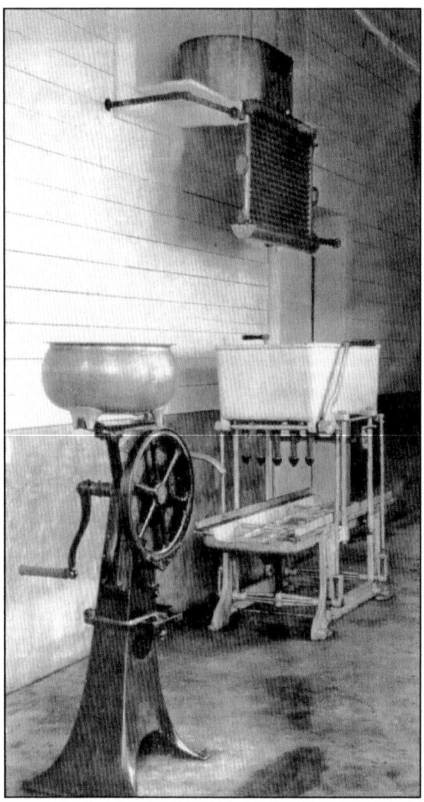

This equipment belonged to the Knapp Dairy in 1920. Milk was poured into the canister on the top shelf. It filtered through a cooling radiator fed by cold water pipes and emptied into the large white tub. The tub apparatus was probably an early bottler. Five nozzles underneath the tub could be fitted into bottles that were then filled with milk. The basin and crank machine (front) was a churn.

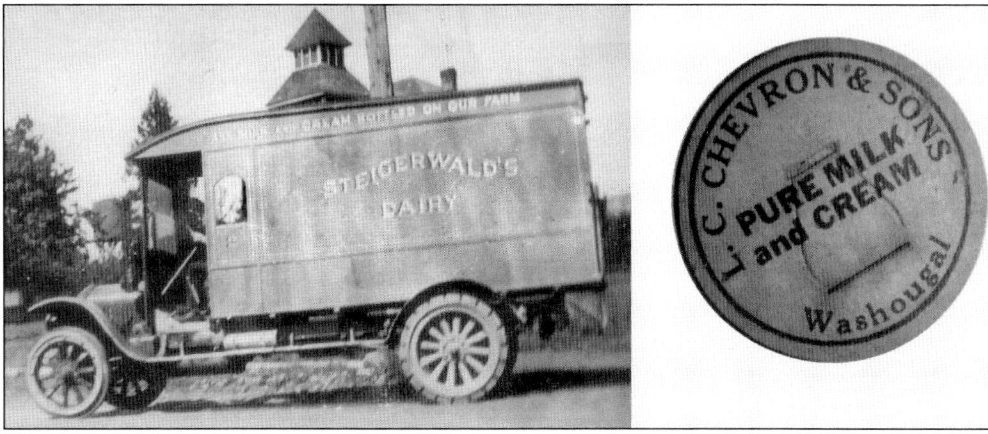

Dairy farmers in Washougal supplied milk to Portland, Vancouver, and internationally. Canned milk products were widely exported, and milk from the Camas-Washougal area supplied Fort Vancouver and the army in both world wars. Local dairies also supplied residents with milk, cream, and butter. Trucks replaced the horse and cart with efficient transport. Bottles were stoppered with chunky corks stamped with the names of dairymen.

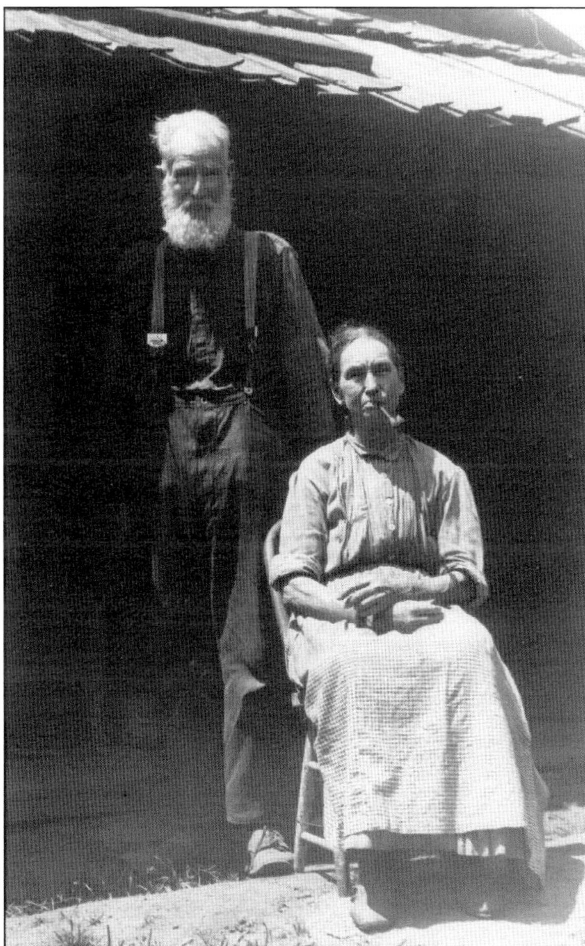

James Knox Polk Jones and his wife lived in Sunnyside along the little Washougal River in the 1900s. Polk was a songwriter and wrote songs during World War I, some of which were published. Jones's neighbor, Anna Kloninger, took this photograph. The Kloningers, Anna and Gustav, emigrated from Germany in 1887 and grew bulbs and flower seeds for the Portland market.

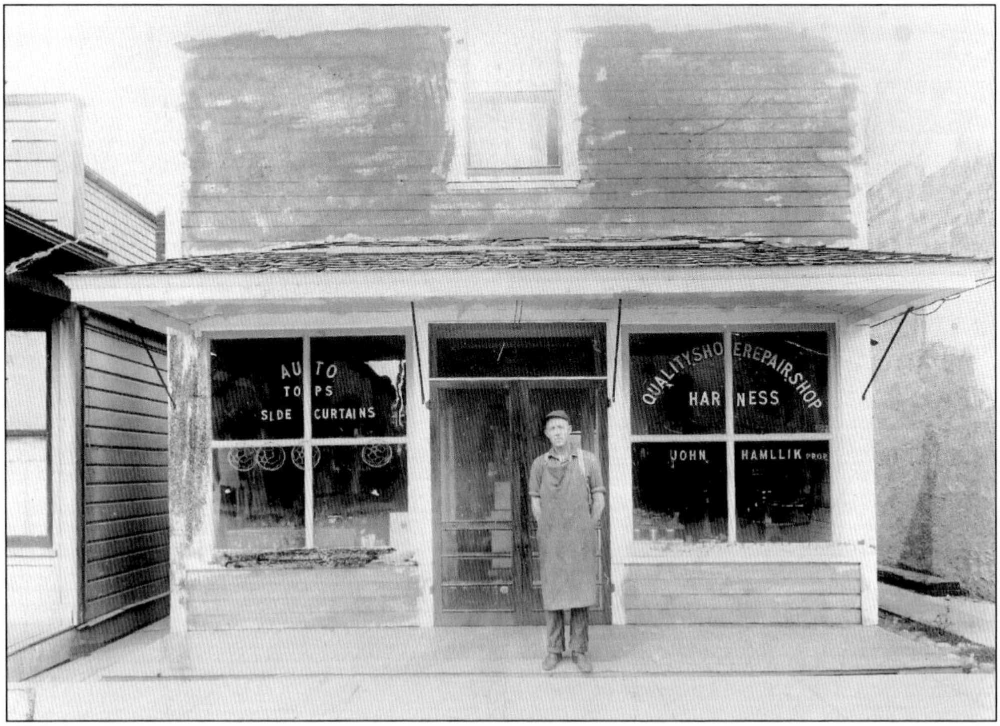

John Hamllik, wearing a sturdy apron, owned a leatherworking shop on B Street during the 1920s. A craftsman, he worked leather for many uses, from gentlemen's boots and ladies shoes to buggy harnesses. The advent of the automobile brought more leather work, and Hamllik advertised automobile tops and side curtains in the shop window. John's son Bill also became a shopkeeper in Washougal.

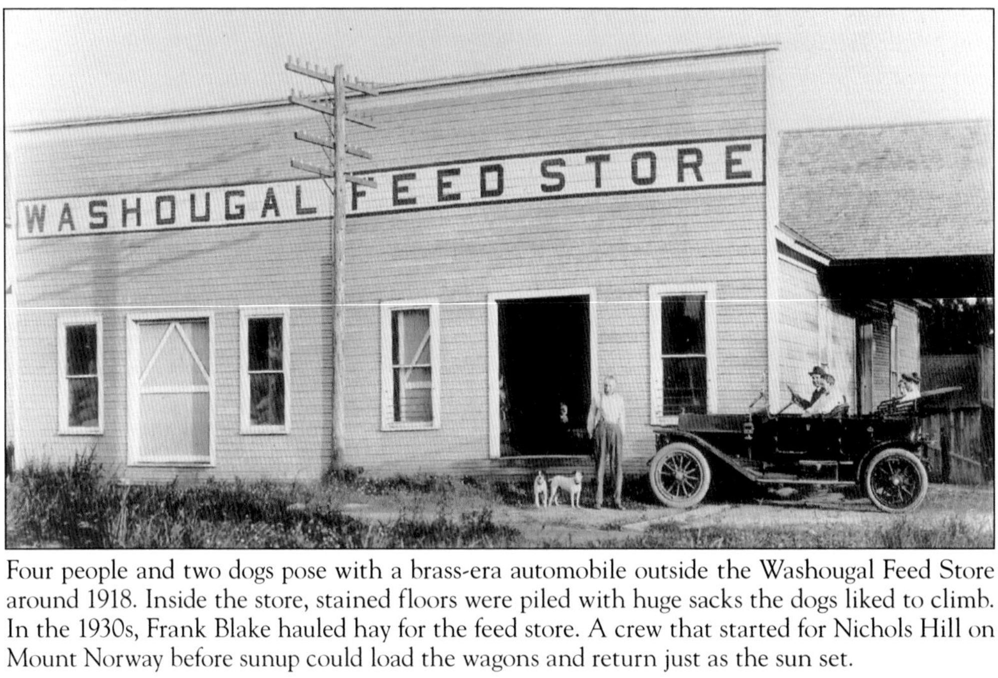

Four people and two dogs pose with a brass-era automobile outside the Washougal Feed Store around 1918. Inside the store, stained floors were piled with huge sacks the dogs liked to climb. In the 1930s, Frank Blake hauled hay for the feed store. A crew that started for Nichols Hill on Mount Norway before sunup could load the wagons and return just as the sun set.

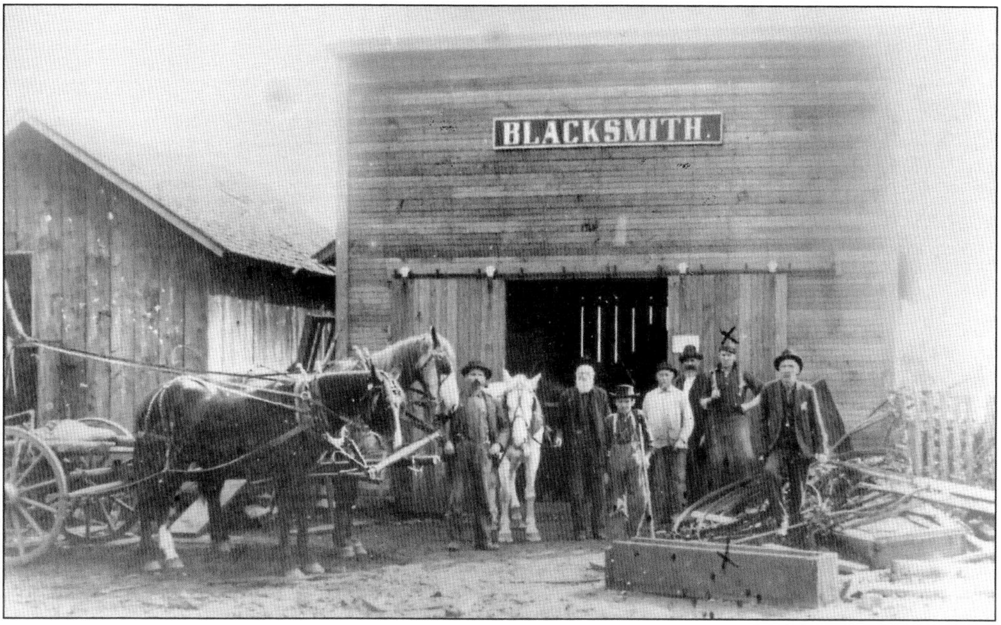

Blacksmith Sam Jones stands (second from right) outside the blacksmith shop he owned around 1900. Located on the corner of Washington and Second Streets behind Jay Baldwin's dry goods store, "the smithy" closed around 1928. The building was converted to housing. Sam and Reggie Jones then ran the soda and lunch counter that Reggie had built adjacent to the old shop around the same year.

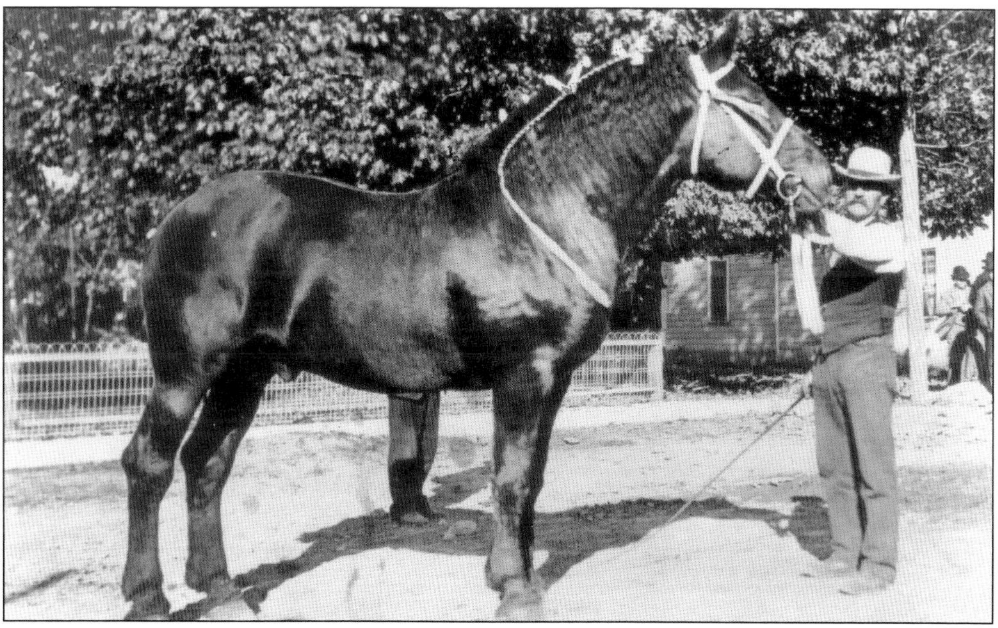

In 1915, 13 businessmen invested a reported fortune of $3,500 to purchase this stud horse, shipped all the way from France. German immigrant Henry G. Sadewasser Sr., pictured here, may have gained an appreciation for horses while serving in the Prussian army around 1880. He and his wife, Christina, brought their growing family to Washougal in 1887. They had seven children: Herman, Lena, Minnie, Albert, Henry Jr., Carl, and Amanda.

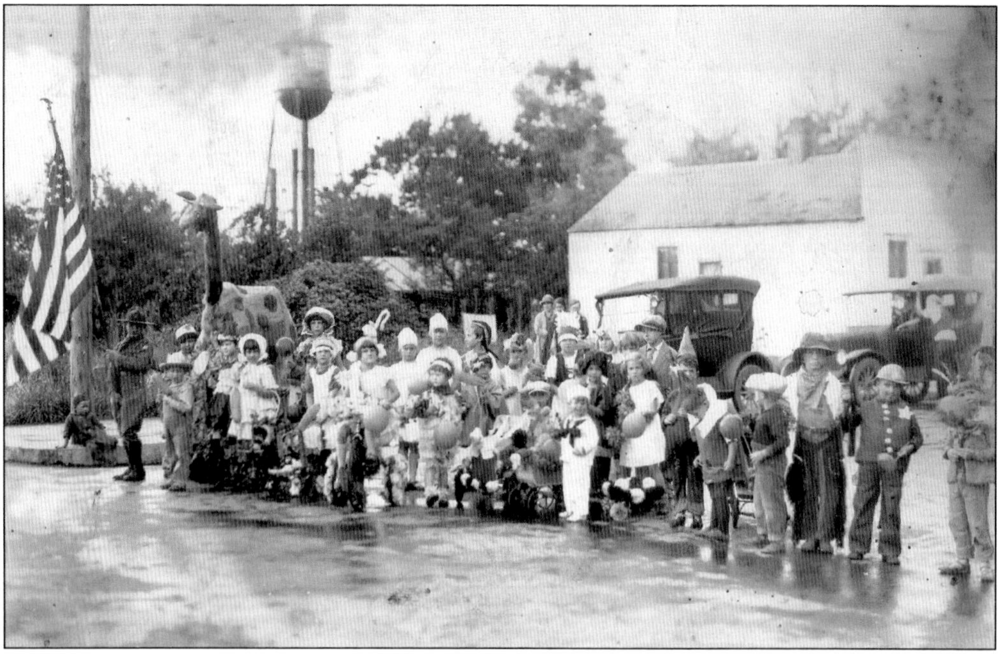

Perhaps the occasion for this *c.* 1928 children's parade is May Day. The kids, dressed as clowns, cowboys, Indians, a sheriff, and little Bo Peep, are garlanded with flowers and carry balloons. Some ride garlanded tricycles, pull wagons, push buggies, or carry baskets of flowers. A small boy rides in a miniature car. Those pictured include Wayland Stayton (with flag), Burt Knutson, Ann Workman (Good), Marie Fitzgerald, and Doris Armstrong.

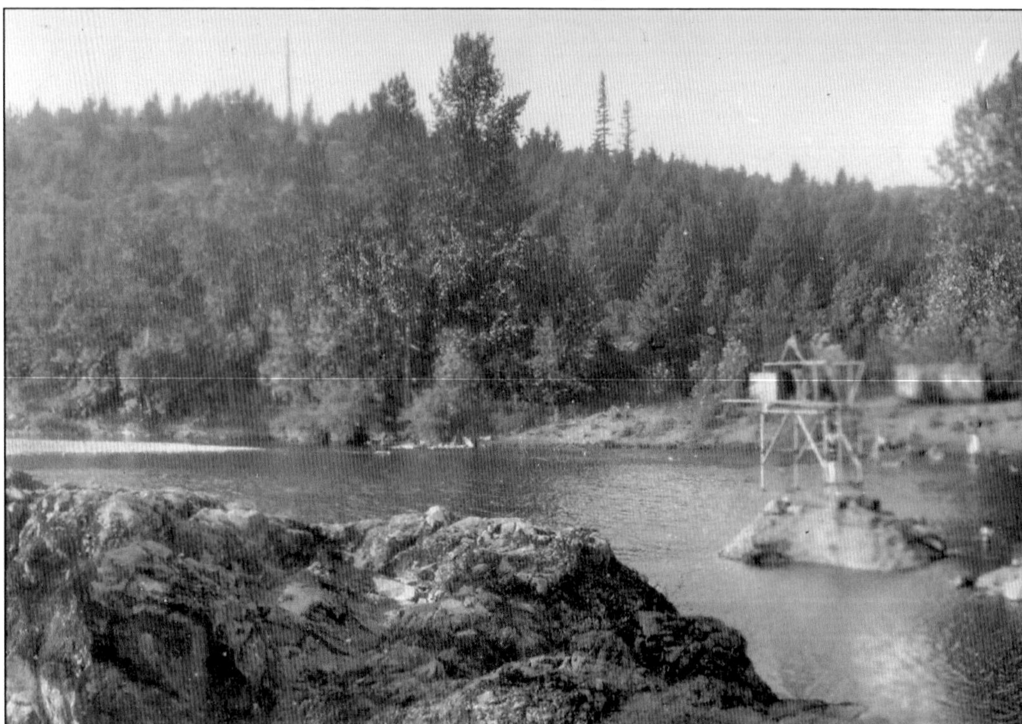

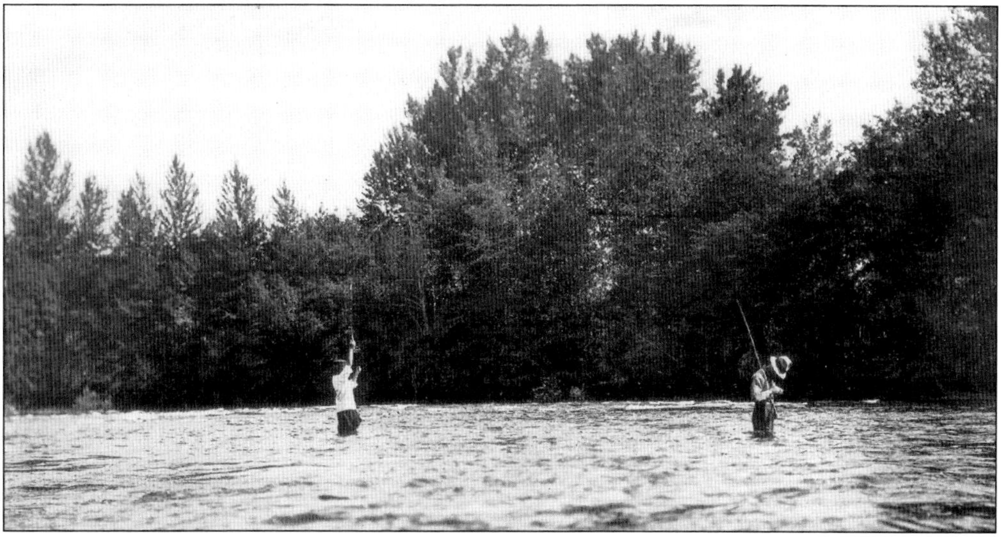

River recreation was not limited to picnicking and swimming. In this undated photograph, schoolteacher Martha Kloninger Ford takes time for fly fishing with an unidentified companion in the Washougal River.

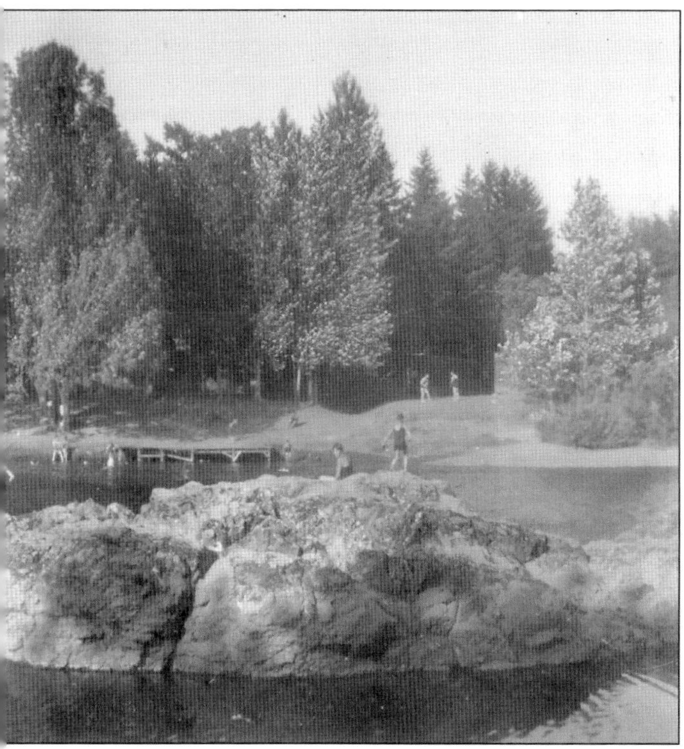

The sandy swimming hole on the Washougal River has, over the years, been a loved outdoor spot, and the Camas Fire Department offered swimming lessons there through the 1940s. Picnics and socials were also held at the river. In one type of social in the 1920s, girls would pack lunch baskets that were then put up for charity auction. Whoever paid the highest price for a basket would get to eat lunch with the girl who packed it and her mother. Generally girls would tell their boyfriends what basket to bid on. But the boys had better be paying attention. According to Thomas Gentry, a witness to the fact, a lot of trouble could ensue if the boy accidentally bid money on the wrong girl's lunch.

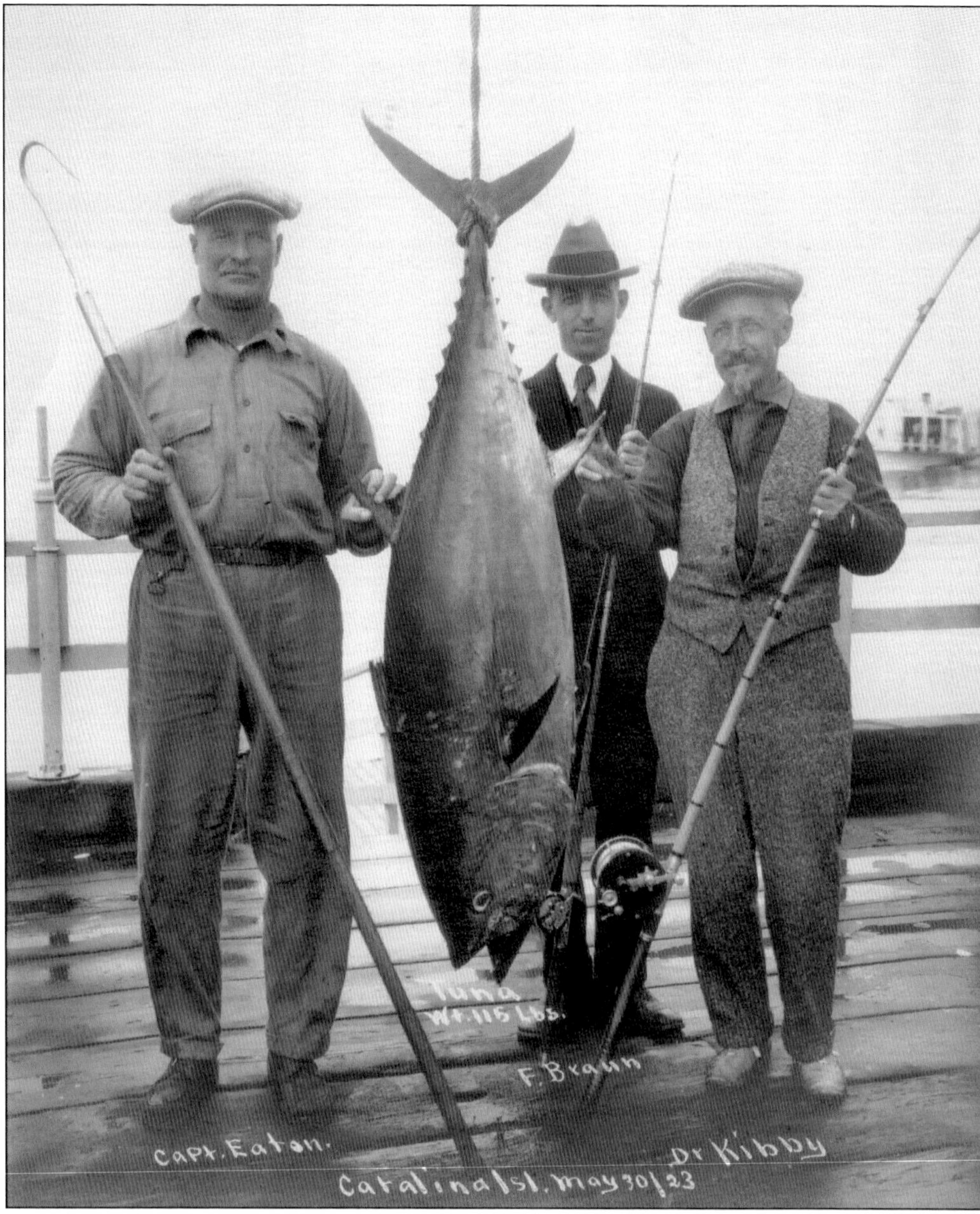

Fritz Braun Jr. poses with a 115-pound tuna next to Captain ? Eaton (left) and Dr. ? Kibby (right) at Catalina Island in 1923. Children raised in Washougal developed an enduring love of river travel, river mammals, fish stories, and fishing. In 1931, a juvenile killer whale swam up the Columbia River. The whale was named Oswald, and many local stories have grown up around this event. According to one story, a Washougal Norwegian immigrant harpooned Oswald after he got stuck in the Washougal slough. This turned out to be a mistake, as the town turned on him in uproar. Oswald was placed in a wooden coffin, complete with metal supports specially made to fit the whale's fins. The whale, coffin and all, was transported up to Livingston Mountain and left above ground. The tale of Oswald the whale has stretched over the years, but at the core, the tale is true. Oswald's coffin, however, was likely a tank of formaldehyde intended to preserve his body for display. (Thanks to Edward Margeson for the whale tale.)

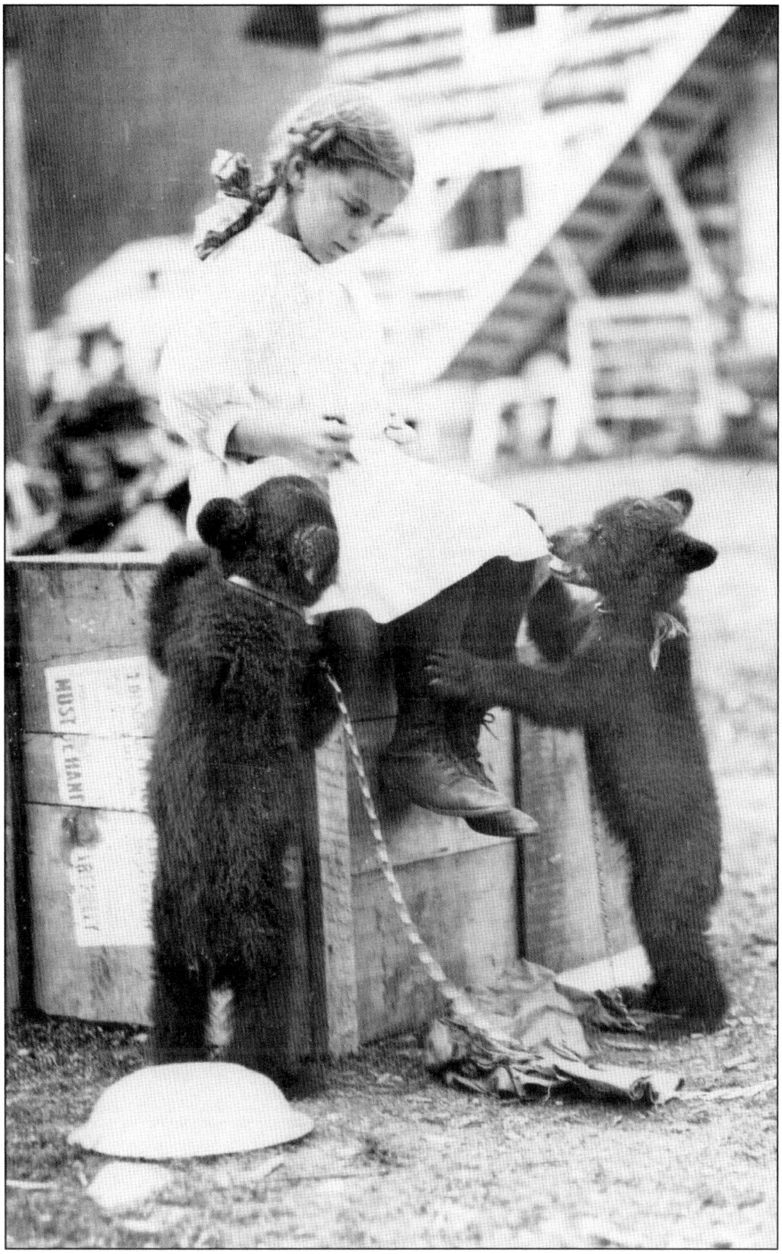

Emily Webber Bright recorded the history of her family and included a story about two baby bears. In 1896, a pair of loggers staying at the Webber's hotel in Washougal killed a mother bear. The men brought the orphaned cubs to the Webber children to look after. Emily recorded that the cubs were playful as kittens and always happy with honey or sugar to eat. Once in their quest for sugar, the cubs got stuck in flypaper, put out to keep the flies away. They were trapped quickly and had to be rescued. Though they were tame, as the bears grew up they became too strong to be playmates for children. The Webber family did not keep the bears after they were grown. Though unusual, it was not unheard of for a family like the Webbers to take in orphaned bear cubs. This photograph of a girl with cubs was taken in Alaska around 1910. (Photograph by Frank G. Carpenter; courtesy Library of Congress.)

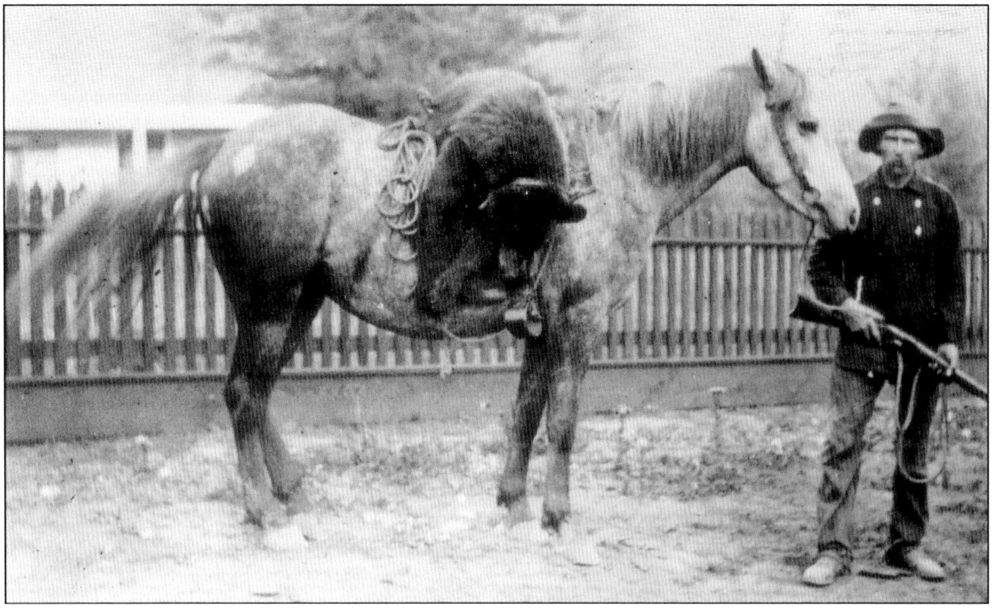

Wild bears were considered dangerous pests, and a dead one usually meant there had been a scary encounter. In 1906, Mr. Linch killed a bear and brought it into town on a horse. Horses are beasts with good sense. In general, a horse will not cooperate with anyone who asks it to carry a bear around, dead or not.

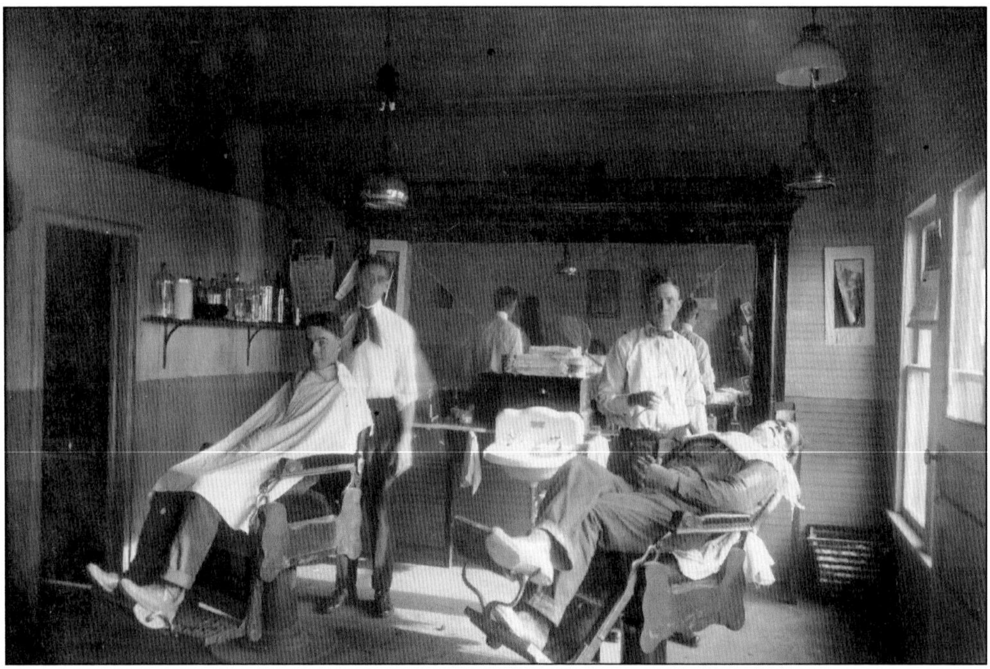

These barbershop customers receive a haircut and a shave in 1916. In the back left corner, a calendar advertises "Cardui" as "a reliable woman's tonic." The men pictured are unidentified. David Nelson "Nels" Gary owned a longtime barbershop in Washougal. During the 1920s, local youths shut a cow in his shop overnight as a prank. Nels released it and cleaned up after it the next morning.

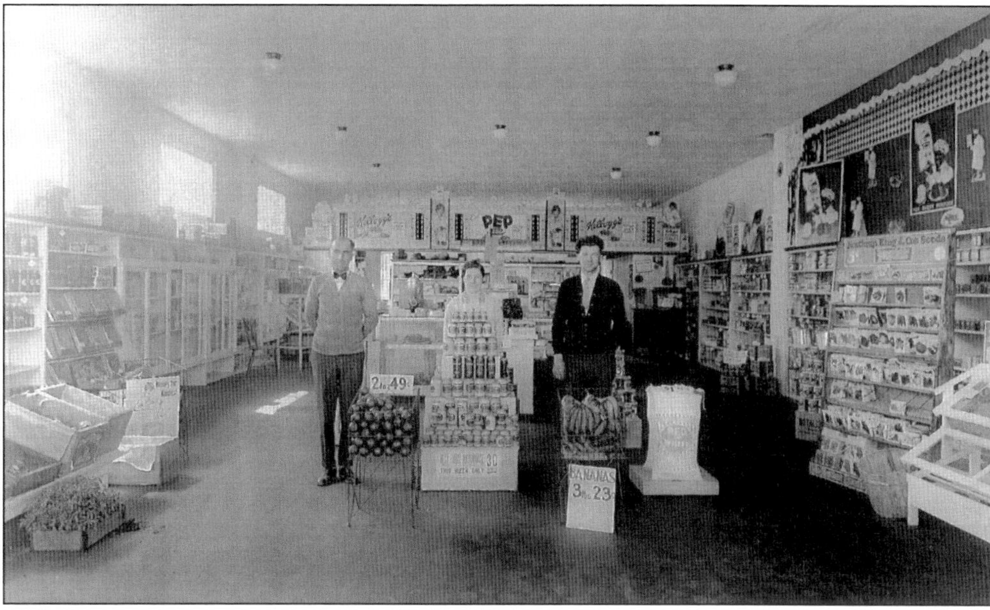

M. J. "Jay" Baldwin and his wife moved to Washougal in 1910. For four years, they lived in Forest Hill, where Jay ran a sawmill. In 1919, Jay purchased a shoe and harness shop in Washougal, expanding the business to include groceries and dry goods and taking his son Everett Lee Baldwin (left) on as partner. Employee Walter Jenny (right) became a partner sometime after 1925. In this 1920s photograph, Mabel Baldwin (center) is also pictured.

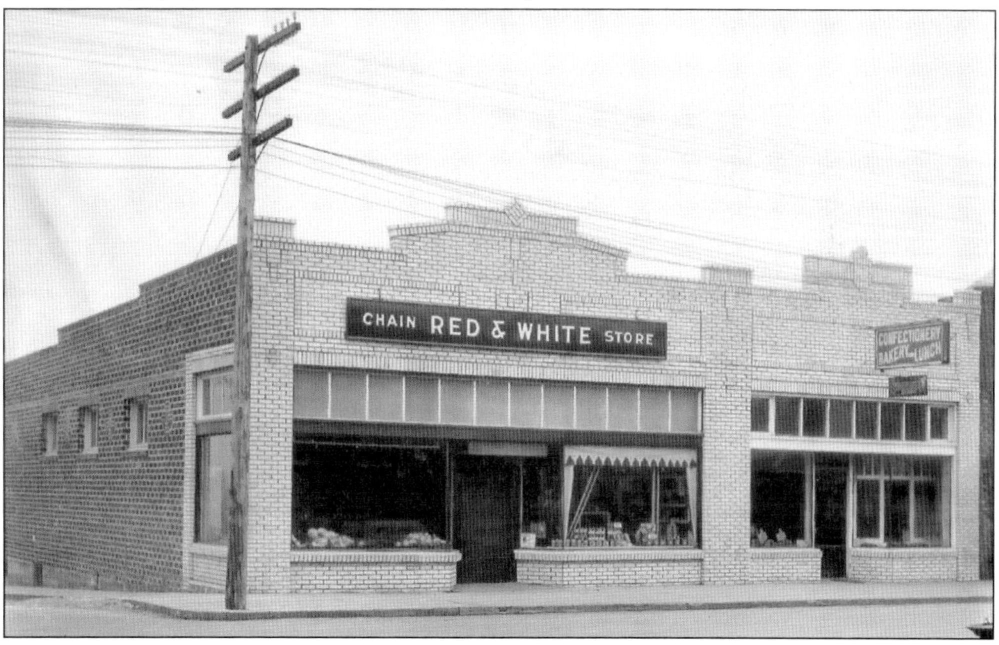

Lee Baldwin married Mary Pauline Prensyger around 1922. Walter Jenny married Sarah Wright in 1927. It is unknown if Jenny was still a store partner when, in 1928, Lee and his father, Jay, built the Red and White store, a franchise for Red and White grocery products. After the Baldwins, store owners included Mr. Holmberg, Pete Gabriel, Jerry Craig, and Pete Puleo. It is now the Fireside Tavern.

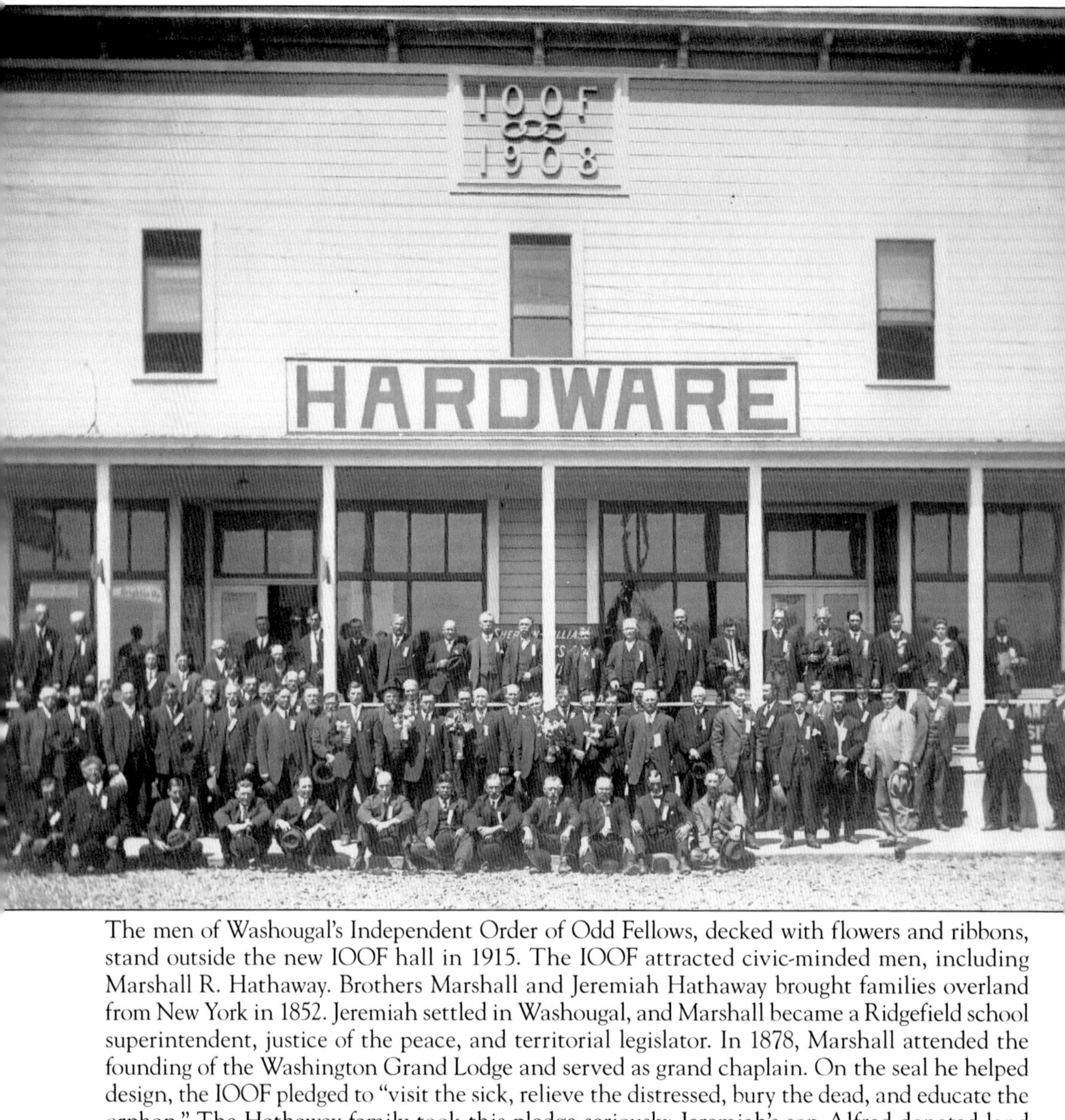

The men of Washougal's Independent Order of Odd Fellows, decked with flowers and ribbons, stand outside the new IOOF hall in 1915. The IOOF attracted civic-minded men, including Marshall R. Hathaway. Brothers Marshall and Jeremiah Hathaway brought families overland from New York in 1852. Jeremiah settled in Washougal, and Marshall became a Ridgefield school superintendent, justice of the peace, and territorial legislator. In 1878, Marshall attended the founding of the Washington Grand Lodge and served as grand chaplain. On the seal he helped design, the IOOF pledged to "visit the sick, relieve the distressed, bury the dead, and educate the orphan." The Hathaway family took this pledge seriously; Jeremiah's son Alfred donated land for Hathaway Park and Hathaway School in the 1920s and 1930s. The IOOF chapters of Camas and Washougal merged around 1990. The building still stands and is one of B Street's enduring historical landmarks.

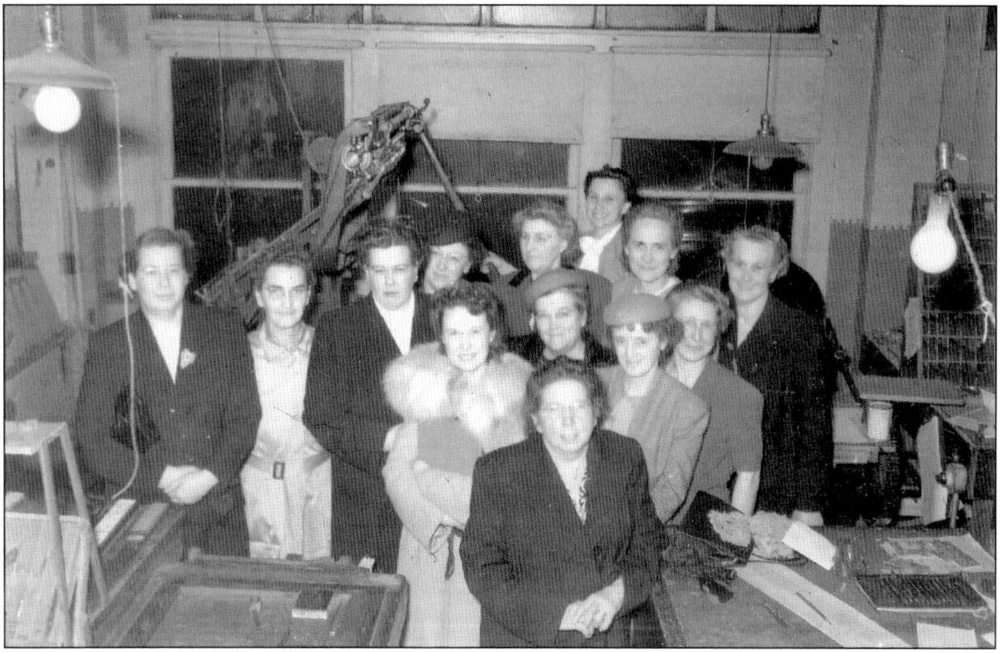

The Washougal Business and Professional Women's Club, first organized in 1924 by Mrs. G. T. Mott, meets here at the *Columbia Valley Advocate* shop in 1944. Pictured, from left to right, are (first row) Jeanette Halling; (second row) secretary Winnifred Minor, Maude Sill, unidentified, Clara Nystrom; (third row) Julia Suver, Maude Teusher, Anne Sault, Martha Ford, Agatha McCuddin, Gudrun Jemtegaard, and Tessie Smead; (fourth row) Stella Vollmar of the *Columbia Valley Advocate*.

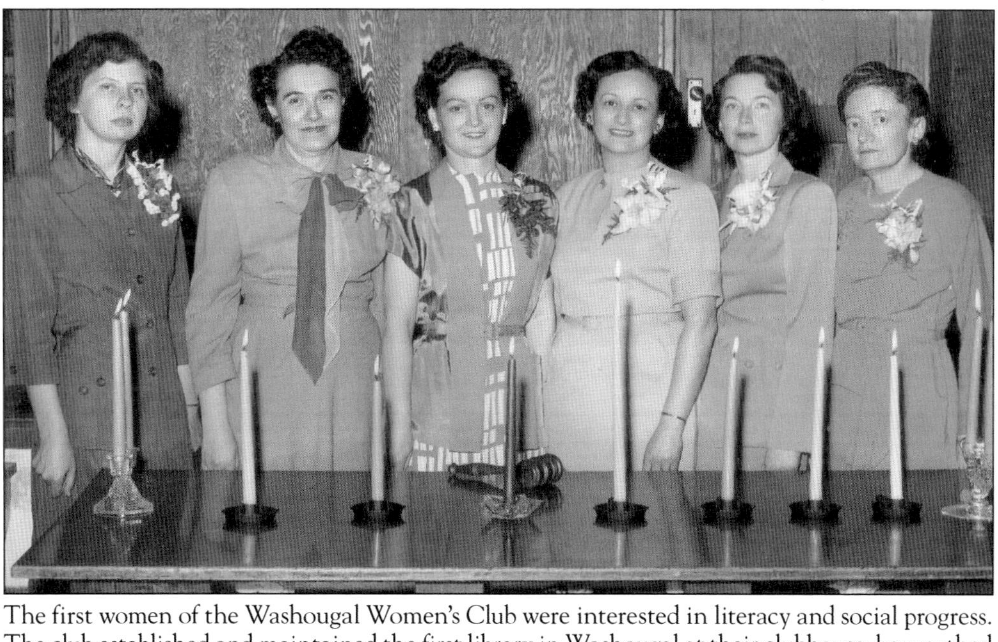

The first women of the Washougal Women's Club were interested in literacy and social progress. The club established and maintained the first library in Washougal at their clubhouse, bequeathed to them by Mable Moody in 1931. Hazel Burris ran the library. In 1951, Washougal's Business and Professional Women's Club members included, from left to right here, Marjorie Blodgett, Arliene Larkin, Ruth Claus, Doris Goff, Wanona Lennox, and Hazel Burris.

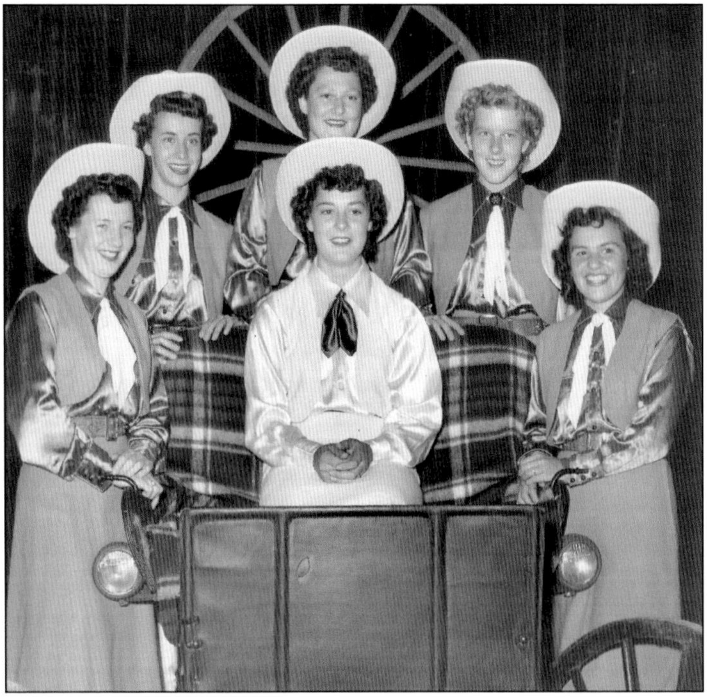

Washougal used to be big on rodeo. The area, though more suburban today, used to be more equestrian. In the 1950s, the Washougal Rodeo Grounds on the Washougal River was the site of many a bucking bronco and corresponding "saddle bronc." Choosing a rodeo queen was part of the fun, and in 1950, Doris Jean Walling won the honor. She sits (center) in her royal buggy, surrounded by princesses.

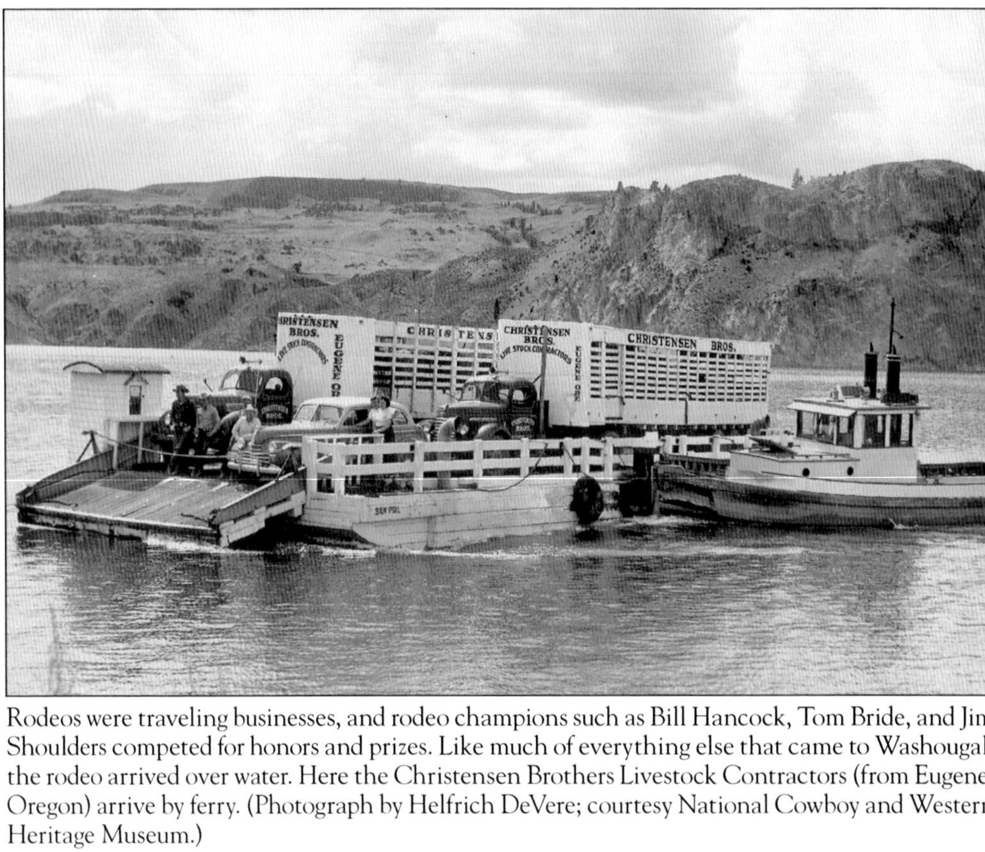

Rodeos were traveling businesses, and rodeo champions such as Bill Hancock, Tom Bride, and Jim Shoulders competed for honors and prizes. Like much of everything else that came to Washougal, the rodeo arrived over water. Here the Christensen Brothers Livestock Contractors (from Eugene, Oregon) arrive by ferry. (Photograph by Helfrich DeVere; courtesy National Cowboy and Western Heritage Museum.)

A rodeo was as much a community event as a visiting enterprise. Local men and women competed in events, brought in their stock for show, and demonstrated their skills with horses and other livestock. These young Washougal women participated as part of the local celebration around 1952. Pictured, from left to right, are Reba Suber, unidentified, Norma Neder, Marie Redwine, unidentified, and Charmalee Allen.

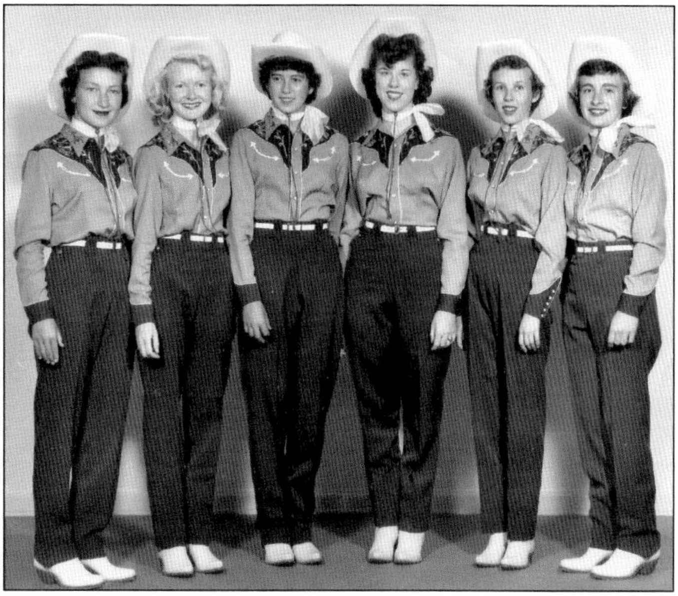

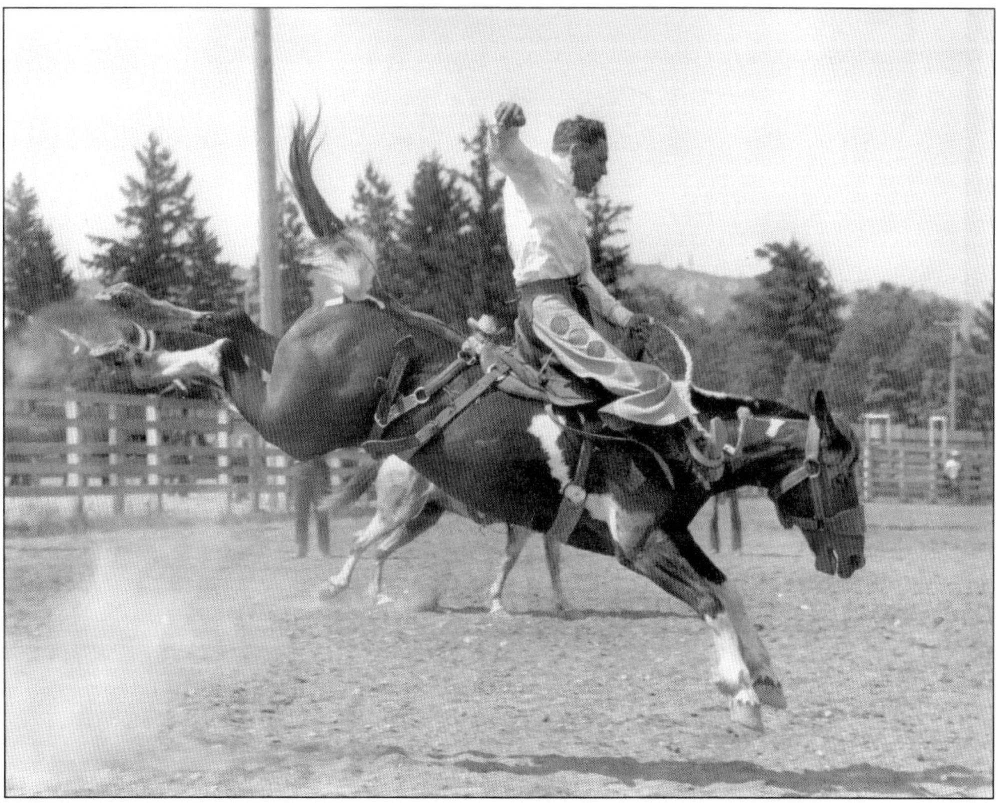

The rodeo brought big names to town. Champion rider Bud Linderman, who is pictured here on Skid Row Sue in Grants Pass, Oregon, was probably among them. Cowboys competed in several events, including calf roping, saddle bronc, bareback riding, and all around. Helfrich DeVere of Klamath Falls, Oregon, took this photograph and is considered by many to be America's foremost rodeo photographer. (Courtesy National Cowboy and Western Heritage Museum.)

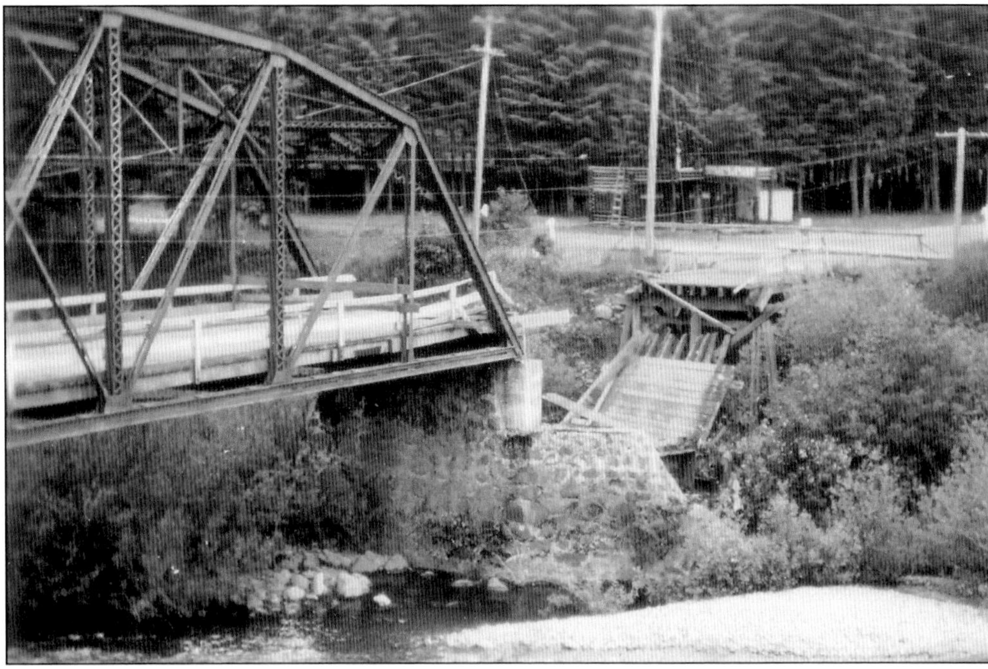

Washougal's first bridges were constructed of wood, including two covered wooden bridges, with one over Gibbon's creek. To accommodate the automobile, many bridges were rebuilt with cement and steel. But the old and the new did not always work well together. In 1929, two men were killed when a portion of the Seventeenth Street Bridge collapsed under Mr. Ammeter's county truck.

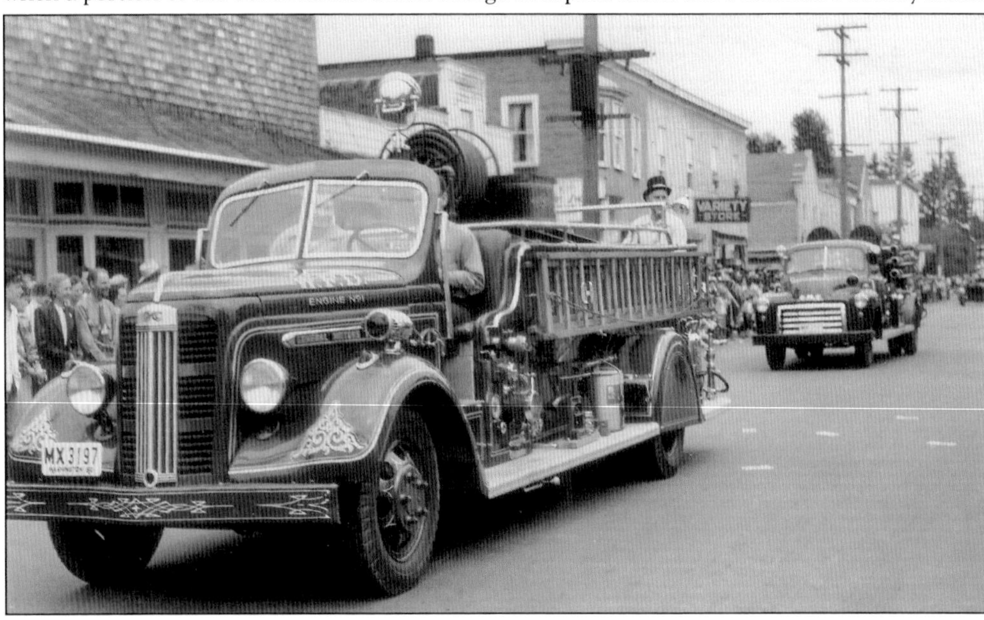

Many of Washougal's firefighters, pictured here in 1951, are volunteers. Search and Rescue crews are also everyday heroes trained to respond to any crisis. Though sometimes there are false alarms. Once after a plea from law enforcement and on a mission of absolute secrecy, Search and Rescue geared up and deployed deep into the forest. Their target? A casserole-munching Sasquatch. A man went down in the search, but no Sasquatch was found. It may still be at large.

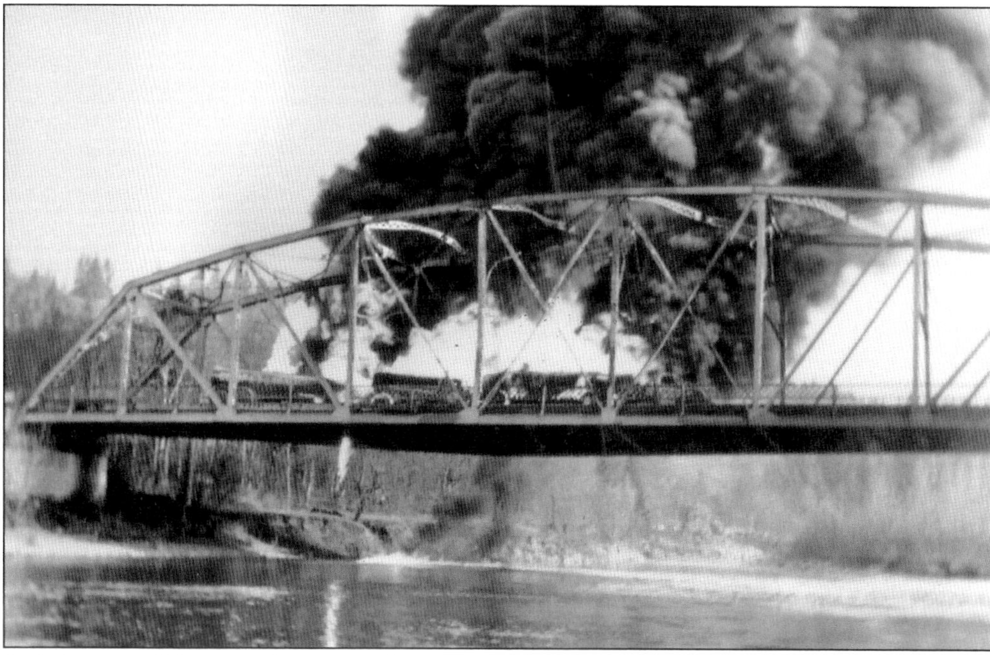

In February 1947, an explosion on Highway 14's Washougal River Bridge caused such a fiery inferno that the bridge collapsed. The fire started when a hay truck sideswiped a truck convoy. The two westbound gasoline trucks and trailers collided, exploded, and burned. The hay truck emerged unscathed. After three hours of intense heat, the bridge fell into the river.

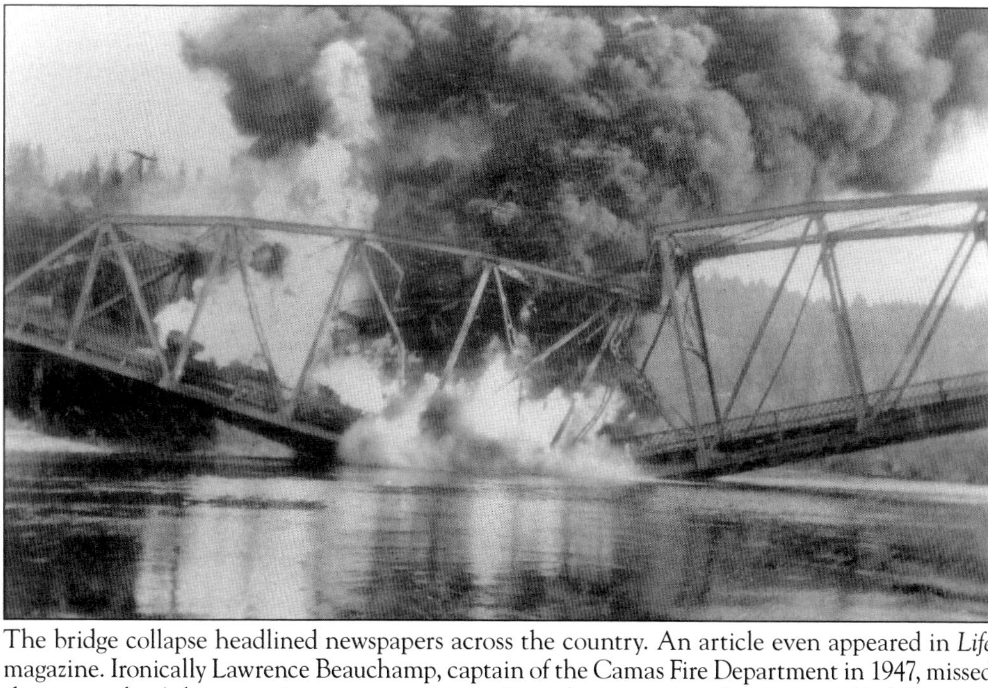

The bridge collapse headlined newspapers across the country. An article even appeared in *Life* magazine. Ironically Lawrence Beauchamp, captain of the Camas Fire Department in 1947, missed the spectacle. A key man in every emergency, Beauchamp was used to being called for every minor incident—yet he never got a call that day. Like "the big one that got away," Beauchamp could not believe he missed it.

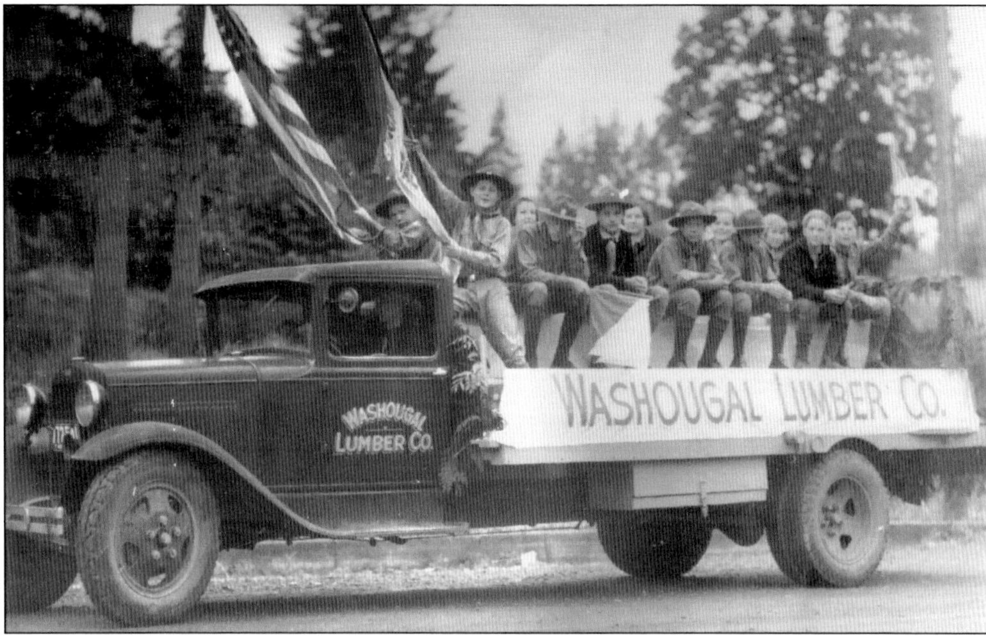

Ray Matlack and E. S. Dubois owned the Washougal Lumber Company in 1924 and sold Nu-Wood, a light, insulating pine. Ollie Wren drives the truck in this *c.* 1934 parade. The passengers, from left to right, are unidentified U.S. flag bearer, troop flag bearer Bob Peery, Sarah Wildon (Dedmore), Leo Baron, Ivan Martin, Corrine Johnson (Farrell), Art Meredith, Virginia Luthy, Stan Nystrom, Alice May Hutchinson, Bob Meredith, and Arnold Martin.

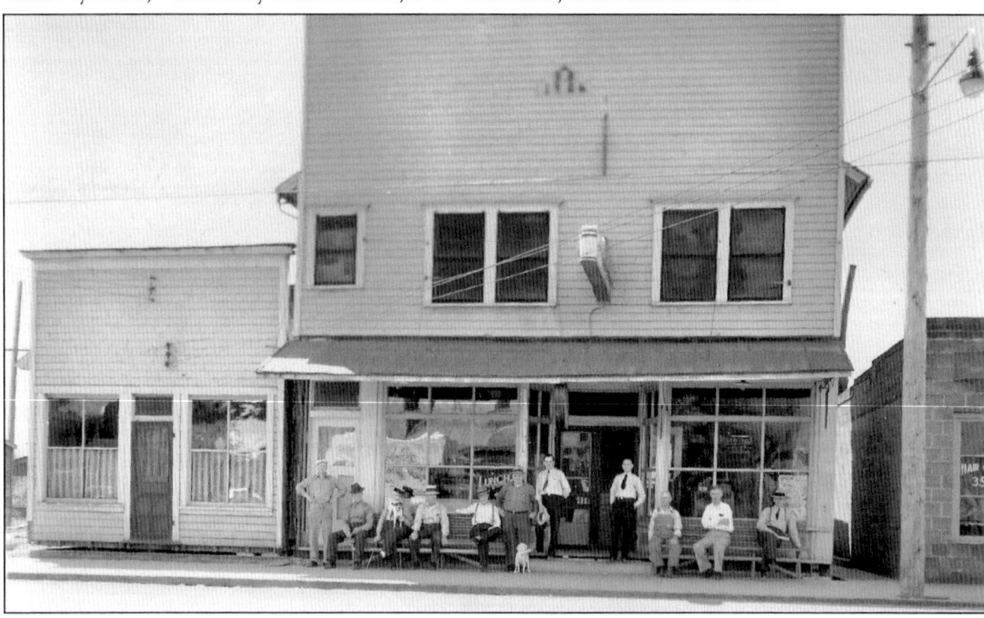

Fritz Braun Jr.'s Smoke Shop was on the southern corner of B and Seventeenth Streets in 1939. Perhaps due to good weather, there is quite a gathering on the stoop, including, from left to right, Mr. Mansfield (the beer man), Bill Ramsay, Jim O'Brian, Pud Durgan, Mort Sayles, Mark Maple, John Shute, Fritz Braun Jr., Walter Fitzgerald, Frank Kaiser, and Mayor George Peery Dibble, a three-time mayor of Washougal. (Photograph by Earl Jones.)

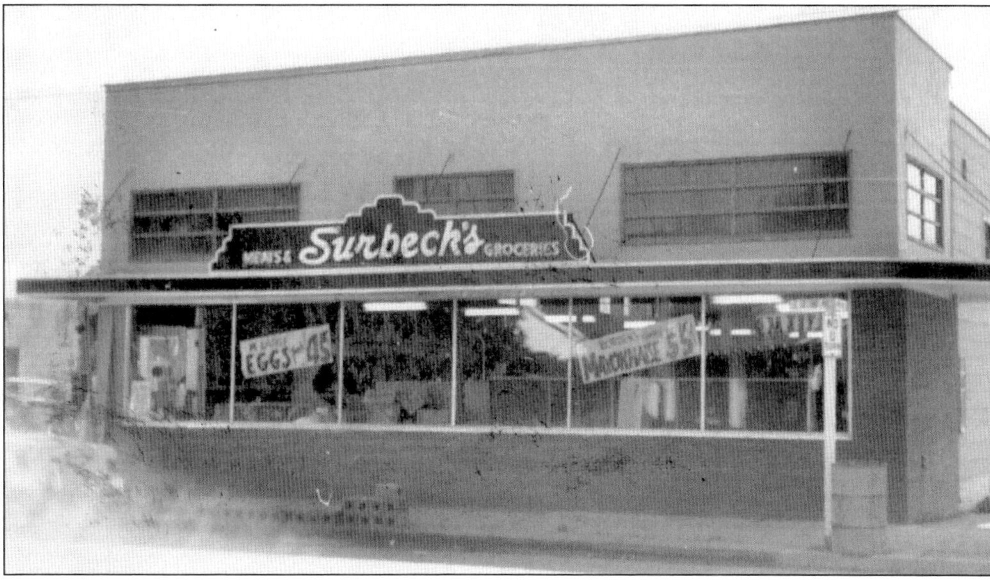

Many shops came and went along Washougal's main streets. Surbeck's Meats and Groceries lasted longer than most. Another long-standing store was Eggbert Nagel and George Dibble's Nagel and Dibble grocery and dry goods store. Other shops included Rundel and Scales, T. W. Pinn's bakery, Greenman and Sons on the corner of Second and Love Streets, H. A. Hill's coal and livery barn, the Smart Shop, and Kimbell's Variety Store.

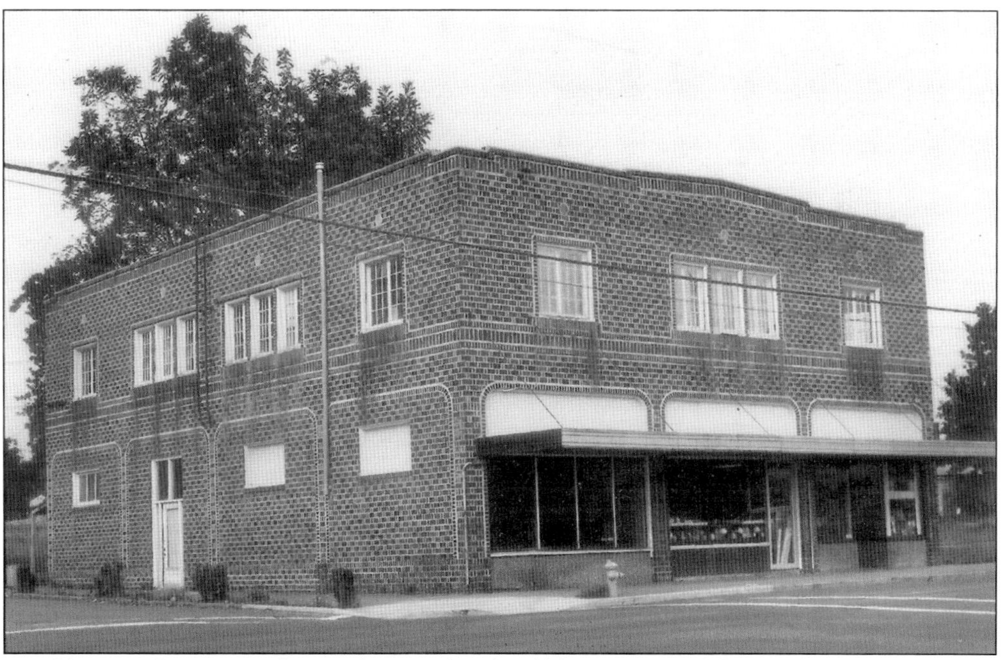

In addition to his partnership in the Nagel and Dibble grocery and dry goods store, at different points in his life the three-time Washougal mayor George Dibble owned a farm, feed store, opera house, and drugstore in the Acheson Building, pictured here. Built around 1927, the Acheson Building is on today's B and Eighteenth Streets.

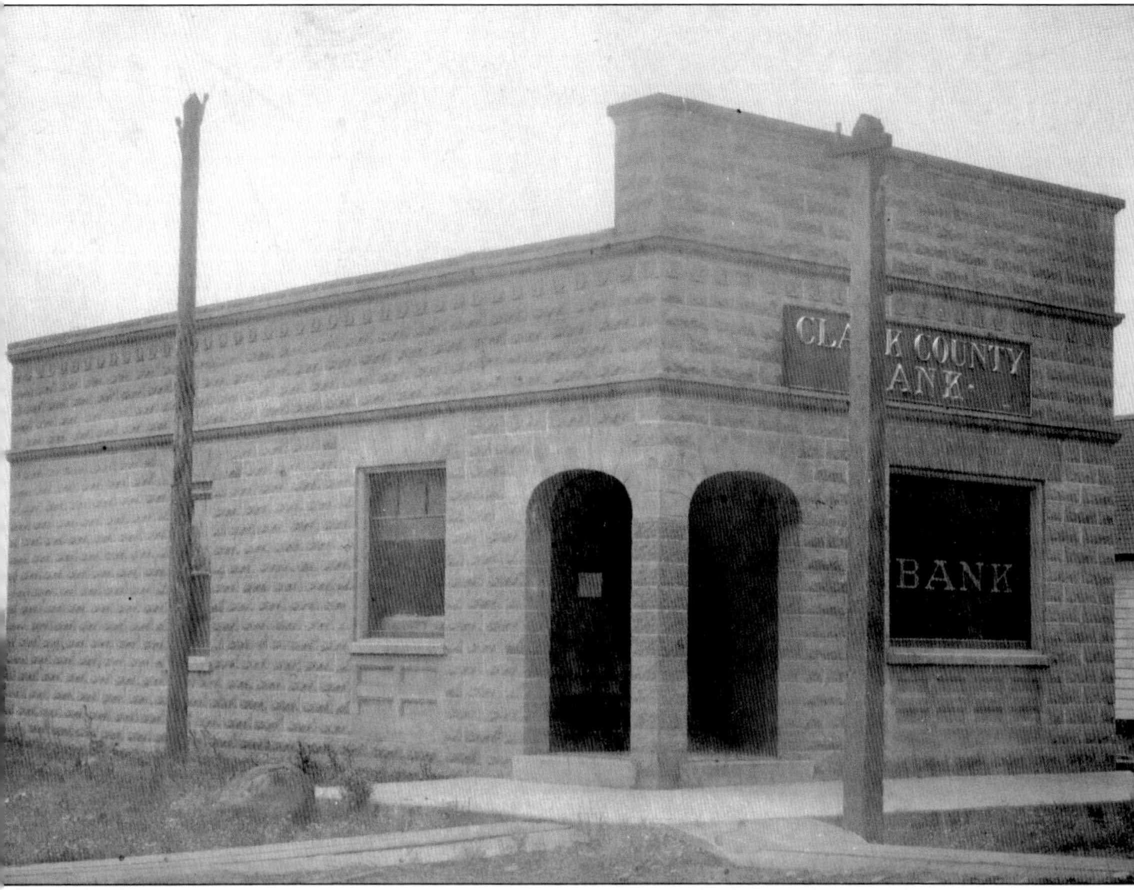

Charles M. Keep built, owned, and managed Washougal's first bank, the Clark County Bank, on B Street. Charles's brother, Tom Keep, was the vice president. In 1918, three men robbed the bank, taking several bags of money. Bank employees Kathryn Keep and Edith Pinn shouted the alarm, and Wes McCallister, a bystander, drove after the men as they sped up Washougal River Road. As if prepared for a pursuit, the robbers threw roofing nails onto the road behind them. Sheriff Til Taylor located the bank robbers at a Cape Horn cabin and took a posse with him to make the arrest, but the robbers fled. Two of them crossed the Columbia River, and when Sheriff Taylor pursued them, confronting the two men on a train in The Dalles, he was shot to death; one of the robbers had concealed a sawed-off shotgun. The murderer was sentenced to life in Salem State Prison. The other served time for armed robbery. The third robber was never found. The bank closed in 1931. The building changed hands and houses Los Jalapeños, a Mexican restaurant.

Five

Port to Port along the Gorge

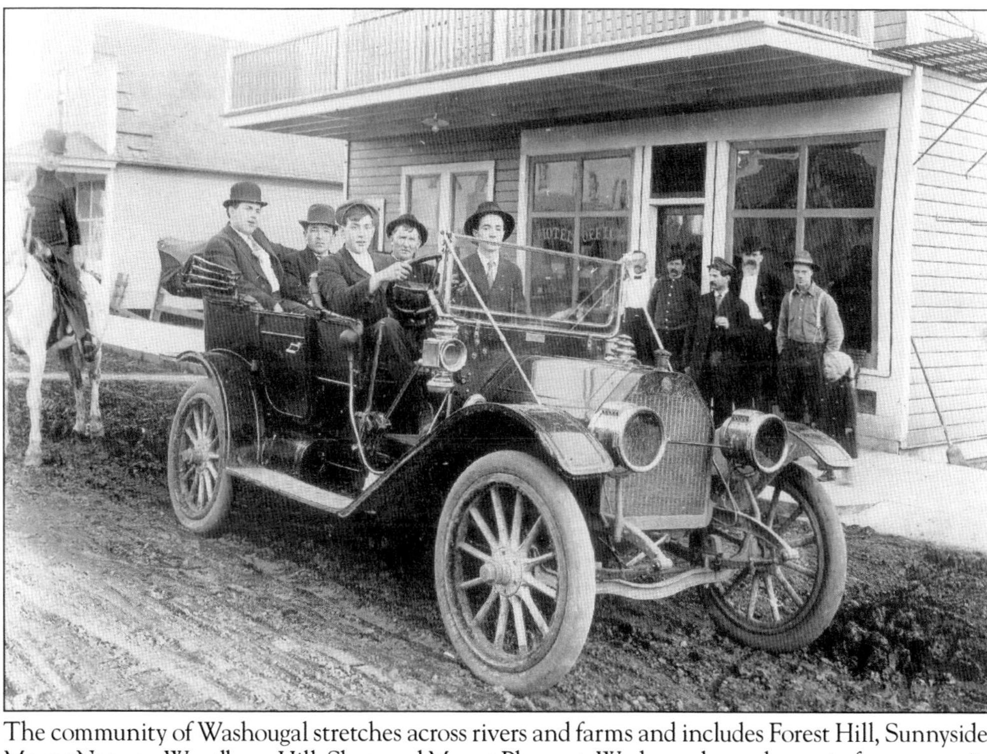

The community of Washougal stretches across rivers and farms and includes Forest Hill, Sunnyside, Mount Norway, Woodburn Hill, Skye, and Mount Pleasant. Washougal was also part of a community that stretched, port to port, along the Columbia River that included Cape Horn, Stevenson, and Cascade Locks. In 1910, Washougal's first car was big news. Cape Horn photographer Fred Froesschle hopped a steamship and took this photograph outside the Commercial Hotel.

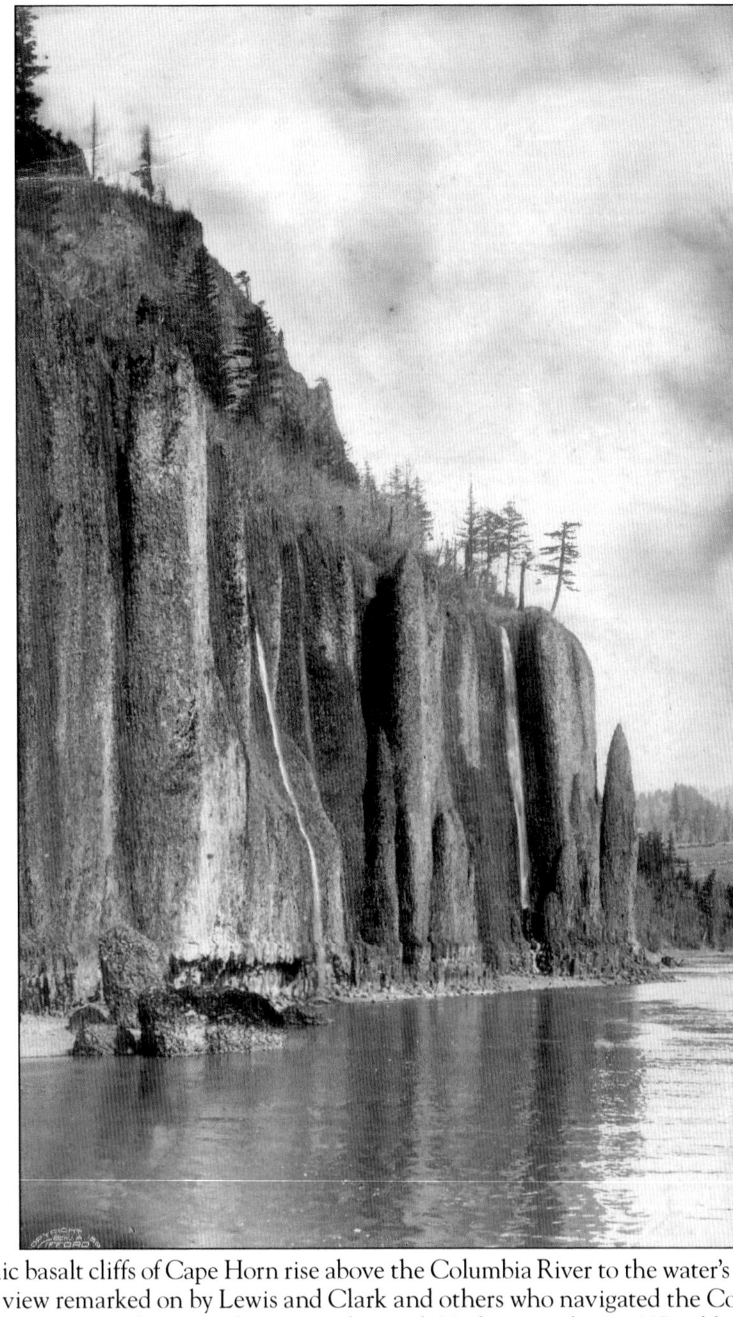

The volcanic basalt cliffs of Cape Horn rise above the Columbia River to the water's edge, creating a stunning view remarked on by Lewis and Clark and others who navigated the Columbia River. This landscape, pictured in 1899, has since changed. Unfortunately in 1927, a blast intended to create a rock shelf for a new highway went terribly wrong. The resulting landslide pushed houses into the river, caused a tidal wave on Oregon's southern shore, and destroyed the cliff face. The slide buried railroad tracks, destroyed fishing grounds, and filled the Cape Horn dock channel. Cape Horn's dock previously had been a busy one. Mining equipment for the Maybee and Skamania Mines and others was brought in by steamship though Cape Horn. Cape Horn was also known for bootlegging during Prohibition. (Photograph by Benjamin W. Gifford; courtesy Skamania County Historical Society.)

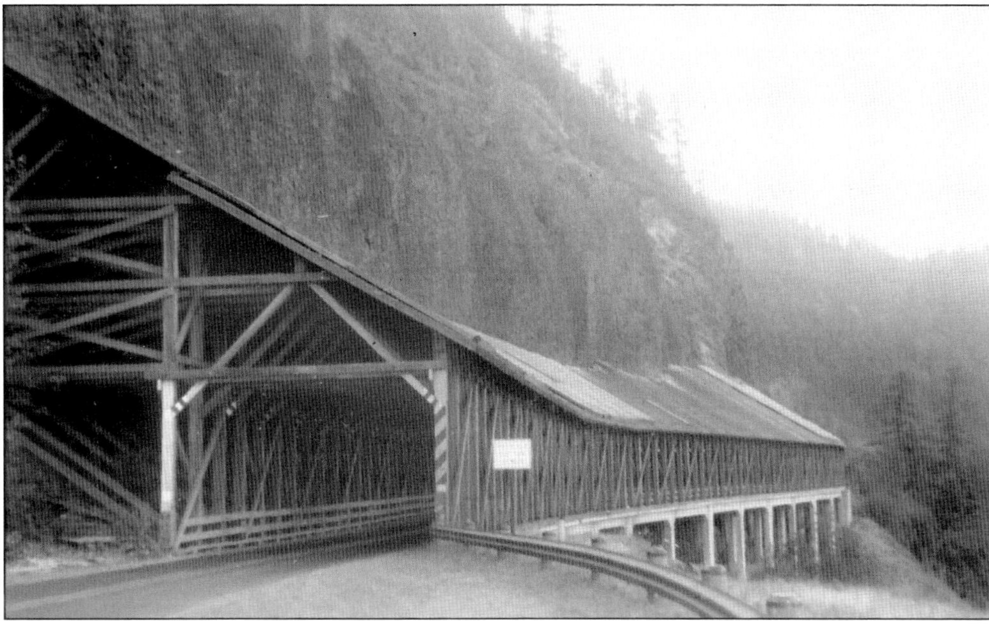

When the rock shelf on Cape Horn was destroyed, contractors had to reinforce the slide area and build the new highway using concrete supports. In 1928, the covered roadway known as "the shed" was completed. It is pictured here in 1940. Prior to the construction of Highway 14, those in the community of Cape Horn traveled to Washougal by boat or over Mount Norway.

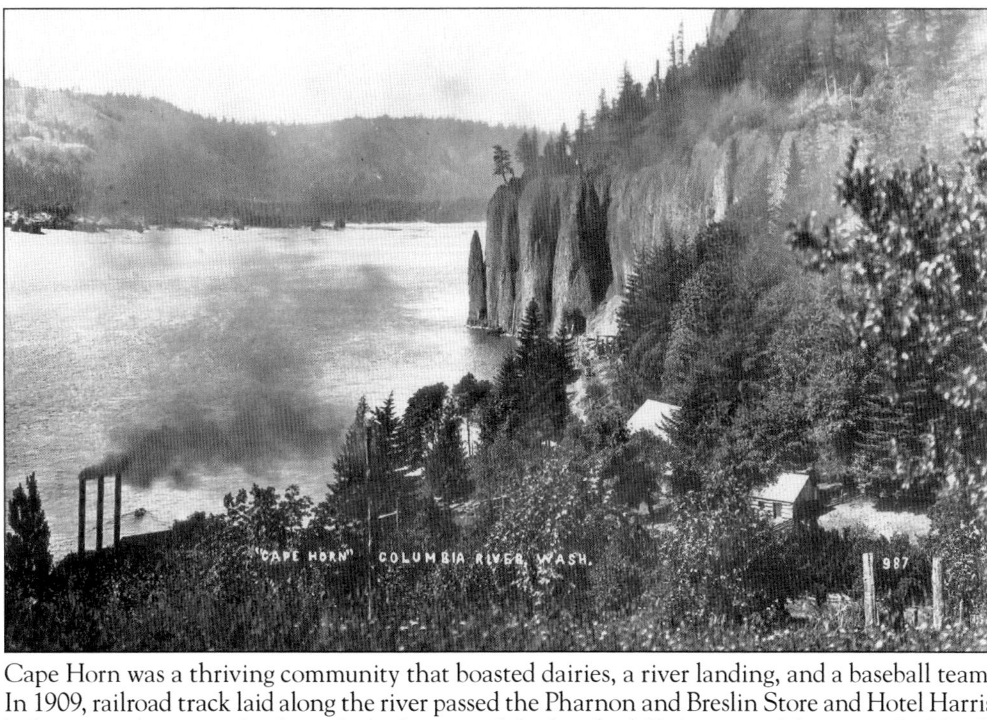

Cape Horn was a thriving community that boasted dairies, a river landing, and a baseball team. In 1909, railroad track laid along the river passed the Pharnon and Breslin Store and Hotel Harris before tunneling straight through the bottom of the basalt cliff. A postcard featuring the North Bank Railroad sent in 1910 declares, "All is well at Cape Horn." (Photograph by K. A. Pierce; courtesy Skamania County Historical Society.)

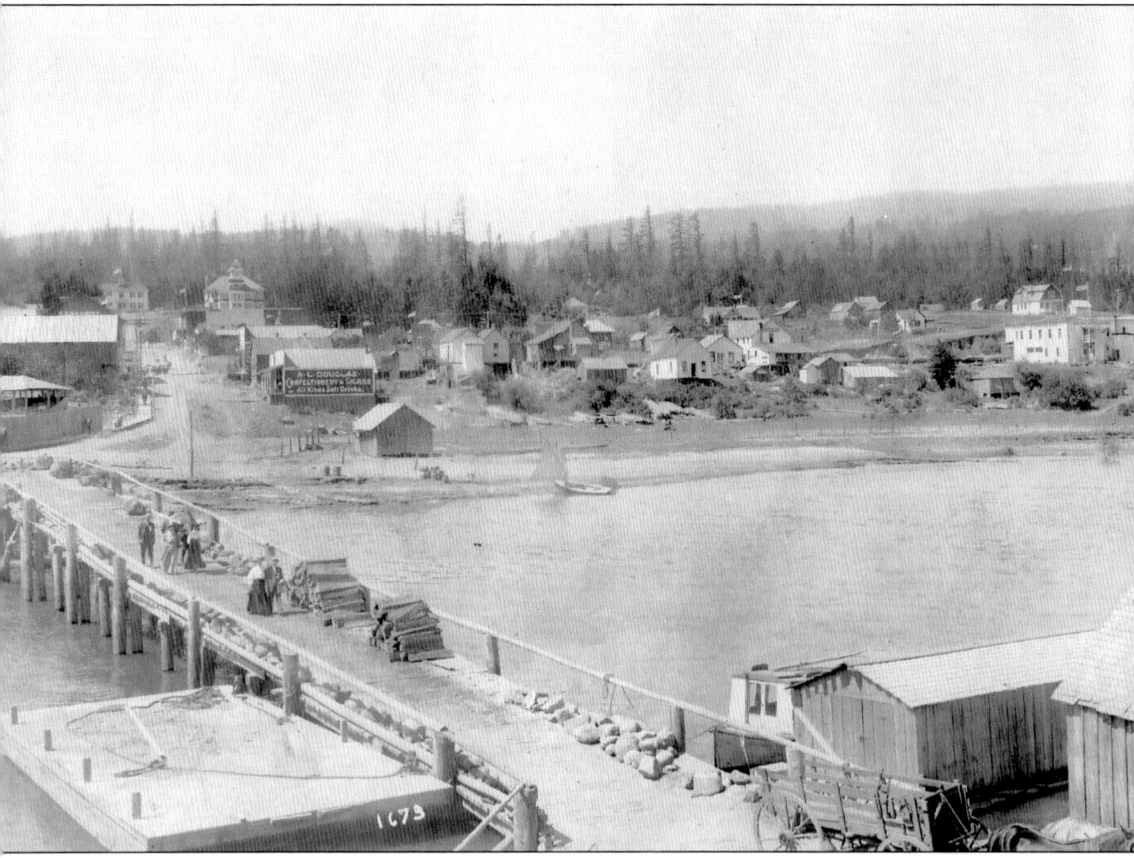

The city of Stevenson, pictured here around 1900, was located above the treacherous grand rapids of the upper cascades on the Columbia River. For immigrants traveling the Oregon Trail, circumventing these rapids marked one of the last hurdles of the long journey overland. At first, the only way around was a muddy path north of the river. This trail, long known by the Cascade and Chinook Indians and used by Lewis and Clark, would eventually give rise to the city of Stevenson. By the 1850s, settlers such as Henry and Lucinda Shepard filed donation land claims in the upper cascades. By 1856, brothers Daniel and Putnam Bradford owned a sawmill, warehouses, and a two-story store. At least 40 settlers, men, women, and children, lived nearby. In 1861, discovery of gold in Idaho fueled improvements in transport conditions. By 1880, locomotives ran north and south of the Columbia River. In 1893, businessman George Stevenson bought land from the Shepard donation claim and platted the city of Stevenson. It would become Skamania's county seat that same year. (Courtesy Skamania County Historical Society.)

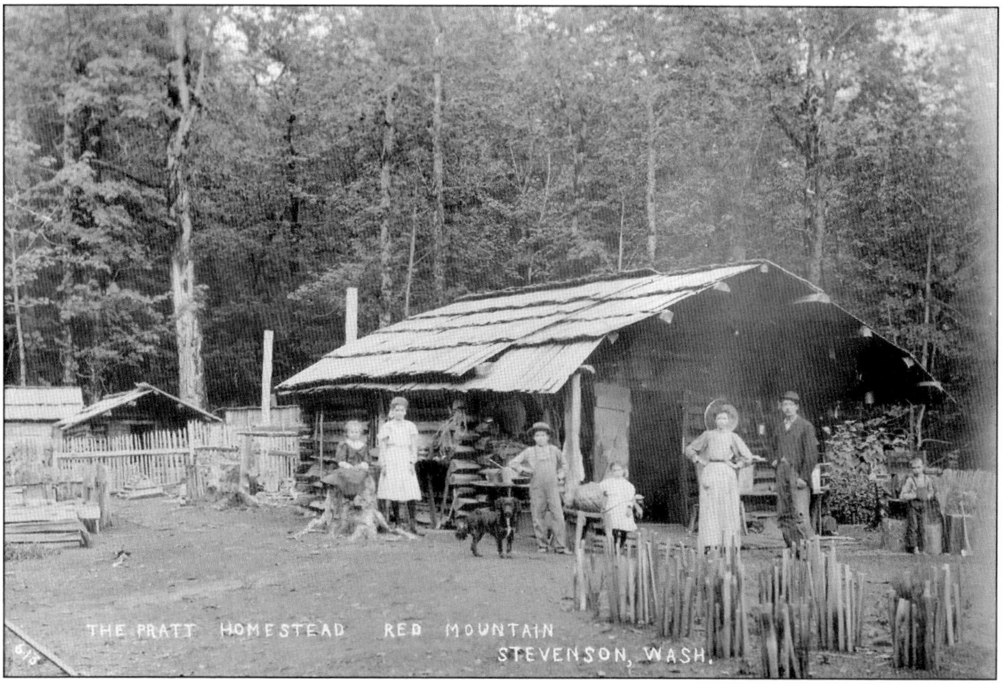

As the timber moved out, homesteaders moved in. The Pratts took a homestead on Red Mountain in 1907. Stakes have been hammered into the ground (foreground) probably to protect young plants. Both the boys in the photograph are barefoot. Pictured, from left to right, are Alice Miller, Dollie Pratt, Russell ?, Blanche ?, Mary Pratt, George Pratt, and Osbourne ?. The dog's name is Queen. (Courtesy Skamania County Historical Society.)

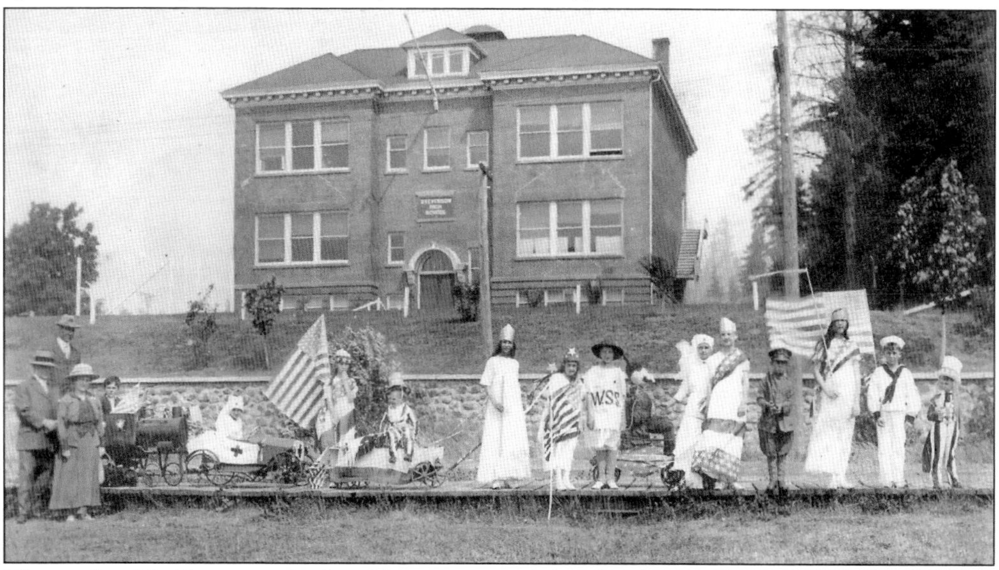

These schoolchildren outside the old Stevenson High School are probably dressed for a Fourth of July celebration. The school complex, pictured here, was in use until at least the 1950s and consisted of a grade school, a gymnasium, and a red-bricked high school. Girls and boys sports included basketball, baseball, and fencing. Boys played football on a wet, muddy field out back. None of the original buildings still exist. (Courtesy Skamania County Historical Society.)

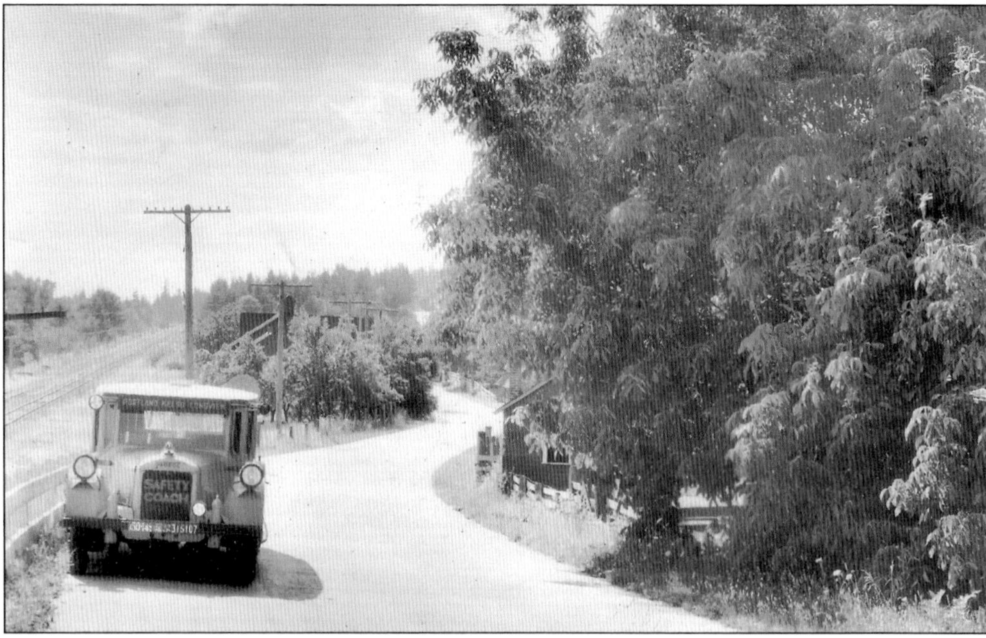

Automobiles replaced the horse-drawn stagecoach by the 1920s. This Safety Coach, owned by a company in Vancouver, went to Portland, Kelso, Longview, and also Beacon Rock. Driver Frank Bunger Simmons drove the route along the old Evergreen Highway past Riverview Farms, pictured here. Riverview Farms was part of the original Simmons land claim. (Courtesy Thomas Gentry.)

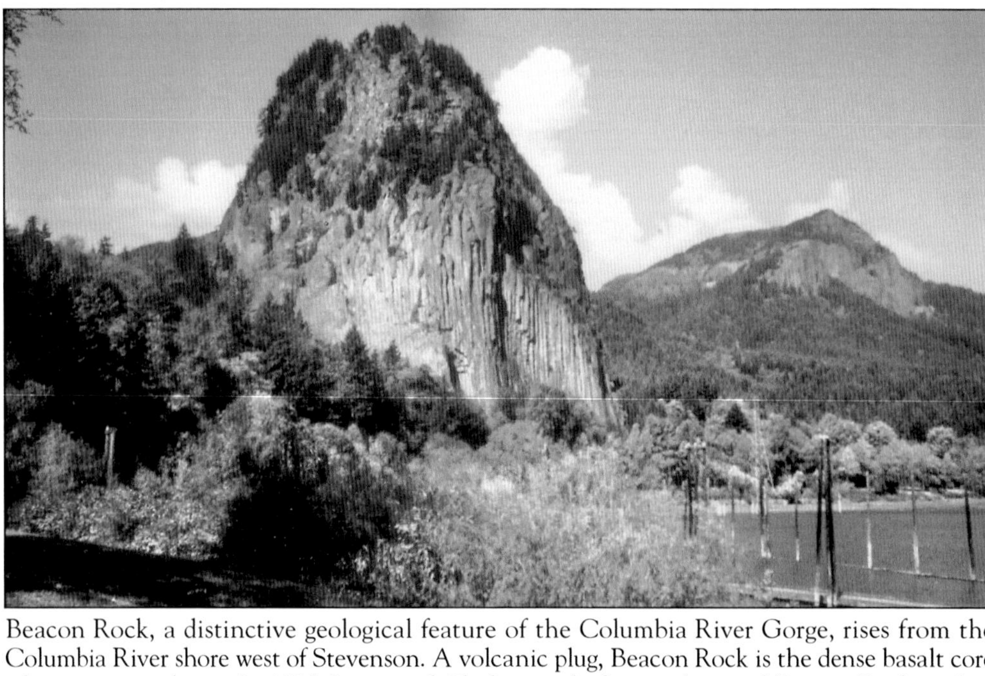

Beacon Rock, a distinctive geological feature of the Columbia River Gorge, rises from the Columbia River shore west of Stevenson. A volcanic plug, Beacon Rock is the dense basalt core of an extinct volcano. In 1805, Lewis and Clark remarked on and named Beacon Rock as they journeyed west. Today visitors to Beacon Rock State Park can hike, bike, camp, rock climb, and even get married. (Courtesy Skamania County Historical Society.)

Henry J. Biddle purchased Beacon Rock in 1915. Determined to build a trail to the top, Biddle hired Charles Johnson as a foreman and employed a team of stonecutters and laborers. The trail was completed in 1918 and featured hairpin turns and a narrow flight of stairs that lead to the summit. Iron railings were the only protection from mishaps. (Courtesy Skamania County Historical Society.)

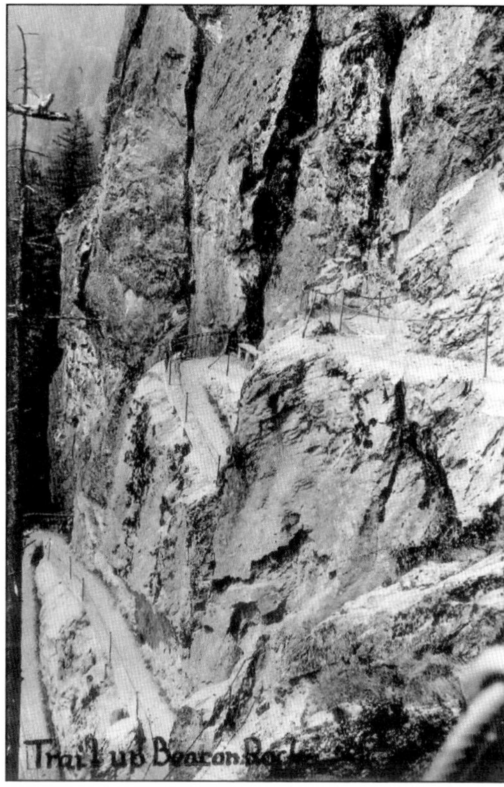

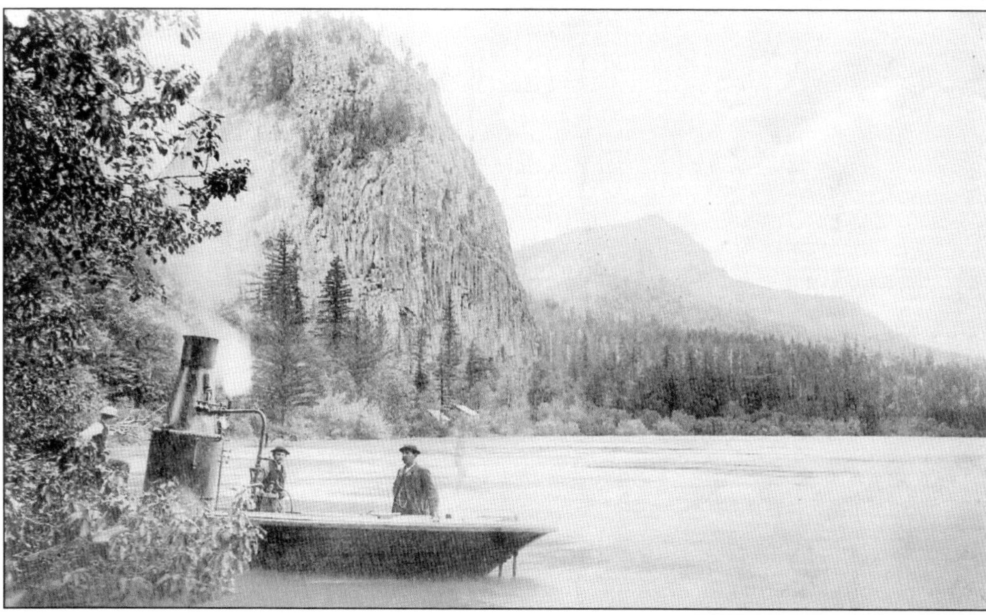

These three unidentified men glide past Beacon Rock in a boat powered by what is probably a homemade steam engine. Many in the Washougal area built their own boats. Thomas Gentry, owner of Gentry's Landing, built his first boat at the age of 16 using wood from a woodpile. The rowboat was for his uncle who wanted to go fishing. Gentry became a boat and engine expert. (Courtesy Skamania County Historical Society.)

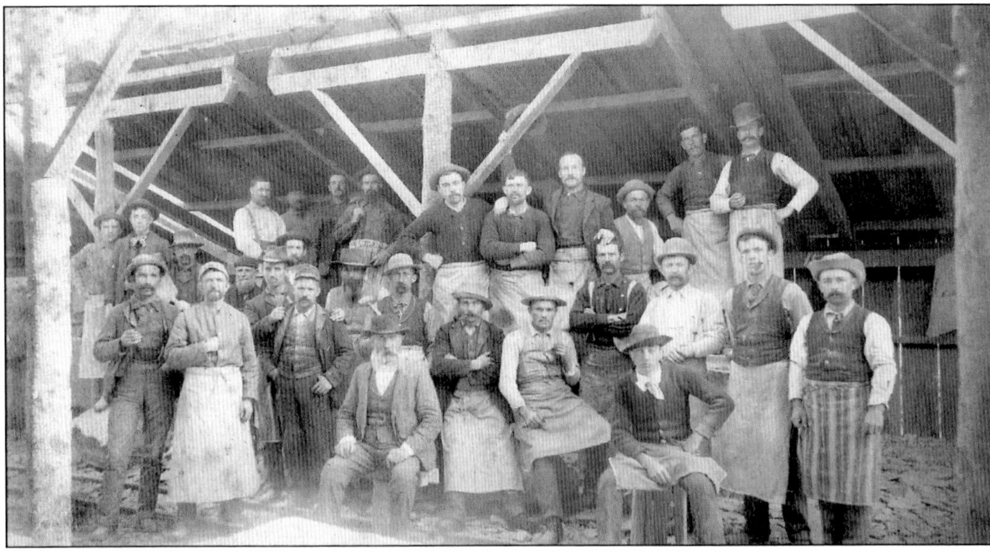

Stonecutters, pictured here in 1878, built the Cascade Locks. The deepwater channel, blasted from solid slabs of basalt allowed steamboats to pass through the Cascade Rapids. Previously steamboats had to stop above the rapids at Stevenson or The Dalles. Everything was then transported six miles by foot, wagon, or narrow-gauge locomotive to another steamboat waiting below. (Photograph by B. C. Towne; courtesy Skamania County Historical Society.)

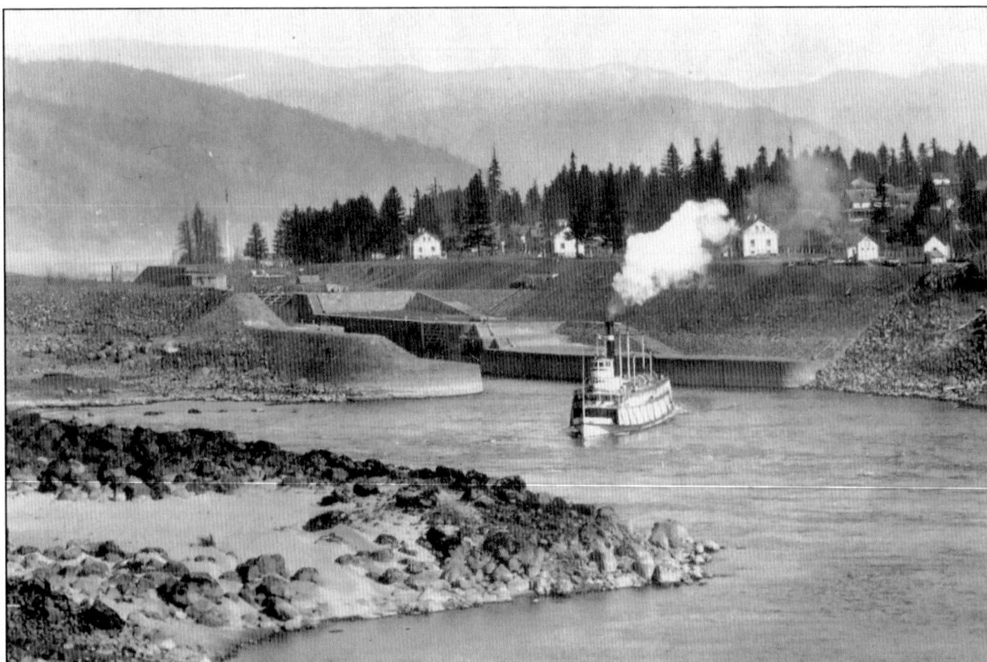

The Army Corps of Engineers completed Cascade Locks in 1896 despite numerous setbacks, including severe winters and the terrible 1884 flood. Yet by then, railroads monopolized transportation inland to the coast. Even so, scores of everyday folks made the trip to see the ships. A 10-year-old Thomas Gentry went to the locks with his grandfather in 1925. He recalled, "It was amazing." (Courtesy Skamania County Historical Society.)

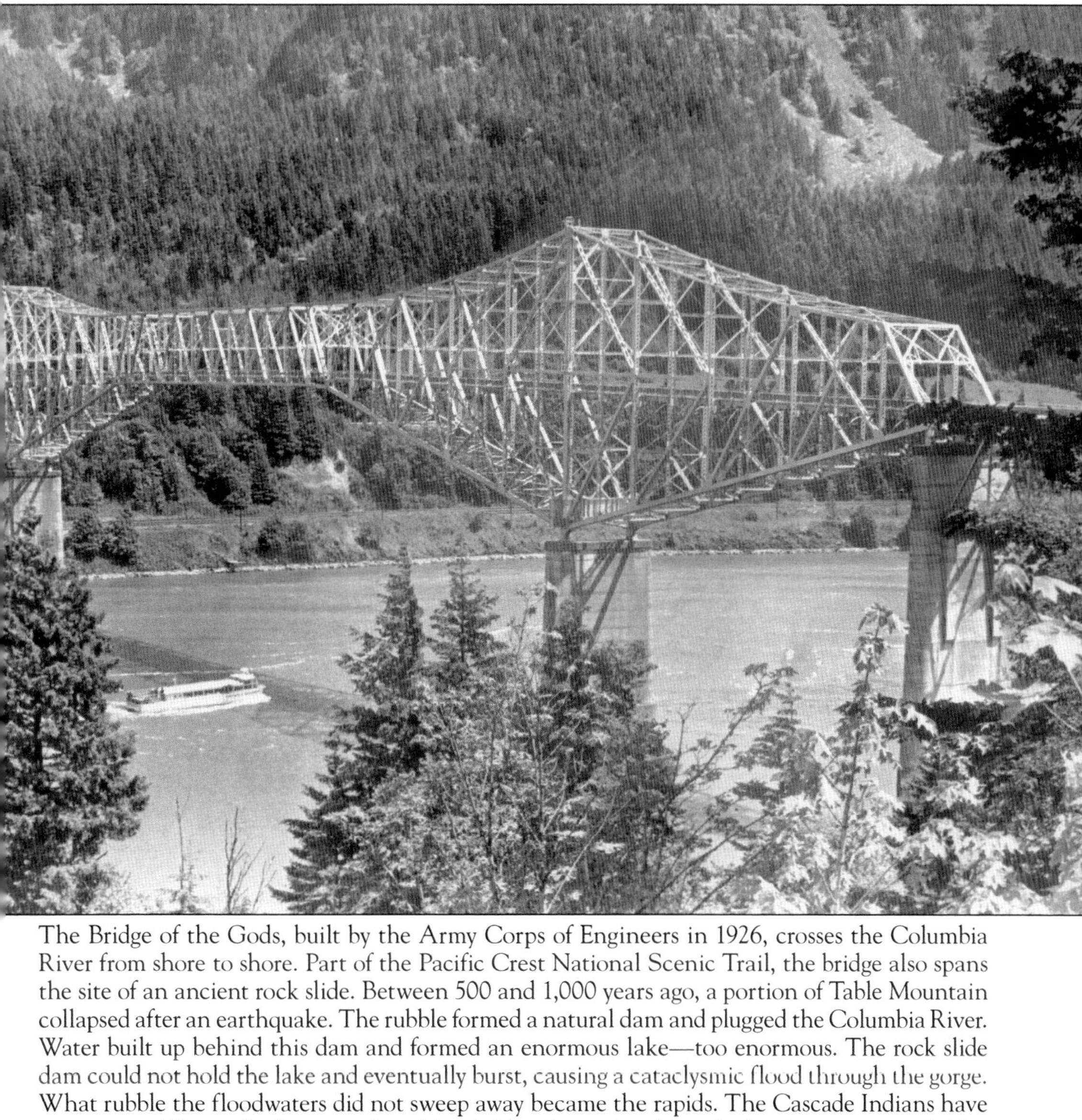

The Bridge of the Gods, built by the Army Corps of Engineers in 1926, crosses the Columbia River from shore to shore. Part of the Pacific Crest National Scenic Trail, the bridge also spans the site of an ancient rock slide. Between 500 and 1,000 years ago, a portion of Table Mountain collapsed after an earthquake. The rubble formed a natural dam and plugged the Columbia River. Water built up behind this dam and formed an enormous lake—too enormous. The rock slide dam could not hold the lake and eventually burst, causing a cataclysmic flood through the gorge. What rubble the floodwaters did not sweep away became the rapids. The Cascade Indians have a story, too. They tell of a natural, arching bridge that existed hundreds of years ago—a bridge of the gods. The tribes used the bridge extensively, especially for trade. That bridge collapsed, and when it did, they say the stony rubble it left behind became the rapids. (Courtesy Skamania County Historical Society.)

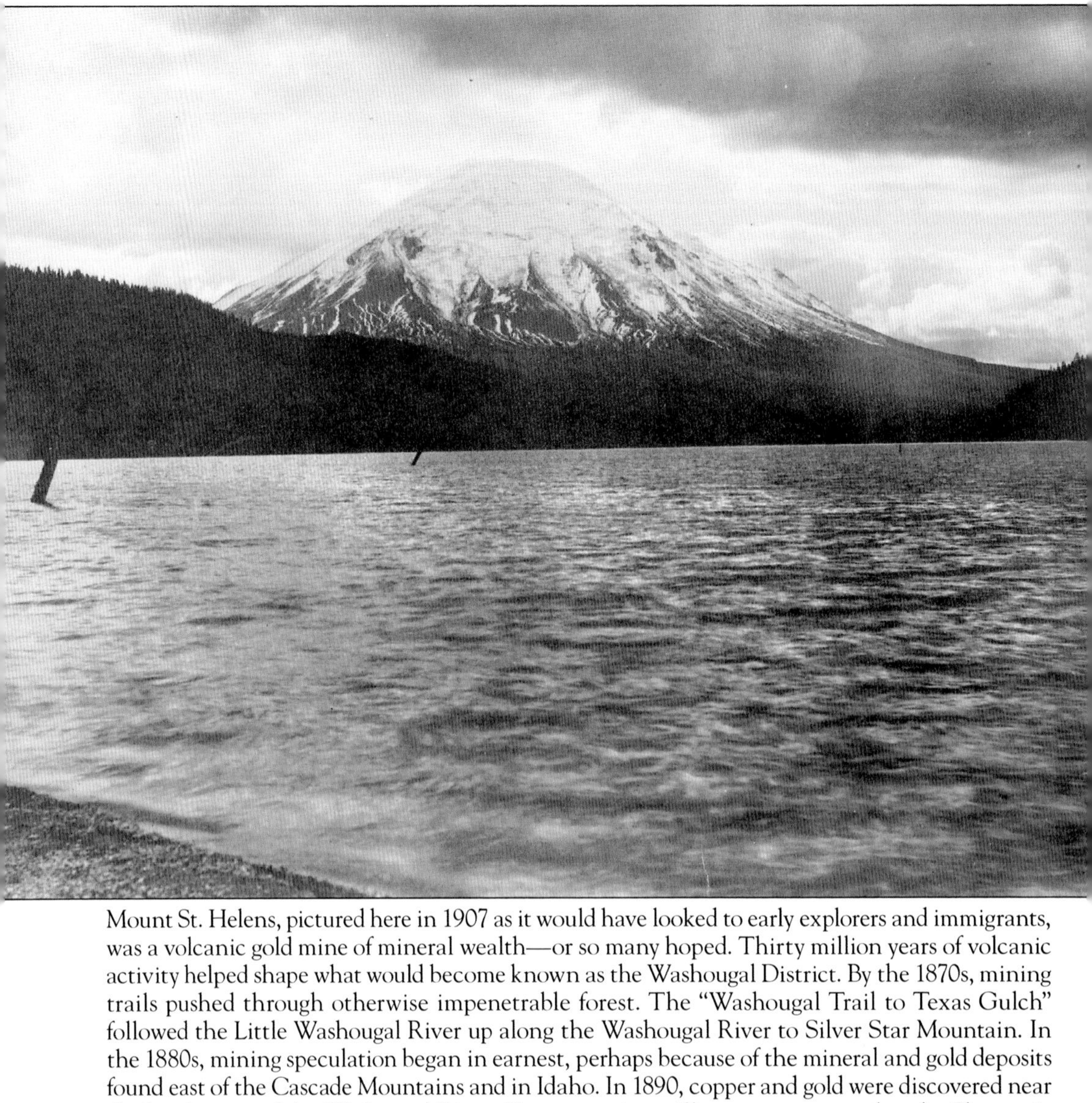

Mount St. Helens, pictured here in 1907 as it would have looked to early explorers and immigrants, was a volcanic gold mine of mineral wealth—or so many hoped. Thirty million years of volcanic activity helped shape what would become known as the Washougal District. By the 1870s, mining trails pushed through otherwise impenetrable forest. The "Washougal Trail to Texas Gulch" followed the Little Washougal River up along the Washougal River to Silver Star Mountain. In the 1880s, mining speculation began in earnest, perhaps because of the mineral and gold deposits found east of the Cascade Mountains and in Idaho. In 1890, copper and gold were discovered near the headwaters of the Washougal River. Concentrating mills were constructed at the Skamania and Maybee Mines and shafts sunk for further exploration. In all, though, it was a sorry tale. The Washougal Gold and Copper Mining Company extracted just a few wagon loads of ore before closing. Sporadic development of the Washougal District after the 1950s, including by the Copper Canyon Mines in Camas, was also disappointing. (Courtesy Library of Congress.)

Harry Dutch and Alex Burgoyne, at the Black Prince Mine in 1904, were just two of the many mining hopefuls in Skamania County. Unfortunately there were no "mother lode" mines in the Washougal District. Mines named "Last Hope" and "Last Chance" may indicate how little luck miners experienced in their quest for riches. In winter, mining camps closed and miners would stay at hotels in town. (Courtesy Skamania County Historical Society.)

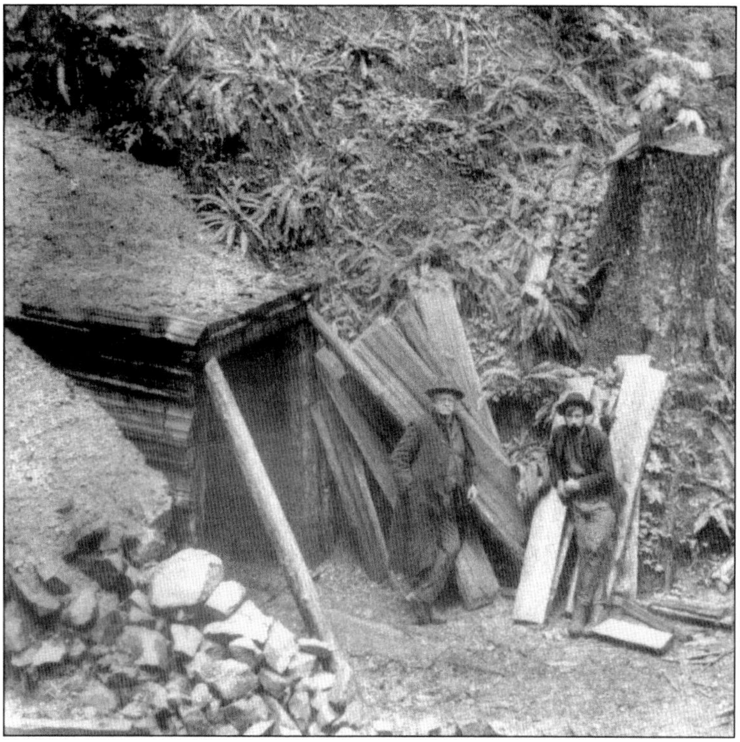

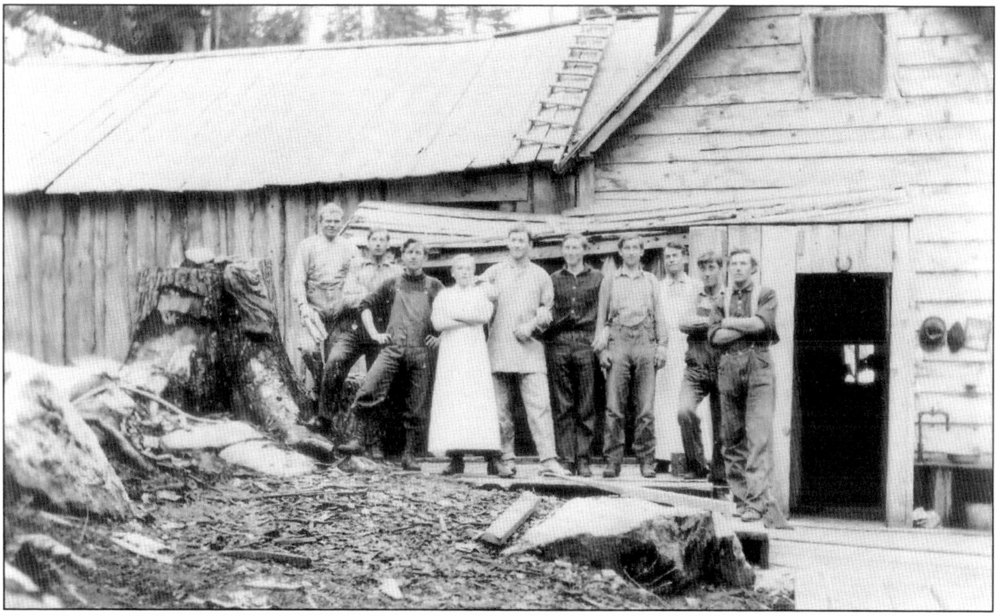

Mining camps similar to this one dotted the Washougal District by 1902. Mining was a hard business, and for many, the raging Yacolt Fire was the end of production. Logger Ben Campen of Washougal remembered explosions behind him as he fled from the oncoming Yacolt blaze. Blasting powder at the Yellow Jacket and Blue Bird Mines ignited and whole camps turned to ash. Few mines were rebuilt. (Courtesy University of Washington Libraries.)

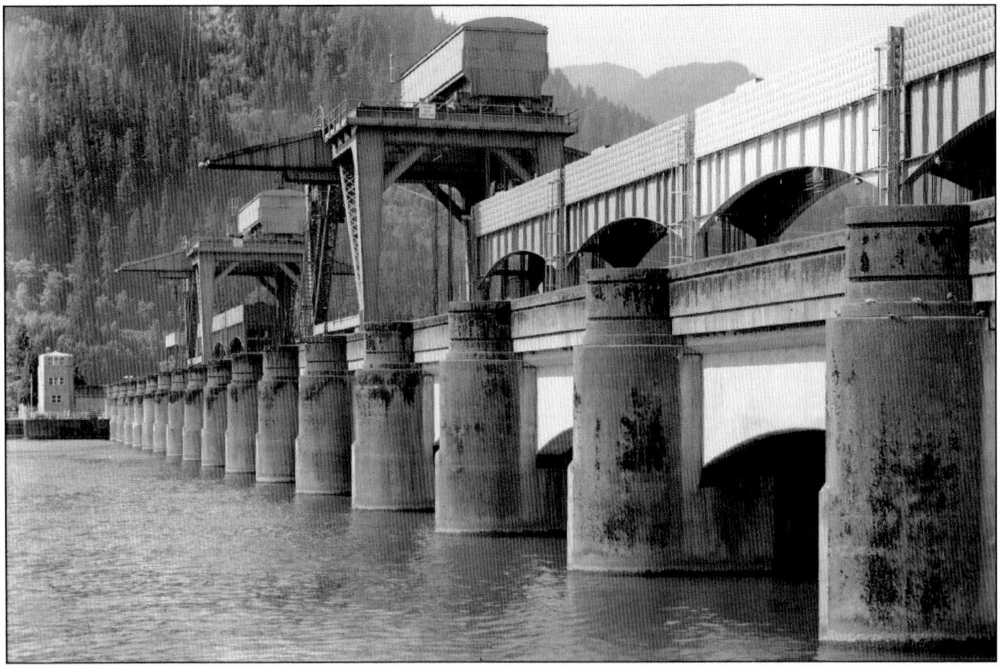

The Bonneville Dam complex is located between Washougal and Stevenson along the Columbia River. This photograph of the spillway under construction shows the Gantry Cranes (center) and gate mechanisms (right). Excavation for the spillway required the monster machine called Monighan. The Monighan was an electric-shovel excavator that weighed in at 441 tons. (Courtesy Library of Congress.)

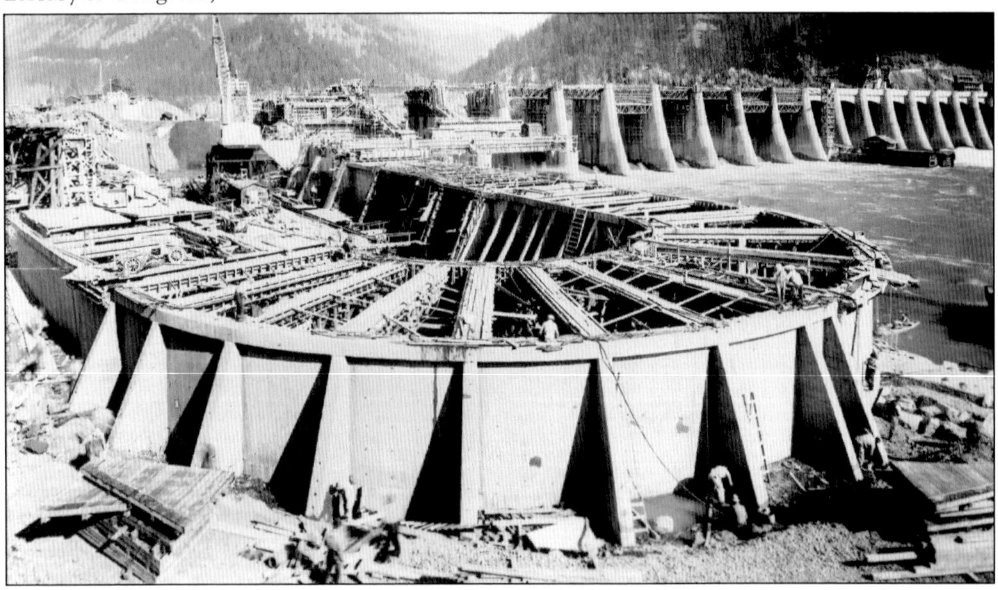

The Washington shore fish ladder was designed to allow salmon and other fish a migration path up the Columbia River to spawn. Ecological and commercial interests were instrumental in making sure the ladder was included in the project. At the time of dam construction, the salmon industry generated revenue of over a $1 million each year and employed over 20,000 people. (Courtesy Library of Congress.)

The Bonneville Dam's structures, while unprecedented in scope, still relied on a basic design developed by the ancient Mesopotamians. The new Navigational Lock Control Room, which was state-of-the-art in 1938, is not impressive by today's standards. This bench board control center, which looks not unlike a washing machine, was an electrical contraption of the industrial age. (Courtesy Library of Congress.)

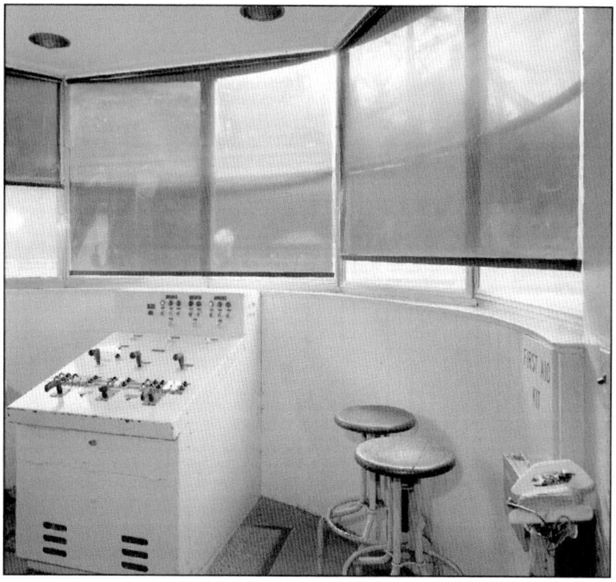

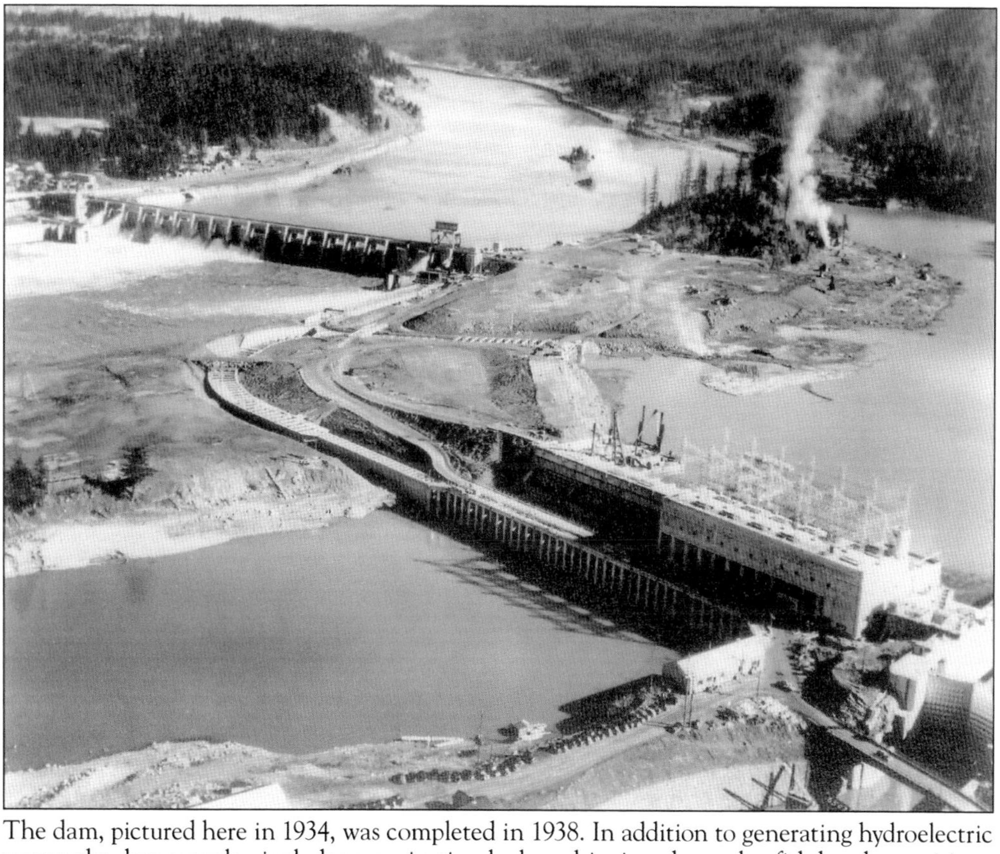

The dam, pictured here in 1934, was completed in 1938. In addition to generating hydroelectric power, the dam complex includes a navigation lock or shipping channel, a fish hatchery, visitors centers, powerhouses, and included the Fort Cascade historic site, the location of a battle between settlers and Cascade and Yakima tribes in 1856. (Photograph by Asahel Curtis; courtesy University of Washington Libraries, UW65027.)

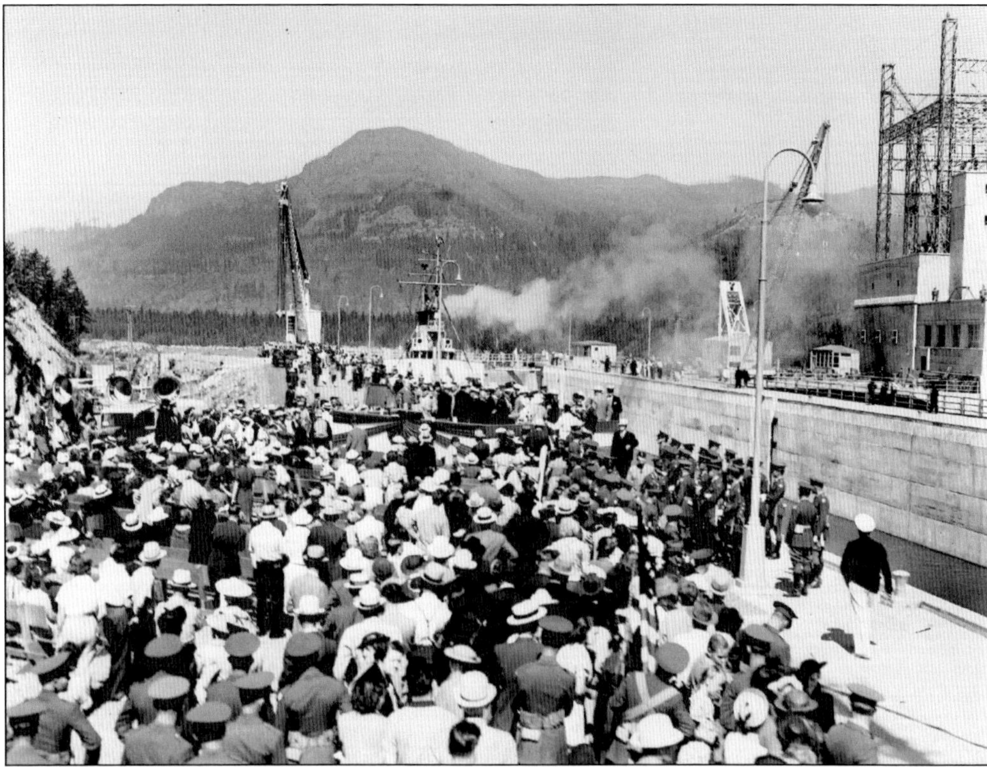

Despite a few controversies, nothing seems to have dampened America's enthusiasm for the Bonneville Dam. Huge crowds gathered to see the first steamer, the *Dalles City*, navigate the locks. Hundreds of thousands of people visit the dam annually, and schoolchildren take regular class trips to see the dam and fish ladders. (Courtesy Library of Congress.)

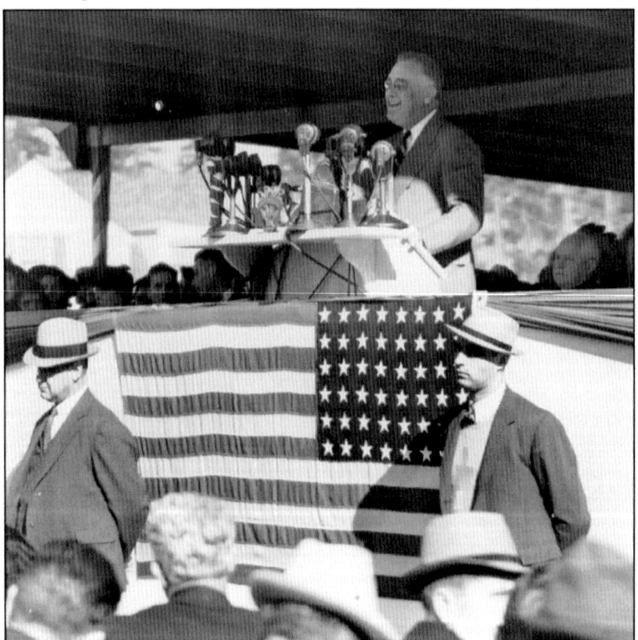

The Bonneville Dam project was part of Pres. Franklin D. Roosevelt's plan to put Americans to work as the country recovered from the Great Depression. Roosevelt visited the Bonneville site in 1934 to inspect designs and blueprints. In September 1937, cheering crowds greeted him when he came to deliver the dedication address. The project cost $60 million to complete. (Courtesy Library of Congress.)

Six

Growing Up and Moving Out

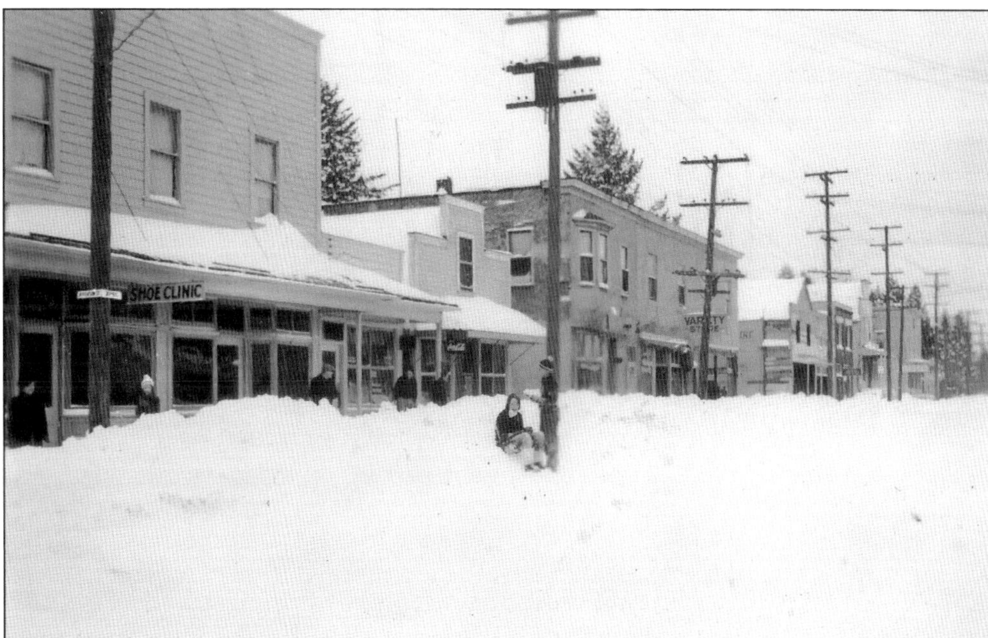

The Washougal community learned early on to withstand freezes. Winters used to be harsher, and snowfall sometimes accumulated four or five feet deep. When the Columbia River froze over, transportation from Lady or Reed Island required a horse and sled. This storm in 1937 dumped 14 inches of snow in 24 hours. The temperature of 18 degrees Fahrenheit, however, does not deter these children at play on B Street.

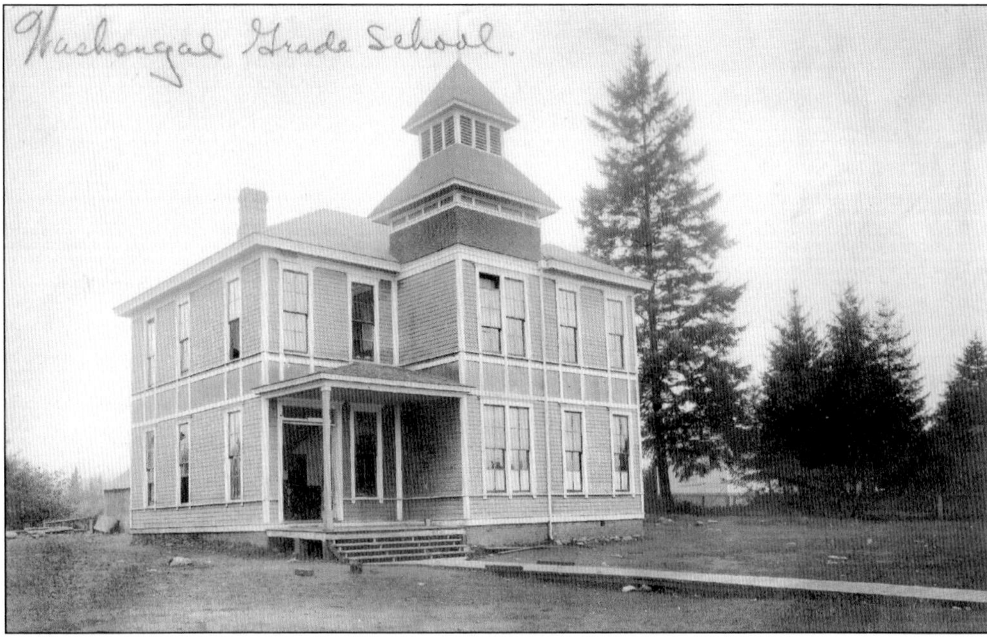

This six-room schoolhouse, built in 1892, was the first official school building for Washougal, whose students had previously studied at the Congregational Church. The school accommodated all eight grades, and Mrs. Long and Mrs. Jacobs were among the first teachers. In 1910, the Washougal Grammar School replaced the six-room school. It was used at least through the 1940s and later served children of junior-high age.

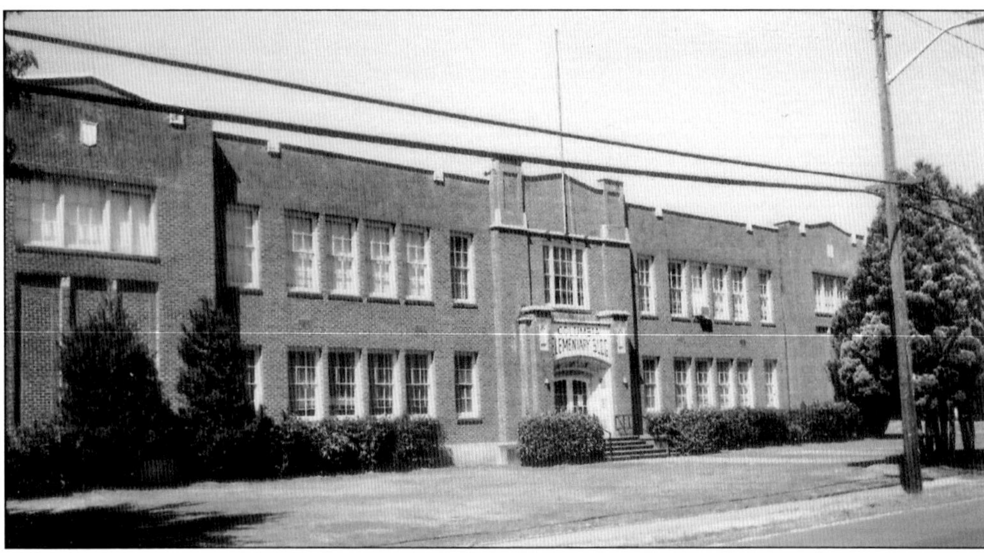

This building, constructed in 1926, served as Washougal's first high school. In 1956, Washougal built a larger high school with a larger field and grounds. This building then became Columbia School. Though still on B Street, the building is no longer used by the Washougal School District. Other school buildings constructed as the district developed included schools for Mount Norway, Skye, Cape Horn, Mount Pleasant, Sunnyside, and Bear Prairie.

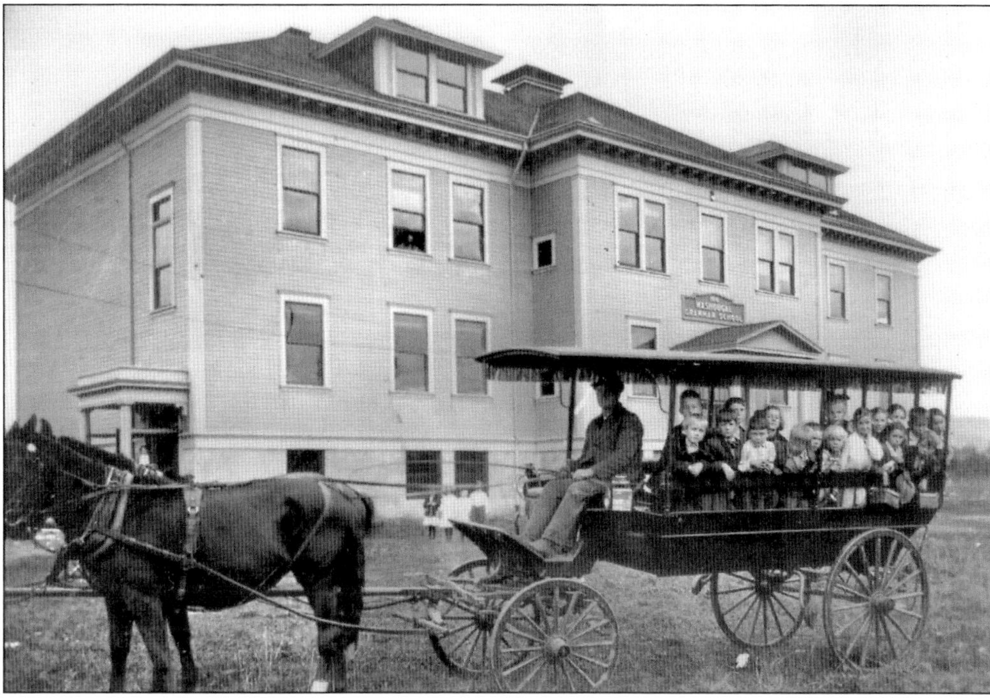

Washougal's first school bus was a horse-drawn carriage from Oak Park to Washougal Grammar School. Driver Henry Stoops would lower flaps to protect riders against bad weather. These bus riders in 1912, from left to right, are (first row) George Lovelace, Willie Drury, Miles ? , Alfred Lovelace, Harriet Davis, Fanny Echolis, unidentified, and Milo Keyes; (second row) Everett Drury, Mabel Wood (Roley), Nita Pickett, Bernadine Davis, unidentified, Sammy Davis, and unidentified.

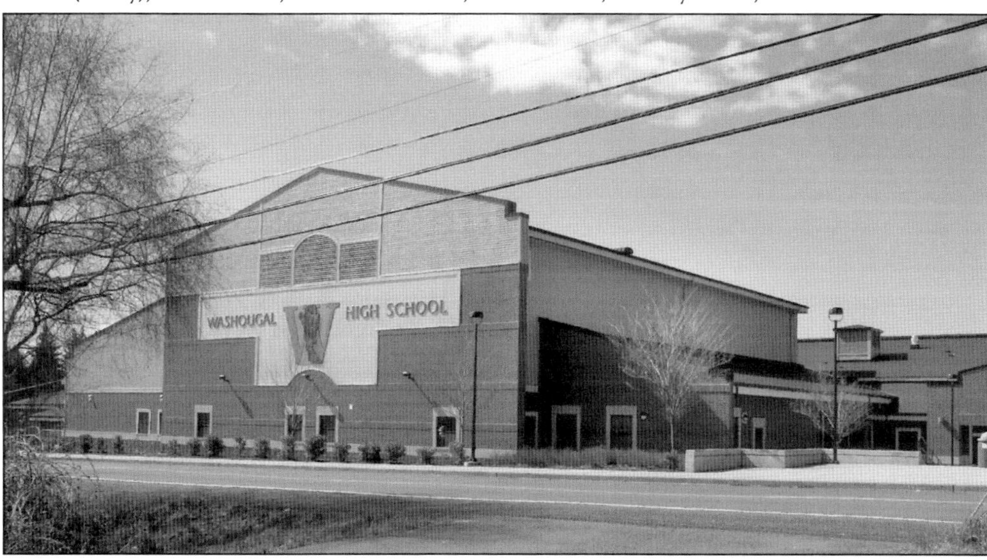

To accommodate a growing population, the 1956 home of the Panthers underwent a 150,000-square-foot renovation completed in 2003. Today's Washougal High School boasts sports teams, art and drama clubs, a debate team, a chess club, and a Japanese club. To accommodate recent population growth, other schools in the Washougal District have also undergone renovation. Its newest middle school, Canyon Creek, came online in 2001.

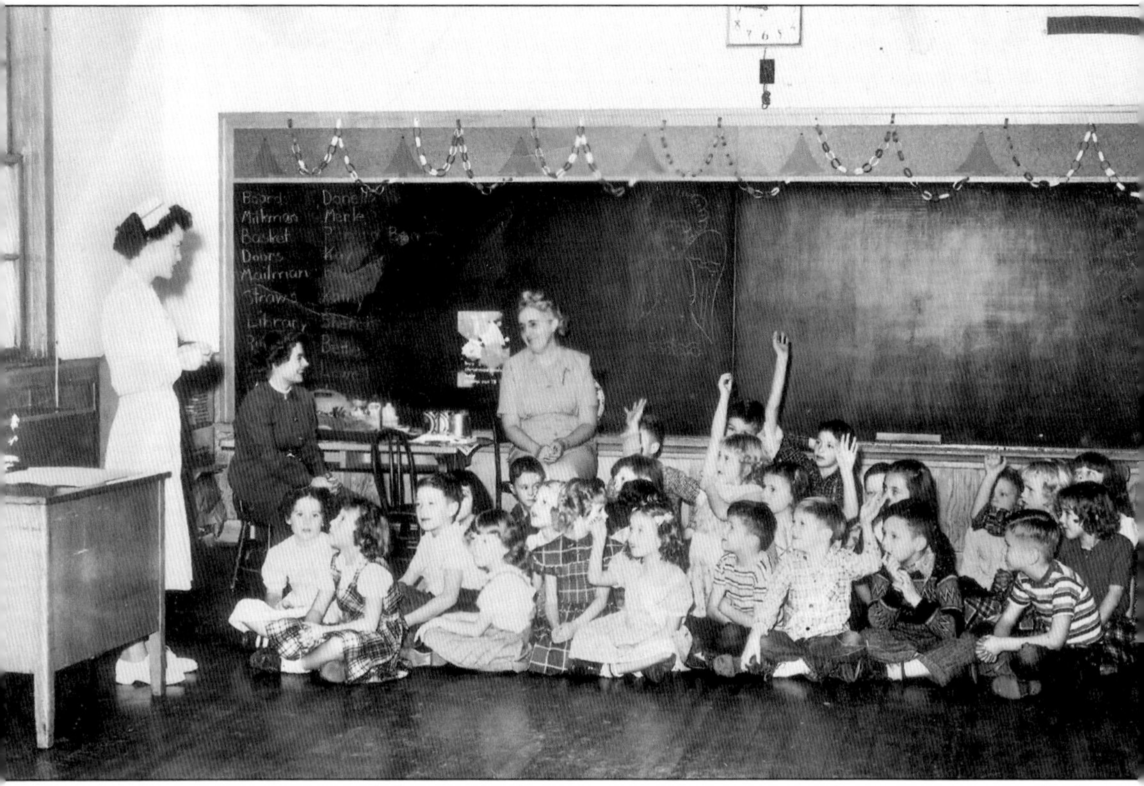

Roberta Stayton's (center) first-grade class engages in a question-and-answer session with the school nurse (left). Edith Kiser (seated right), a former girls high-school basketball champion, was a teacher before she became a school principal. Written on the blackboard are class jobs and the name of the child responsible for that job, a list that includes milkman, mailman, straws, library, and boards. Washougal's first schoolchildren attended classes in small, one-room schools, churches, or grange halls. Classes went only through the eighth grade. Those students who wished to attend high school had to go to Vancouver or across the river to Portland. Emily Goot, who lived on Lady Island, attended Portland High School. She commuted by rowboat every day the weather allowed. Martha Kloninger (Ford) of Sunnyside also attended Portland High School. In 1909, Martha studied mathematics, science, composition, history, English, Latin, German, and drawing.

Washougal's first graduating high-school class was in 1914. The four graduates, clockwise from left to right, are (seated front) Margaret Keep, Lois Hathaway, George Carpenter, and Rosa Kiser. Rosa studied civil government, grammar, geography, history, orthography, physiology, reading, writing, and arithmetic. Her grades were an average of 88 percent. Washougal's High School class has grown since 1914. In 2005, Washougal graduated 151 students.

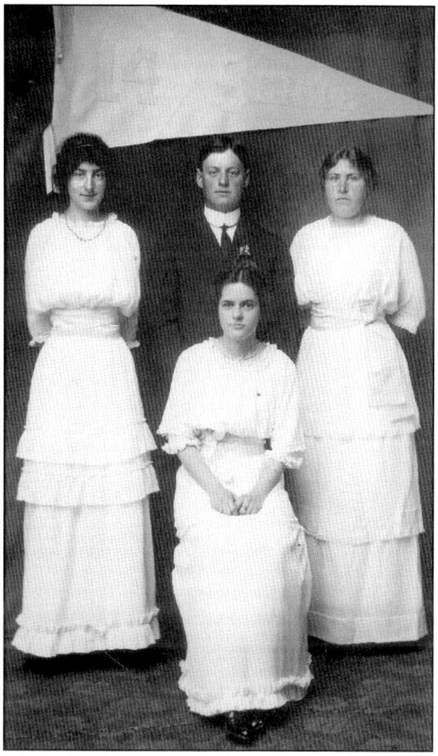

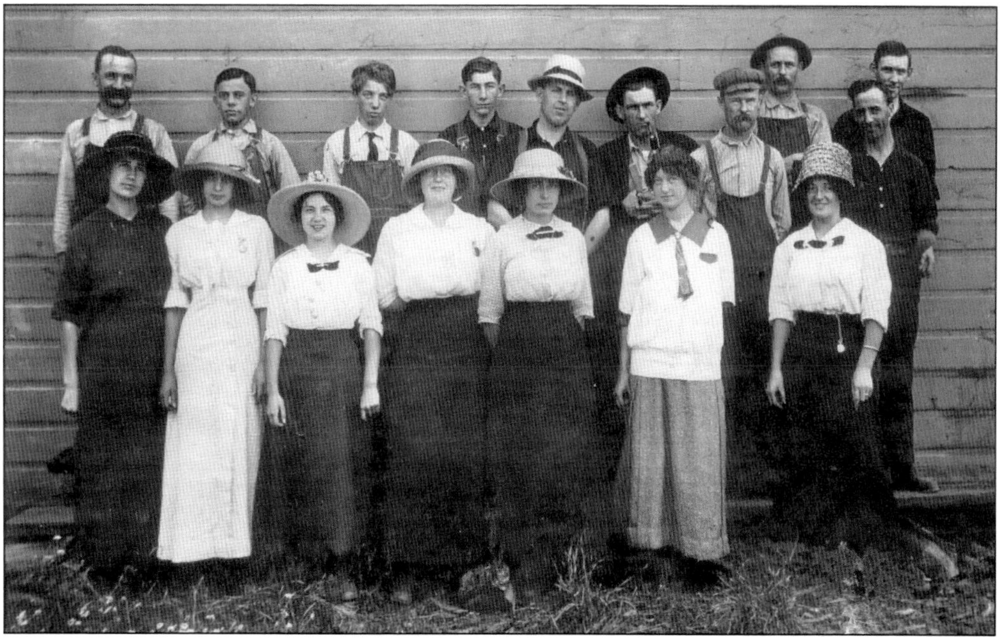

These teachers and staff from the Washougal Grade School in 1908, from left to right, are (first row) Nettie Brown Smith, Lillian Alson, Laura Fleming Tidland, Lillian Nagel Tice, Nelle Brown Steele, Bertha Dibble McNama, and Mayme Hickey Wright; (second row) Tom Roth, Raymond Richi, unidentified, Earl Hathaway, Stub Stayton, unidentified, unidentified, unidentified, Charles Roth, and Charles Stoops.

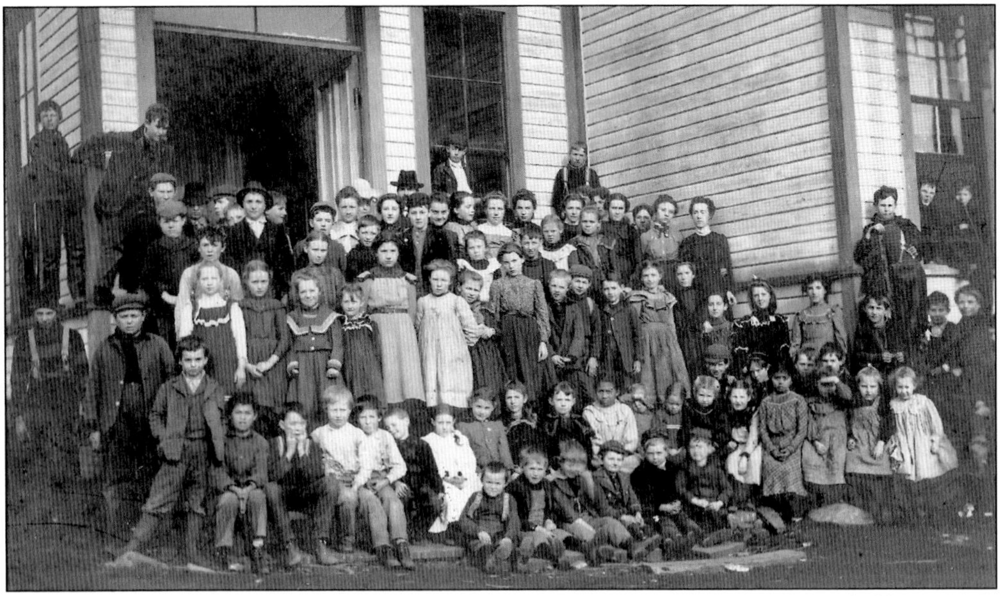

Attendees of Washougal Grade School in 1900 included a few Native American children. Some had parents or grandparents of both European and Native American ancestry. Of those children, some, like the Oughs, were part of an important local family. Those who did not have that protection sometimes suffered from discrimination. Dolphe Gilbreath remembers she was not allowed to befriend native-descended children at school—though she did, anyway.

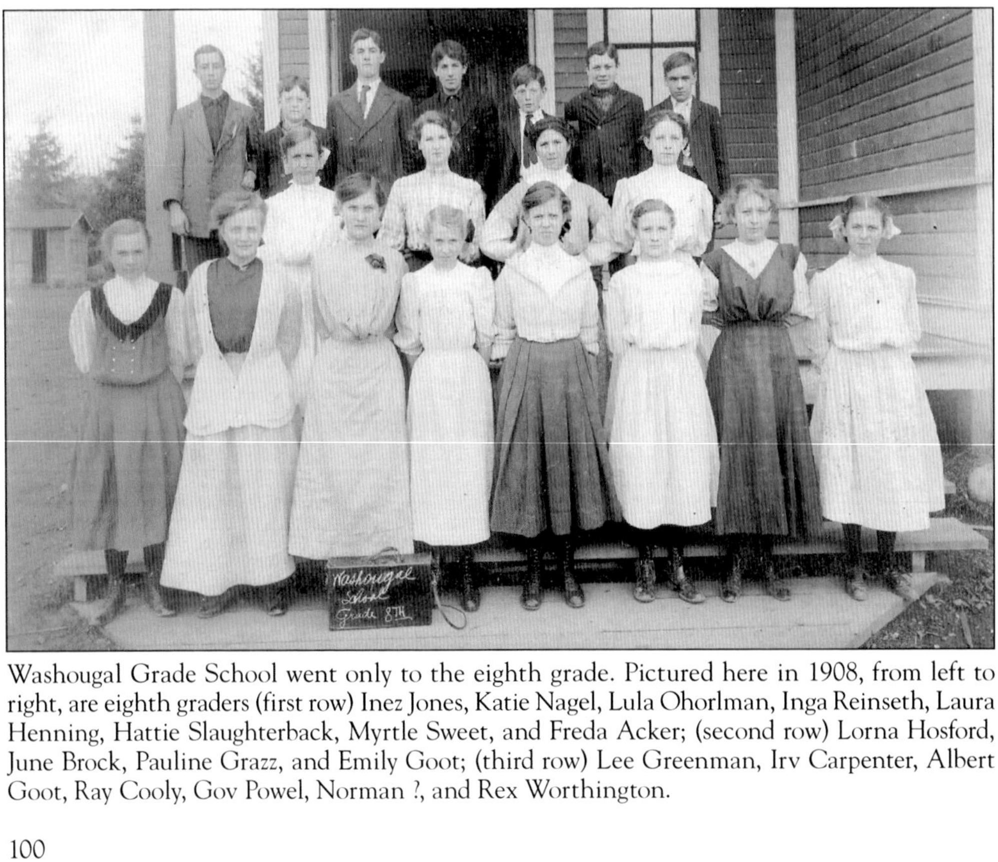

Washougal Grade School went only to the eighth grade. Pictured here in 1908, from left to right, are eighth graders (first row) Inez Jones, Katie Nagel, Lula Ohorlman, Inga Reinseth, Laura Henning, Hattie Slaughterback, Myrtle Sweet, and Freda Acker; (second row) Lorna Hosford, June Brock, Pauline Grazz, and Emily Goot; (third row) Lee Greenman, Irv Carpenter, Albert Goot, Ray Cooly, Gov Powel, Norman ?, and Rex Worthington.

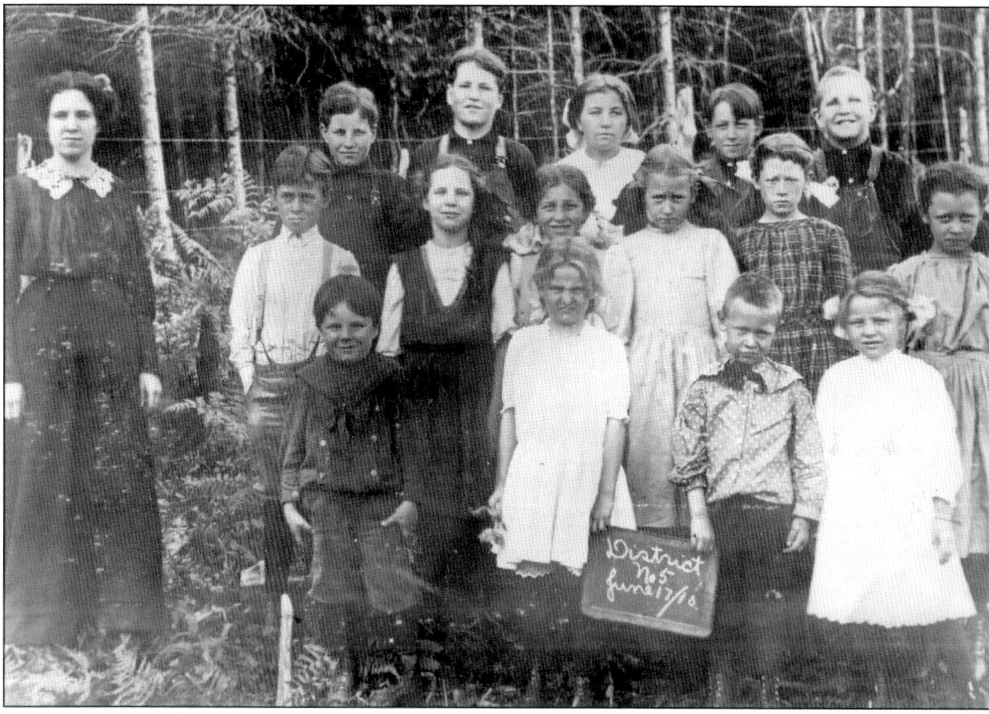

Mary Daugherty (left) taught at the Forest Hill School in 1910. Rural schools were usually one room and heated by a single stove. They were open only three months of the year, during winter; the other months they helped their families on the farm. Rural teachers were often young, unmarried girls not long out of school themselves. In the early days, all who passed the eighth grade could take an exam that, if they passed, qualified them to teach school.

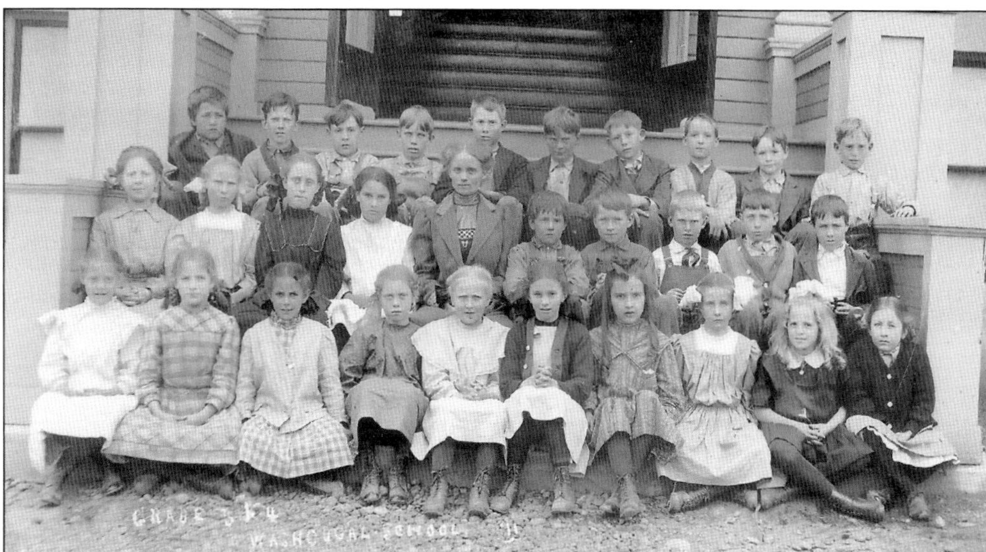

These children on the steps of the new Washougal Grammar School in 1911 are probably fourth graders. Just as now, bad words were not allowed in school. If a student cursed in school, the teacher was likely to send the culprit to a neighboring house for laundry soap. The soap was lathered into a washcloth and used to "wash out" the offender's mouth.

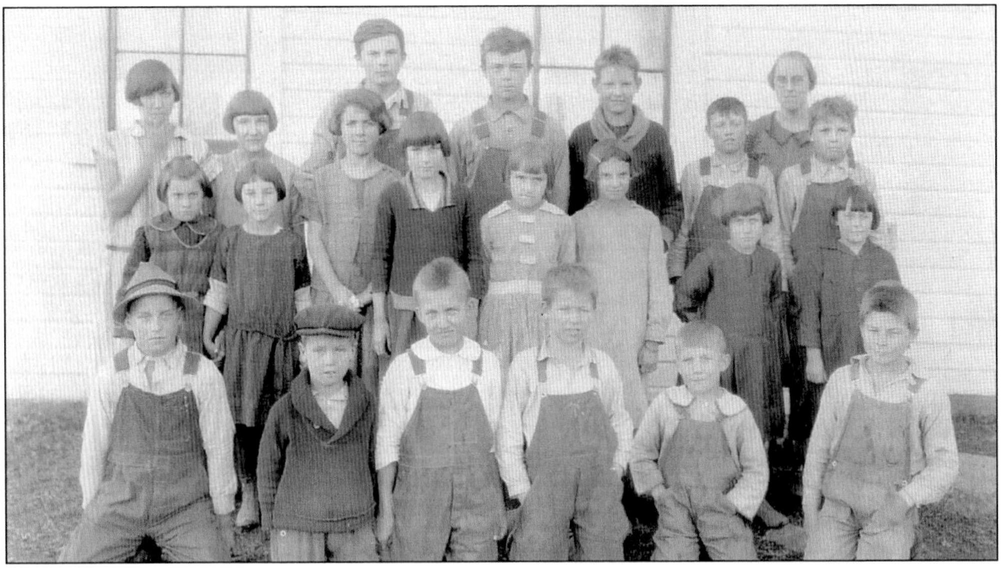

These children of Sunnyside School in 1925, from left to right, are (first row) Johnny Ammeter, Albert Dahlgren, George Broscheit, Walter Dahlgren, Walter Broscheit, and Otto Sunberg; (second row) Frieda Ammeter, Margaret Sunberg, Florence Krohn, Elsie Dahlgren, Alice Broscheit, Katherine Crowson, Marie Schlegal, and Mary Hudson; (third row) Ruth Wolfe, Gladys Brascheit, Elmer Beckman, Victor Beckman, Harry Crowson, Jerry Crowson, Miss ? Erickson (teacher), and Billie Beckman.

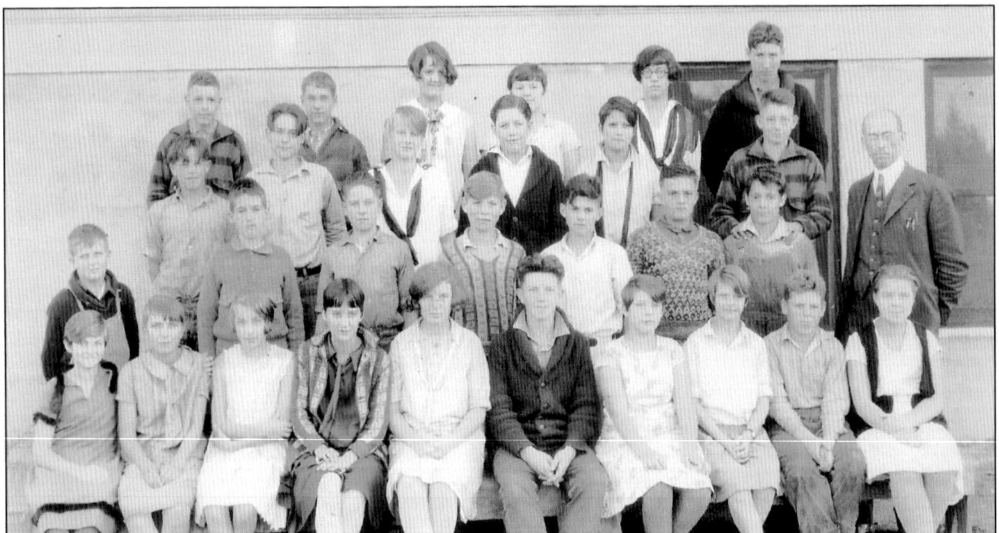

These students are probably seventh or eighth graders at Washougal Grammar School in 1926. Their teacher is J. H. Moore. The students, from left to right in the first row, are Lola Fox, Helen Erickson, Margorie Surbeck, Nellie Woodman, Arvine Nash, Roger Sherman, Mildred Johnson, Irene Barchus, Hyland Stayton, and Dorothy Meredith. Also included in this image are James Catto, Eddie Dahlgren, Wallace Wood, Roy Brown, Leland Fine, Lillian Johnson, John Grell, Boyd Jossy, Orville Masxwell, George Arthnell, Vernon Campen, Gilbert Starr, Roy Brown, Harold Acker, Lillian Johnson, Ethel Horsey, George Clearwater, Florence Carpenter, Ethel Jernigan, Frances Bedell, and Ross Duncan.

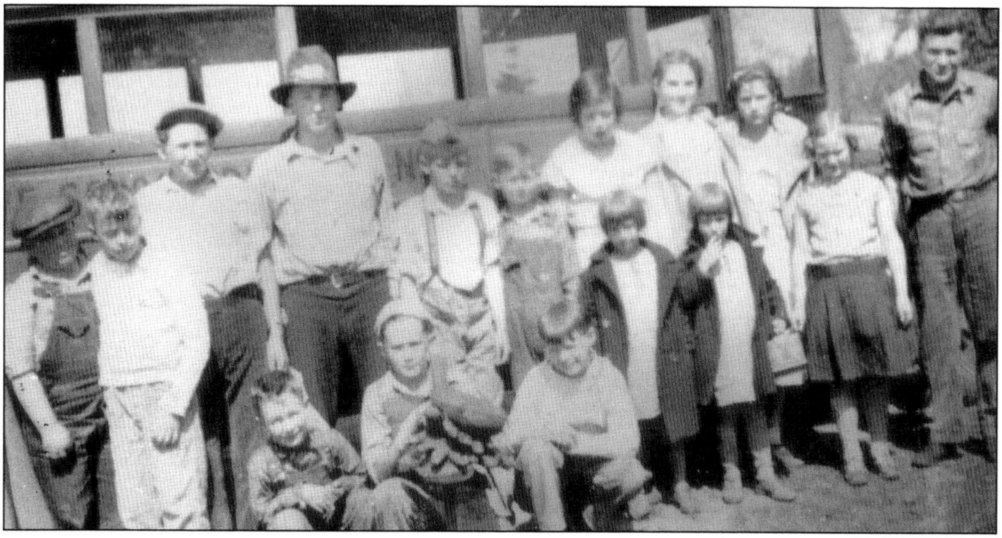

Bill Black drove a school bus at Skye School in 1931. A boy in the front row poses with his baseball bat and at least one baseball glove. In those days, everyone was crazy for baseball and every school, town, hamlet, and even businesses had baseball teams. The paper mill in Camas employed professional ball players, giving them paid afternoons off to practice.

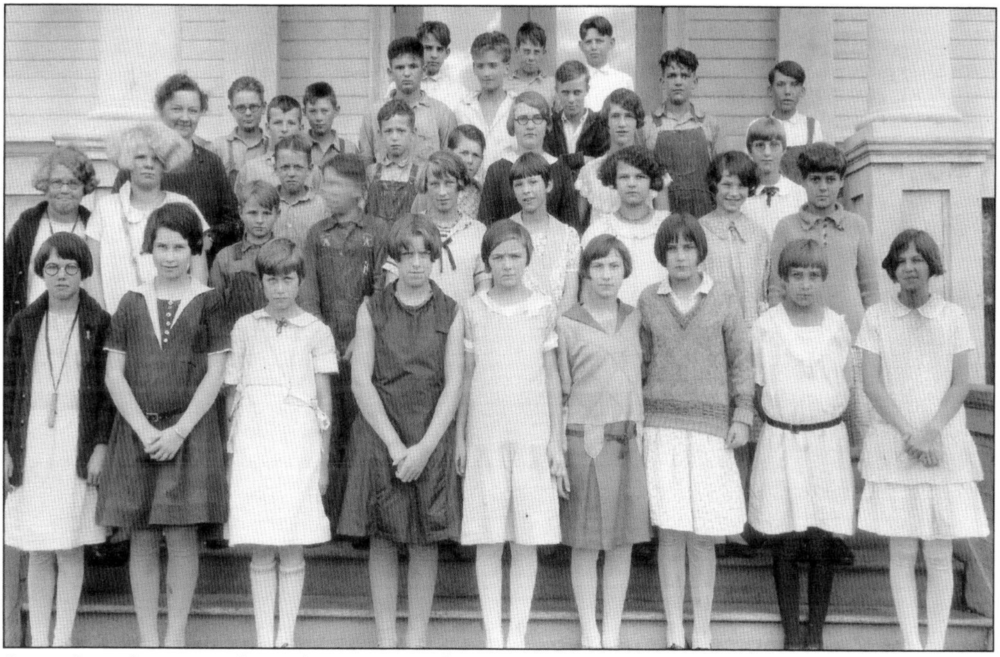

Seventh graders at Washougal Grammar School in 1927 are (first row, in no particular order) Olive Lester, Dorothy Brown, Arla Roth, Mildred Martin, Arline Bruce, Elsie Dahlgren, Ethel Liedtke, Muriel Spoon, and unidentified; and, from left to right, (second row) Elva Lester, Millie Mills, Ernest Cornelius, Harvey Rancore, Marie Barnhill, Joy Smith, Althea Talt, Louisa Holterman, and Mary Jane Woodings; (third row) unidentified (teacher), Howard Henning, Leo Mayer, Roma Benbow, Marjorie Wren, Helen Johnson, and Margery Hutchinson; (fourth row) Vern Raven, Lloyd Wing, Woodrow Brown, Stanley Benson, John Liedtke, Lester Woodman, Claude Wren, Robert Giesler, Francis Vail, and Hubert Bedell.

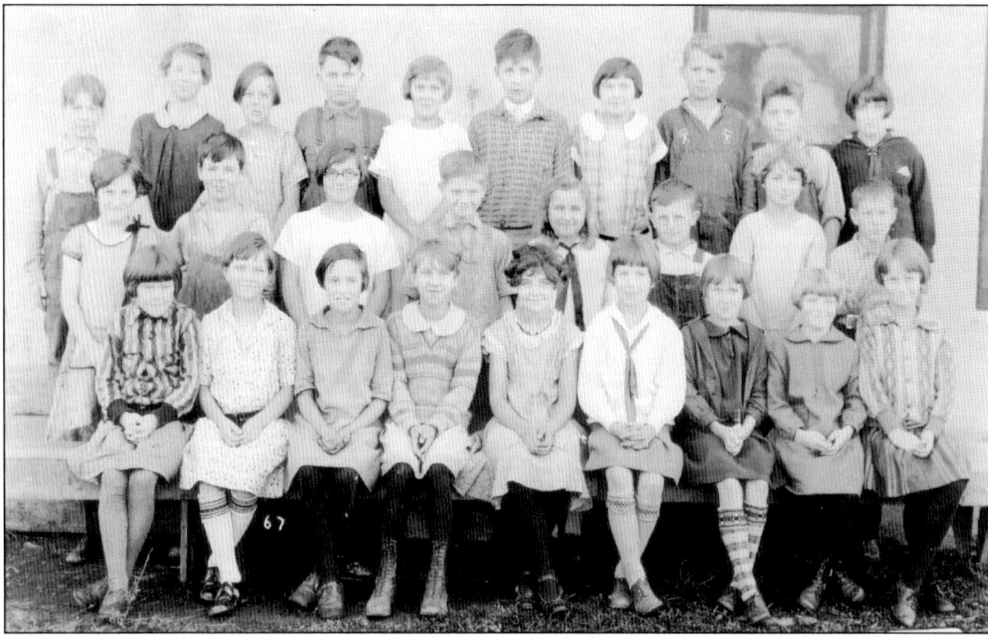

These grade schoolers may have attended the new Hathaway School. Pictured in 1935, from left to right, are (first row) Lena May Mack, Dorothy Gill, Helen Munch, Frieda Scherpf, Nora White, Ella McClain, Jean Catto, Josephine Dole, and Dolly Woodman; (second row) Frances Rasmussen, Bruce Babcock, Jean Flanagan, Bobby Bollinger, Daphne Lowe, Forrest McIntyre, Doris Woodings, and Clarence Dahlgren; (third row) Homer Baldwin, Clara Naillon, Jennie Wren, Roy Howard, Martha Krieves, Wesley McCallister, Marion Martin, Everett Smith, Alvin Guyll, and Claire Waggener.

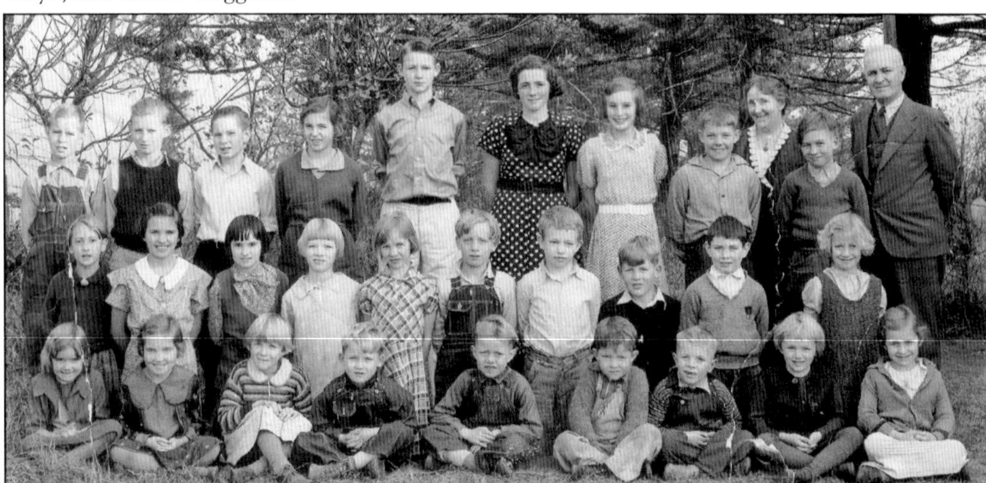

These are students of Mount Pleasant School in Skamania County. Posing for this 1936–1937 school photograph, from left to right, are (first row) unidentified, Carol Knapper, Jean Knapp, John Knapp, Don Burris, unidentified, unidentified, Virginia Cowan, and Cleo Knepper; (second row) Lois Piontek, Lois Knepper, Leah Mae Bethany, unidentified, Ida Mae Dedmore, Ronald Corey, Bill Cowan, Bob Knapp, Duncan McDonald, and Beverly Burris; (third row) George Williams, Bud Knapp, Harold Smead, Annie Mickas, Ray Nordstrom, June Byers, Grace Williams, Ken Ferguson, and Gale Dedmore. The teachers are unidentified. (Photograph by Leo's Studio.)

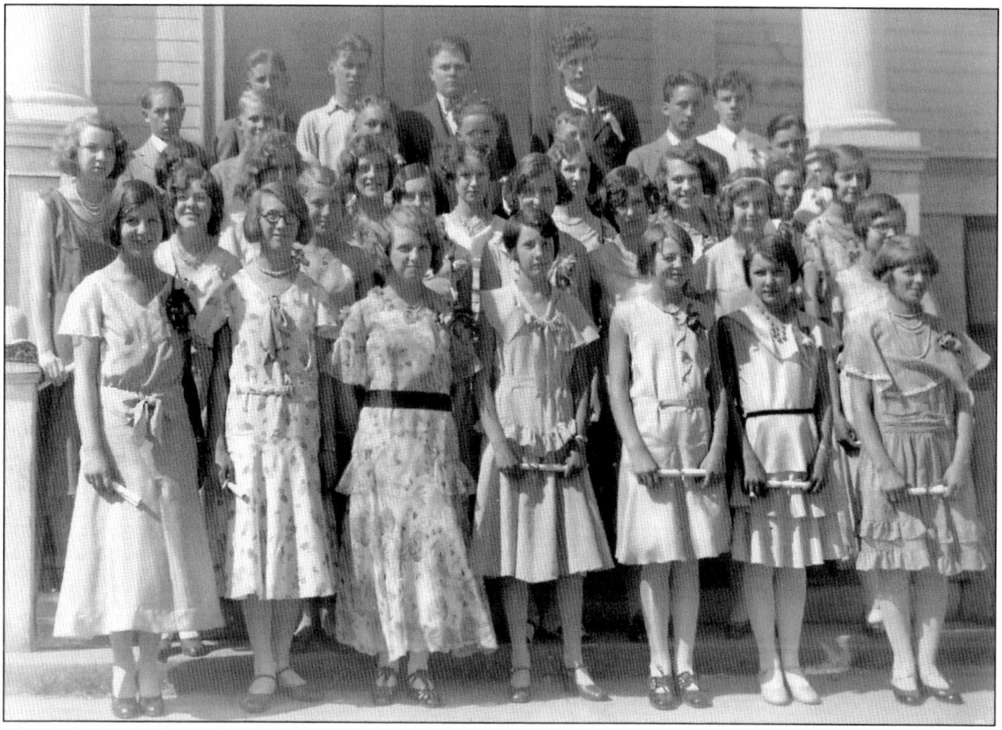

This photograph of the Washougal High School graduating class of 1931 was probably taken on the steps of the Washougal Grammar School. With 35 graduates, Washougal was growing up and its traditions were becoming established. High-school clubs included boys and girls glee clubs, manual-arts training, and sewing. In 1921, graduating senior Ruth Adeline Byers bequeathed her "darling little nose" to underclassman Leah Sherman.

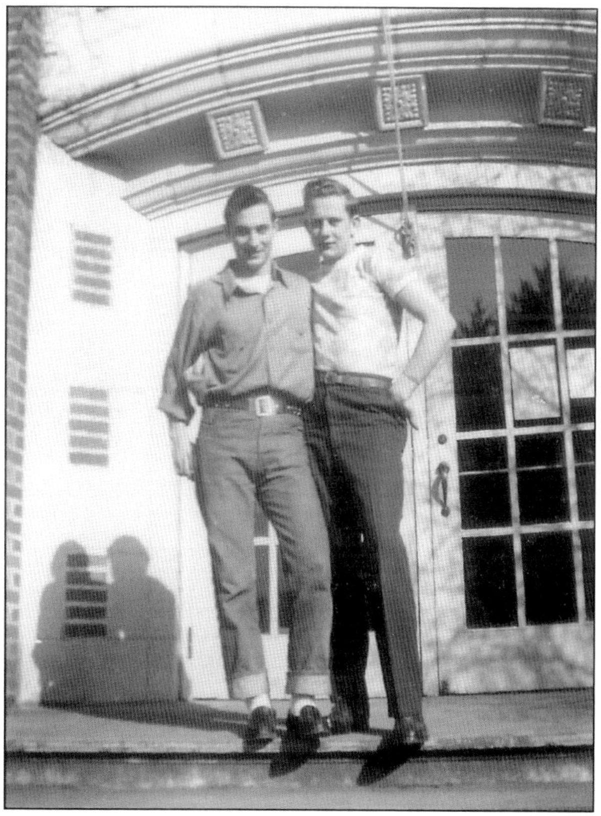

Dennis "Denny" Schroeder and Jerome "Buck" Kiederowskie stand together on the steps of the old Washougal High School Building on B Street in 1947. Denny and Jerome played together on the football and basketball teams and were best friends. After high school, Jerome worked at the paper mill as a machine inspector.

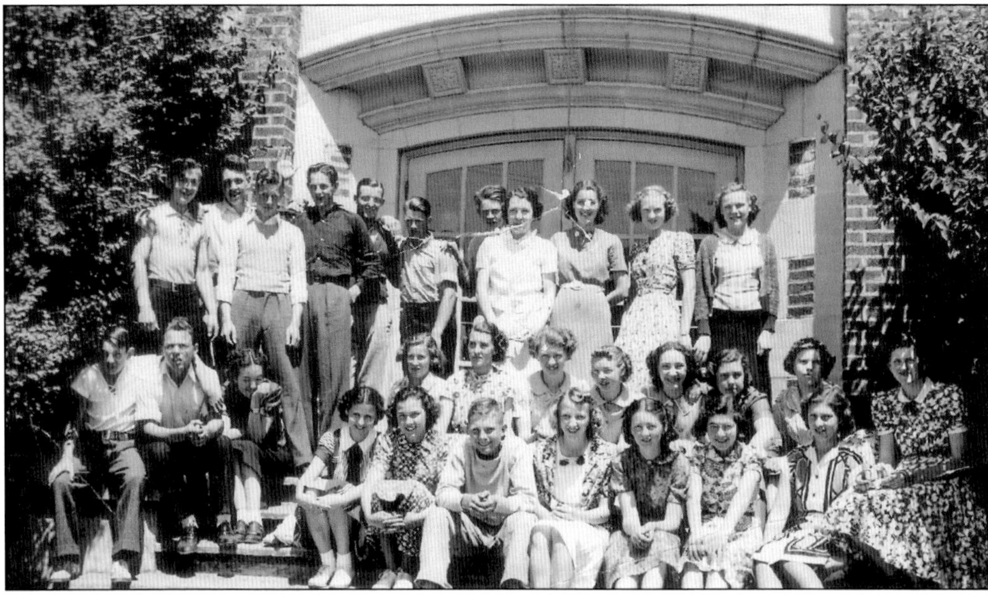

Students from a high-school class or club pose together on the front steps at the old Washougal High School. Pictured here, from left to right, are (seated, first row) Naomi McDowell, Betty Higham, Willis Britton, Dorothy Poser, Mary Josephine Thrailkill, Kathryn McCallister, and Lily Mickes; (seated, second row) Alfred Roley, Sydney Wellman, Genevieve Roley, Sarah Dale Howard, Alberta Bedell, Helen Knapp, LaRita Ferguson, Eleanor Warren, Helen Bemis, Virginia Sooter, and June Rainey; (standing, third row) Bob Meredith, Bob Stump, Don Dahlgren, Bob Peery, Harvey Packer, Floyd Margeson, Art Meredith, Lea Baron, Margaret Blaisdell, Alice May Hutchinson, and Rose Krohn.

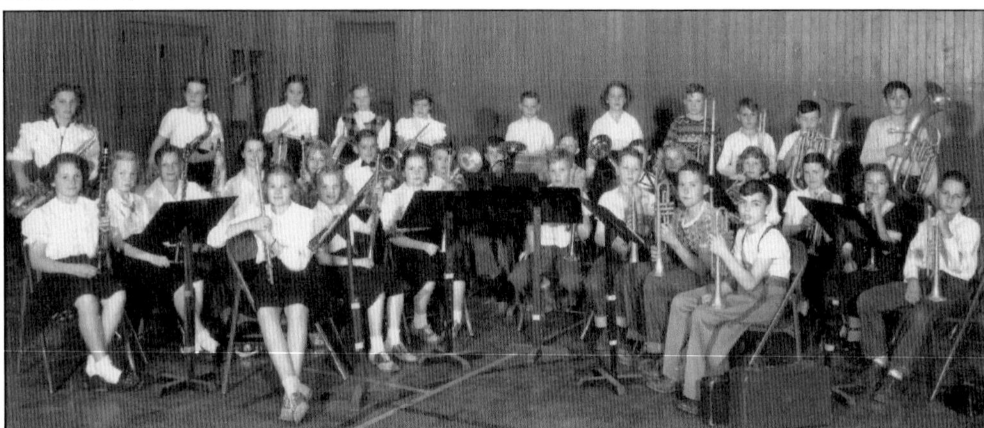

These *c.* 1935 students, likely fifth graders beginning band classes, are part of a celebrated musical tradition in Washougal. Some of these kids went on to be part of the Washougal Drum and Bugle Corps. The band members, from left to right, are (first row) Diana Gabriel, Jacquline Bjorensen, Karen Newby, Jimmy Rodgers, Morris Munch, Bob Bedell, and Teddy Lightheart; (second row) Patsy Malcome, Mary Caroline Stuhr, Fred Straub, Phillis Erickson, unidentified, unidentified, unidentified, Skipper Bolger, Bob ?, YaVonne Rassmussen, LaVine Potter, Marilou Aslin, Mary Denton, Annice Rodgers, and Jerry Wagner; (third row) Betty Garland, Sharon McKinney, Rochelle Walling, Coco Hendrickson, Jackie Whitley, Larry Jones, Diana ?, Dick ?, Vincent Loman, Allen Clark, and unidentified.

Gudrun Jemtegaard (left), pictured here with Minerva Tarleton, was born in Norway and emigrated with her parents by steamship across the Atlantic Ocean. The family settled in Mount Pleasant. Gudrun graduated from Washougal High School and attended university before returning to Washougal and the Washougal School District. Gudrun, a leading Washougal teacher and citizen, served her community both as an educator and a community leader.

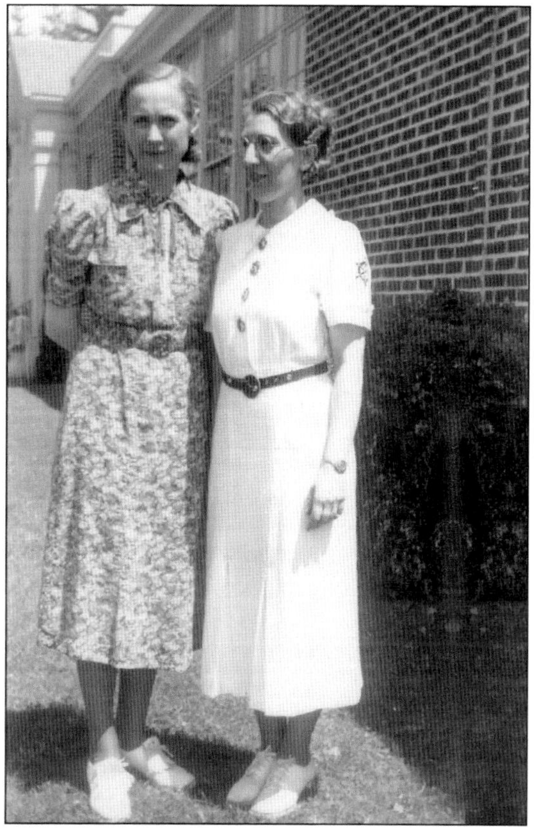

Over the years, hundreds of men and women have served the community of Washougal as educators both inside the classroom and out. The Washougal High School faculty, pictured here in 1950 on the steps of the old Washougal High School, includes school secretary Mrs. White (second from left, front row), principal Terrell Lauren (fifth from left, back row), and Gudrun Jemtegaard (second to last row, fourth from left).

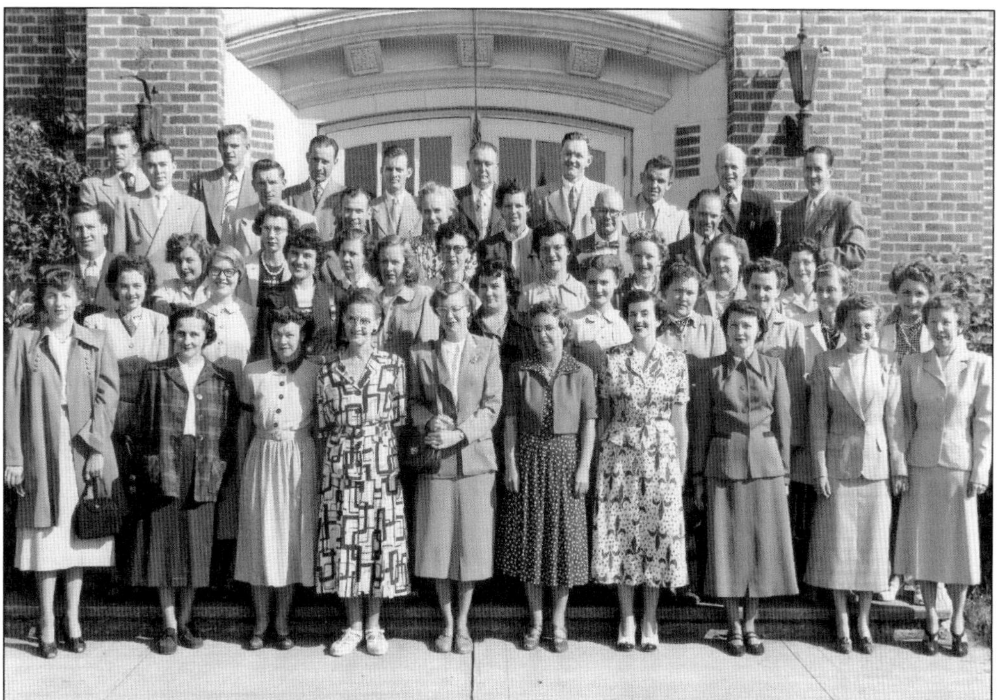

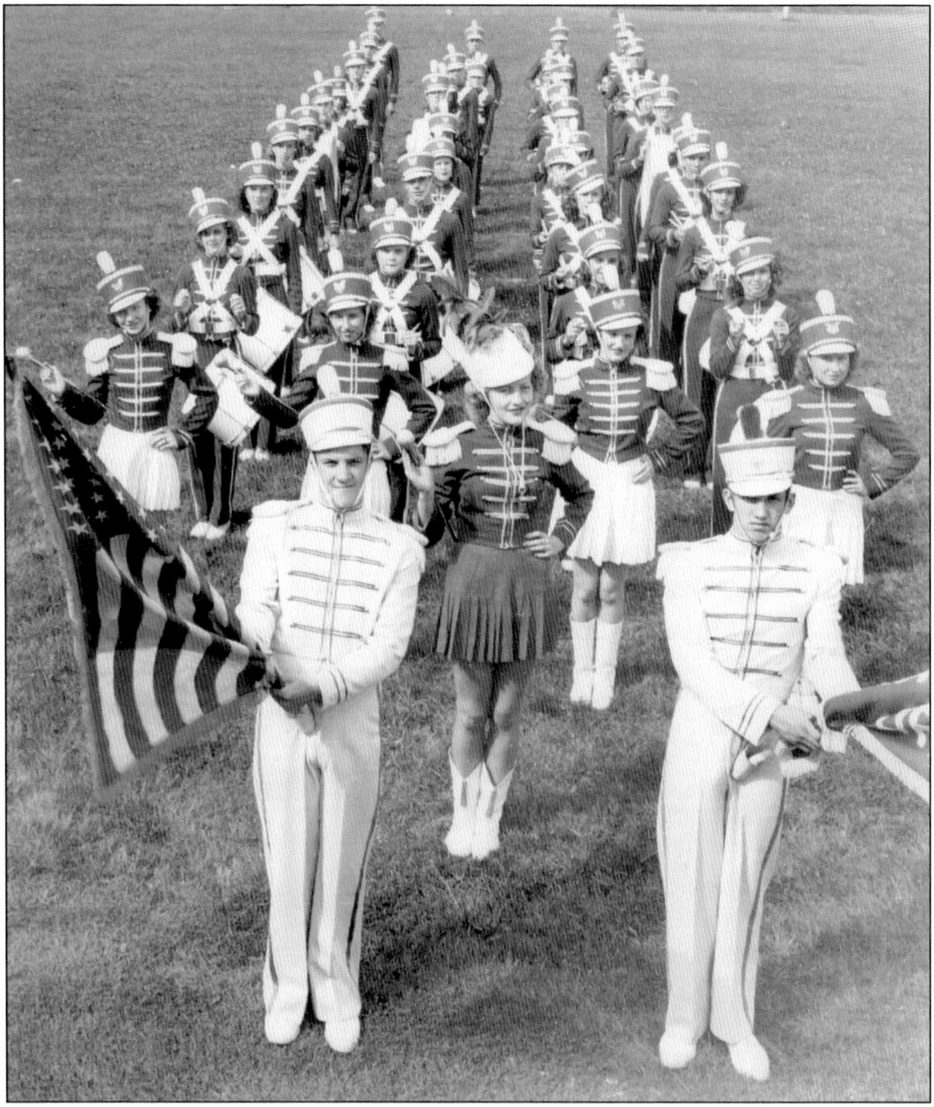

The Washougal Drum and Bugle Corps kept their promise to "take the inland empire by storm" during the 1930s and 1940s. Directed by Eldon Phillips, the members of the corps in 1940 included (majorettes) Yyvonne Duncan, Idell Ernst, Dalphyne Krubeck, Beth Madison; (drum corps) James Dean, Corrine Dixon, Dorothy Ensworth, Joyce Fletcher, Ann McNett, Starla Poulsen, Glen Radford, Jean Rogers, Arlean Taylor, Shirley Tuttle, and Joan Scott; and (band) Marie Beck, Ward Buzan, Bill Cooper, David Cox, Barbara Dean, Bill Dixon, Don Kronholm, Robert Peake, Fred Tidland, Wes Varney, and Doris Walling. Members in 1939 included (majorettes) Bernice Brown, Ruth Foster, Laura Heintz, Edra Jett, Joanne "Joan" Jett, Louise Luthy, Barbara Nickel, and Eileen Richardson; and (drum and band) Donna Alexander, Joy Alexander, Allan Armstrong, Franklin Blair, James Britton, Wilbur Britton, Milton Brown, Ross Brown, Doris Bruce, James Bruce, LuRae Carlson, Helen Case, Billy Cox, Everett Cox, Garth Duncan, Neff Duncan, Billy Farrell, Leslie Fleming, Dedra Flohr, Earl Flohr, Boyd Gibson, Tom Gibson, Wayne Halling, Harlan Hemm, Jack Harkin, Leif Leifson, Allan Lightheart, Junior Margeson, James Martell, James Mays, Elton Nystrom, Viola Packer, Dale Pederson, Glen Reavis, Don Recdolf, George Seeley, Loren Smith, Keith Stoops, Clyde Walling, Curtis Whetzel, Wayne Whetzel, and Ernest Wilson.

Majorettes, including Louise Luthy (left), pose on the parade grounds during a competition in 1940. The spirited, award-winning corps became the pride of the community. In 1939, the Camas-Washougal Kiwanis Club paid their expenses so they could compete at the Kiwanian Convention. The corps also won the Hill Military Academy's Marching Prize and Honorable Mention at the Portland Rose Festival Parade.

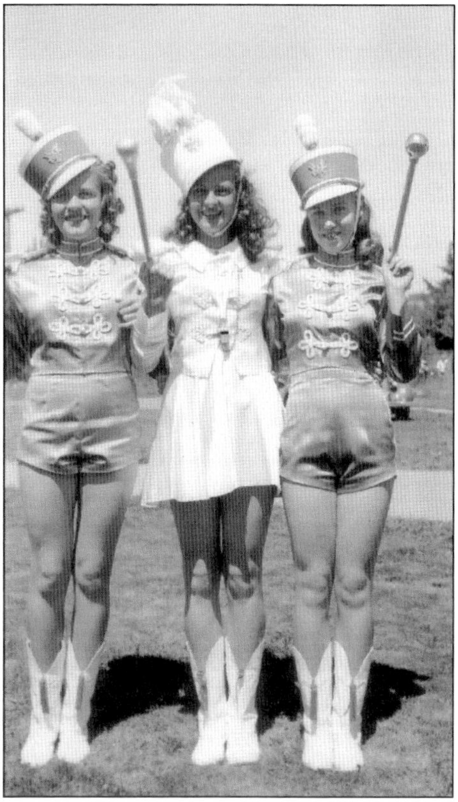

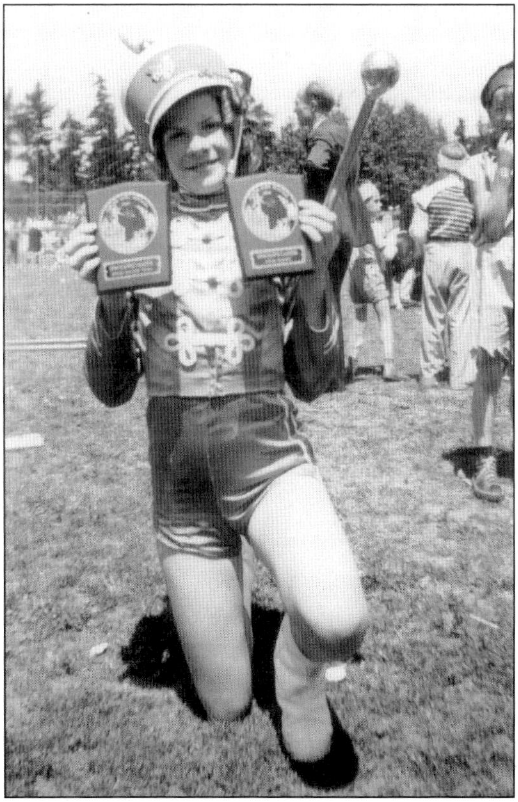

Washougal Drum and Bugle Corps majorette Ruth Foster displays Sweepstakes prizes won by the corps in 1939. In 1938, the Pendleton Woolen Mills donated materials and tailoring assistance to the corps for their new uniforms. Clarence M. Bishop, in a letter to Eldon Phillips, writes, "Our company has always felt a distinct pride in the success of the Corps," which represented "the enterprise and spirit of the community."

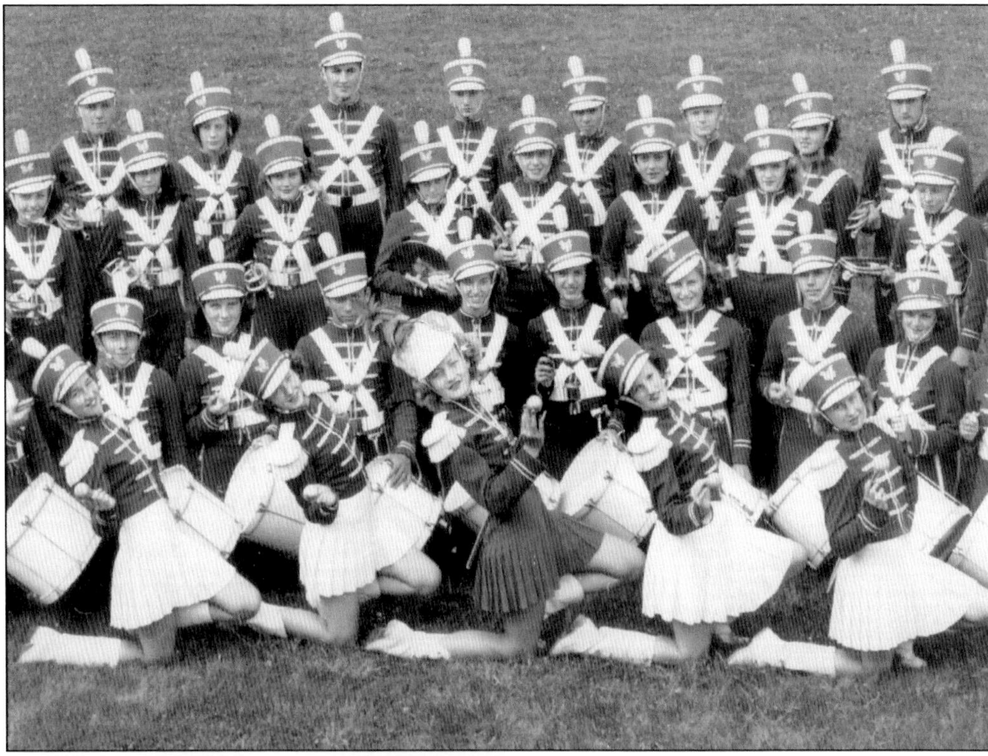

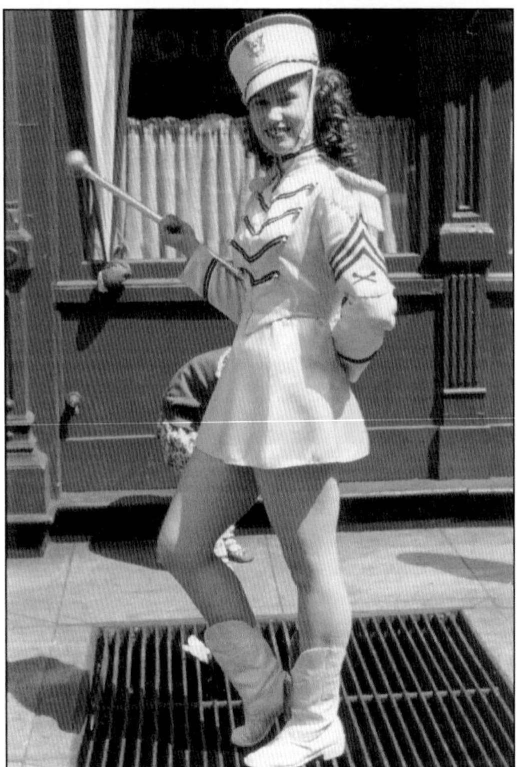

The corps, pictured here again in 1939, benefited from local support and sponsorship. Booster buttons raised money for a planned trip to the American Legion State Convention in Spokane, where the corps took the state championship and garnered four first place prizes, one each for the corps, the majorettes, individual majorette Edra Jett, and individual drummer Wayne Halling.

The majorettes and baton twirlers competed with the band, but they also had their own separate competitions. Like the rest of the drum corps, the baton team in 1941 was a championship team. Joanne "Joan" Jett, pictured here in 1941, was an award-winning member of the team.

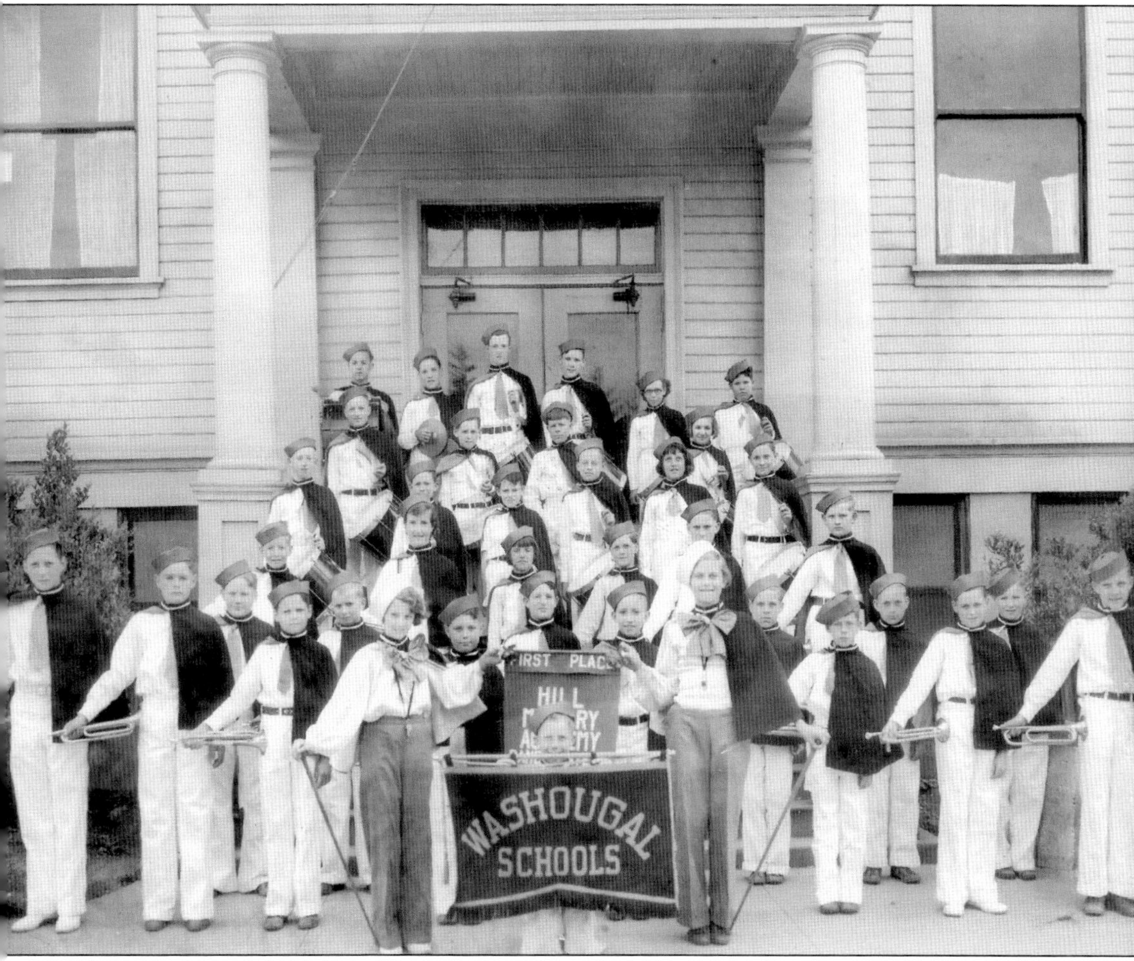

Washougal High School did not have a monopoly on first-place prizes. Washougal's Junior Drum Corps, pictured here in 1940, won their share of awards, including the 1936 Best Junior Drum Corps at the American Legion State Convention in Longview, Washington. In all, they won three junior state championships. During the 1930s, the Junior Drum and Bugle Corps won the Junior Rose Festival three years in a row. Eldon Phillips became a local hero for his leadership with the students of the Drum and Bugle Corps. Phillips came to Washougal in 1935, beginning as a fifth-grade teacher. He would stay in the district for 40 years and become a school principal. His wife, Irma, also taught school in Washougal.

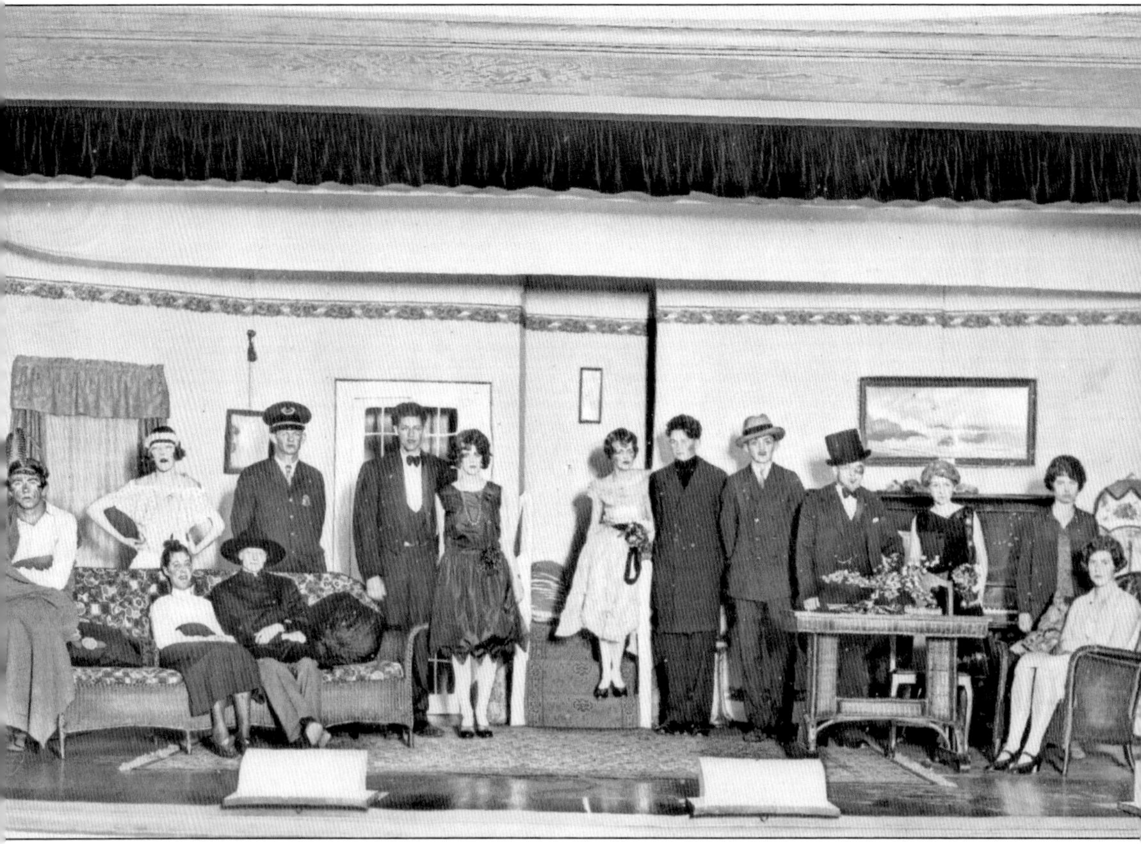

In 1925, the class of 1928 staged *What Happened to Jones* by playwright George Broadhurst. The play opened on Broadway in 1897. It featured a bridegroom who, when caught gambling by police, dresses in women's clothes and escapes into a women's bathhouse. Needless to say his bride is not pleased and does not accept his explanation of events. The play had been made into a silent, black-and-white movie in 1920 and perhaps that inspired the class to do the show. The players, from left to right, are Otto Scherff as Bigbee, Daphne ? as Helma, Lella ? (seated) as Alvina, Ray Andrews (seated) as Bishop, Earl Schafer as Halder, John Brantner as Richard, Leah Sherman as Marjorie, Vaiden Durgan as Cissy, Delbert Wilson as Jones, Leo Gallant as Fuller, Owen Owens as Mr. Ebenezer Goodly, Helen Russell as Mrs. Ebenezer Goodly, and Charlotte Wooding (seated) as Minerva. Miss Hatley directed the show.

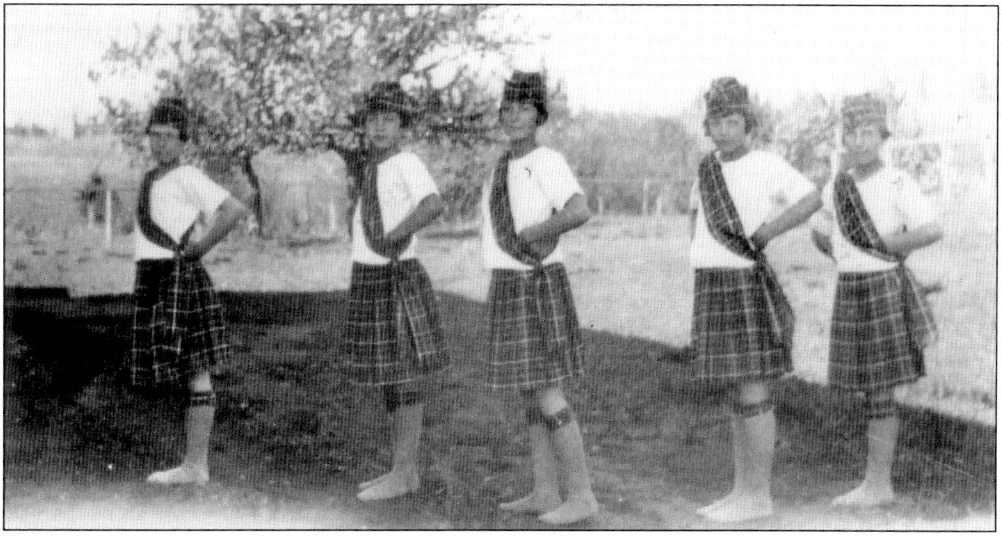

In 1927, the Highland Flins, a dance group at Skye School, featured Ella Huckins, Lillian Buhman, Louise Buhman, Stella Pohl, and Ivy Pohl. Many Washougal children had parents or grandparents who had emigrated from Europe to America. Once naturalized, these immigrants kept their old-country traditions alive with dance and music performed during local events and festivals. Some of the largest immigrant groups came from Norway, Sweden, Poland, and Germany.

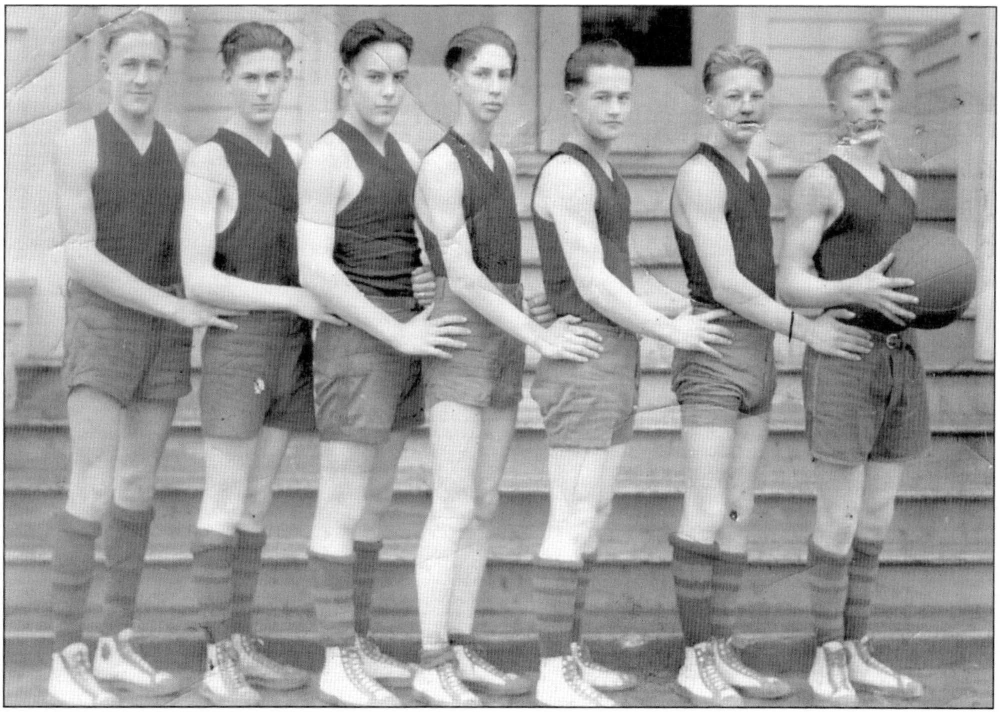

Athletics and sports teams were enormously popular and enjoyed tremendous community support. More than a few Washougal teams won championships, including the girls basketball team in 1909. In the 1920s, it was popular for young people to use nicknames. Only these nicknames are recorded on this 1920s photograph of the Washougal boys basketball team. These boys, from left to right, are Walt, Bob, Barcy, Spoon, Tubby, Bernard, and Happy.

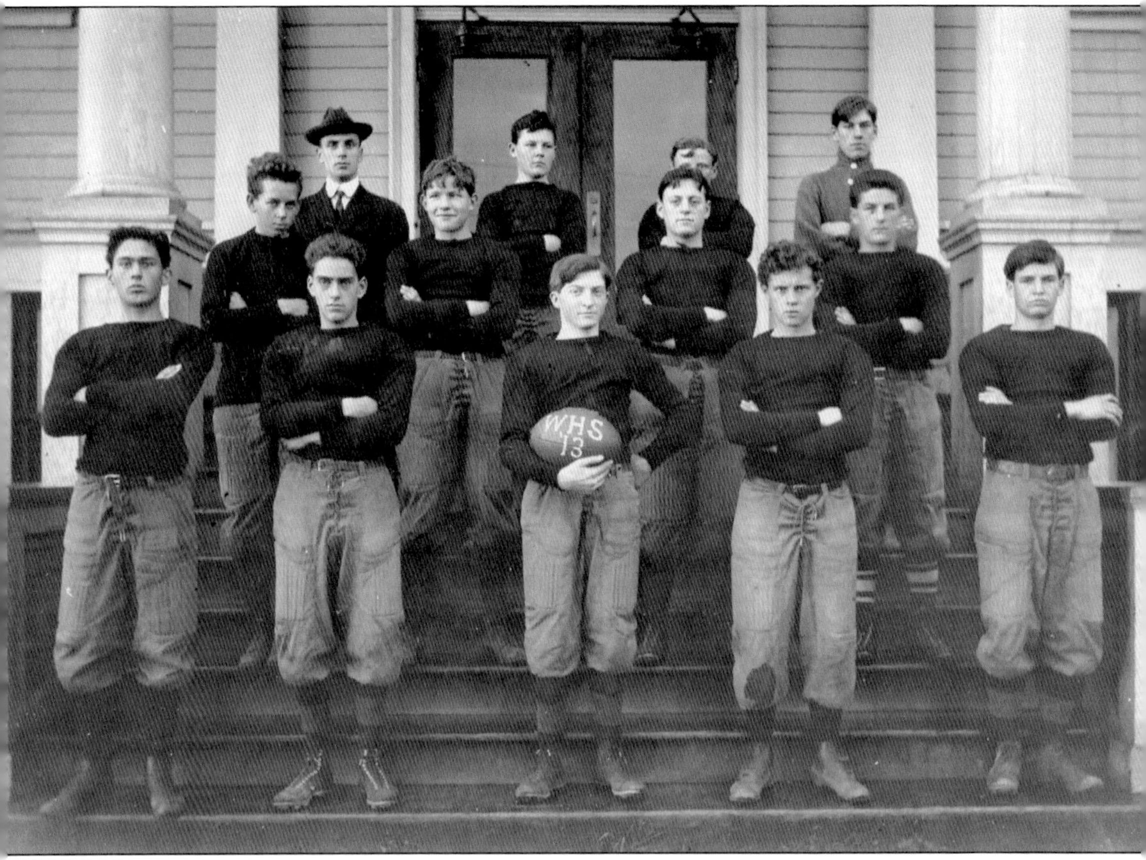

These boys comprised Washougal's first football team in 1913. They wear the football uniform of their era, which is quite different from the attire today. The biggest difference was that many teams did not wear helmets. What helmets existed were more like thick leather caps with ear flaps that tied under the chin. Leather was the best padding material available, and it was stuffed and quilted for use as shoulder padding. The jersey could also be reinforced with quilted padding. The Washougal team wore thigh pads and may also have worn shin guards, which were heavy fabric or leather pads tied around the calf. Pictured here, from left to right, are (first row) Oral Neal, Chester Sappington, Wallace Weger, Loren Cochran, and Harland Brock; (second row) Ed Reinseth, Loren Cochran, George "Cook" Carpenter, and Carl Goot; (third row) H. B. Ferrin (coach), Dick Smith, Clarence Powell, and Laurence Clark.

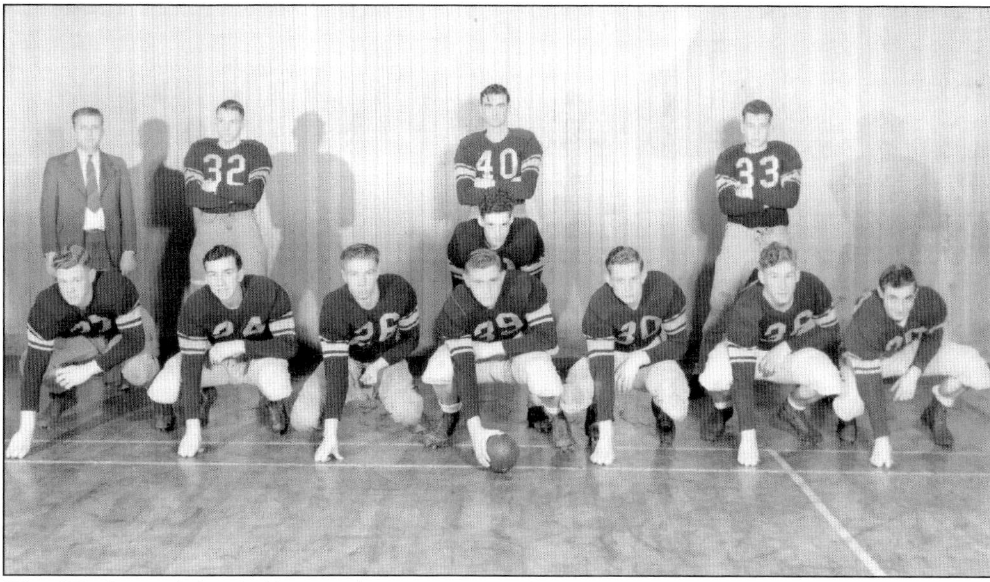

The Washougal football team by 1946 wore shoulder pads and sturdy leather helmets, perhaps with a hard plastic shell. Tough plastics would be in general use for gear by the 1950s. These team members, from left to right, are (first row) Robert Loeffel, Gerald Jendro, Albert Rasmor, Allan Otto, Jerome "Buck" Kiederowski, Loren Rhodes, and Dennis Schroeder; (second row) Wes Hutchinson; (third row) ? Maroney (coach), Wayne Spellman, Ken Devaney, and Ronald McChesney.

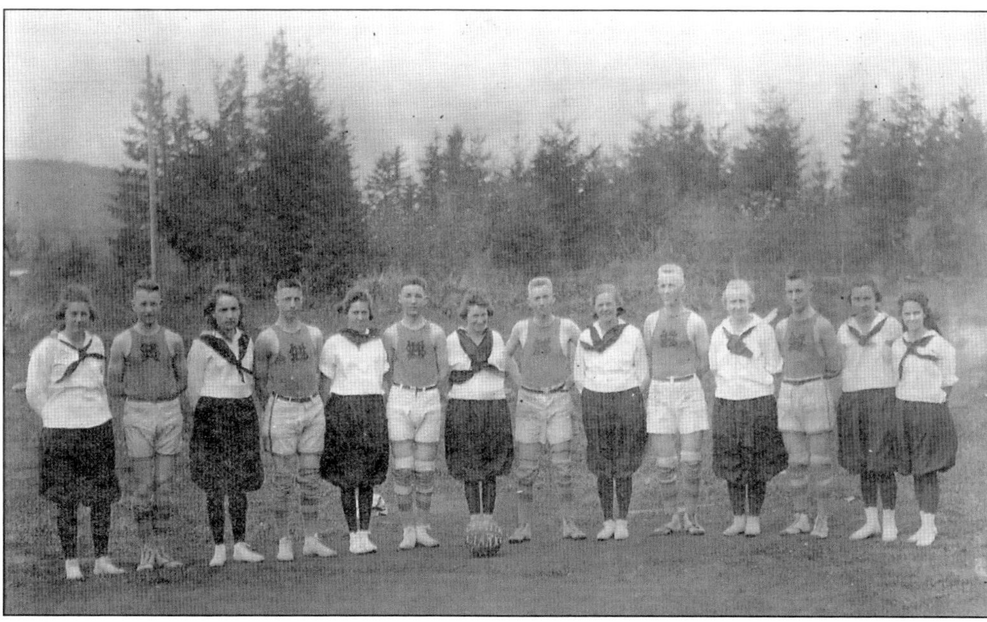

Both the girls and boys basketball teams were champions around 1922. The boys wore similar uniforms as today, though the shorts were belted. The girls wore serge bloomers, a garment they generally detested. Both team's players, pictured here from left to right, are Inez Dunn, Cecil Roley, Edith Kiser, Glen White, Ada Dibble, Paul Clearwater, Grace Dibble, Loren Beatty, Velma Freeland, Lester Strong, Freda Nagel, Mordeci Sayles, Gracia Ough, and Eleanor Keep.

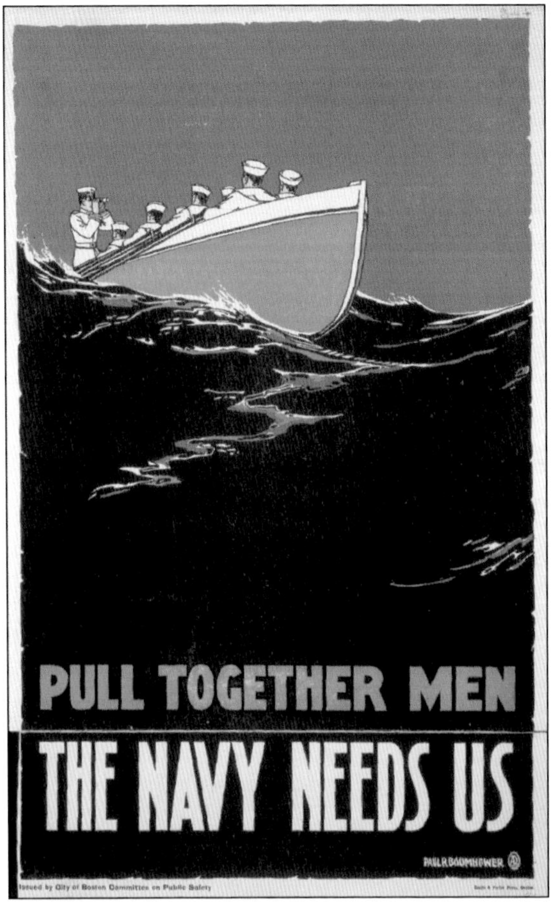

During the world wars, many of Washougal's boys signed up for the navy or coast guard. The navy was part of America's "first line of defense" and posters like this one encouraged enlistment and troop support. A number of Washougal's world-war enlistees joined up with friends or brothers, and thankfully most of them came home. Although some, like Otto Acker, would feel forever changed. (Courtesy Library of Congress.)

Small-town bands were common and popular at the turn of the 20th century. The Washougal Military Band in 1914 was a brass and drum outfit, with tubas, trumpets, and trombones far out-numbering the three clarinets. The all-male players in the band ranged in age from boys, perhaps aged 12 or 13, to grown men.

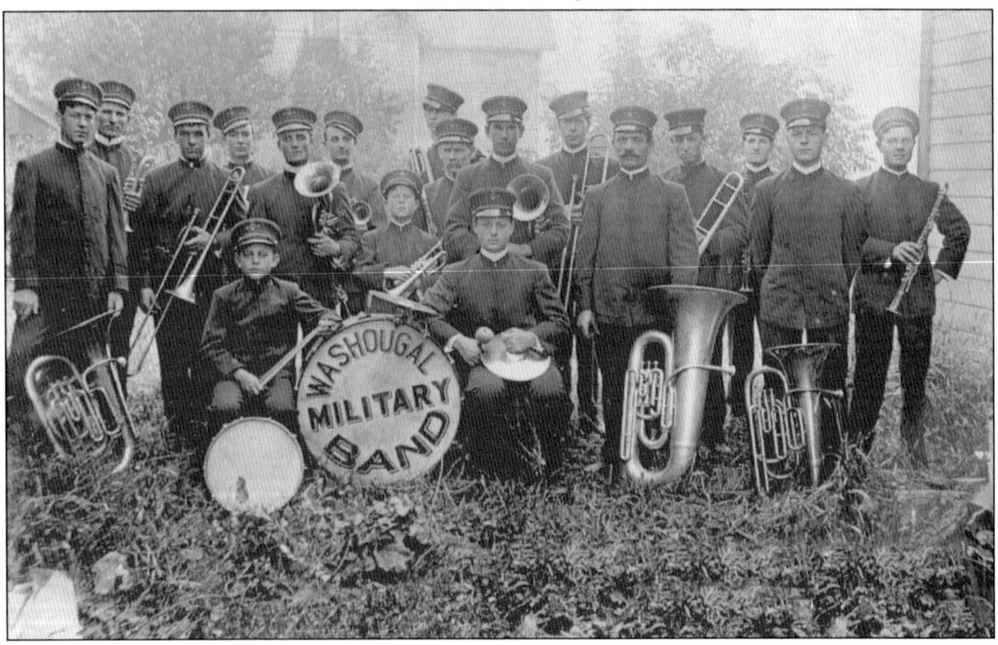

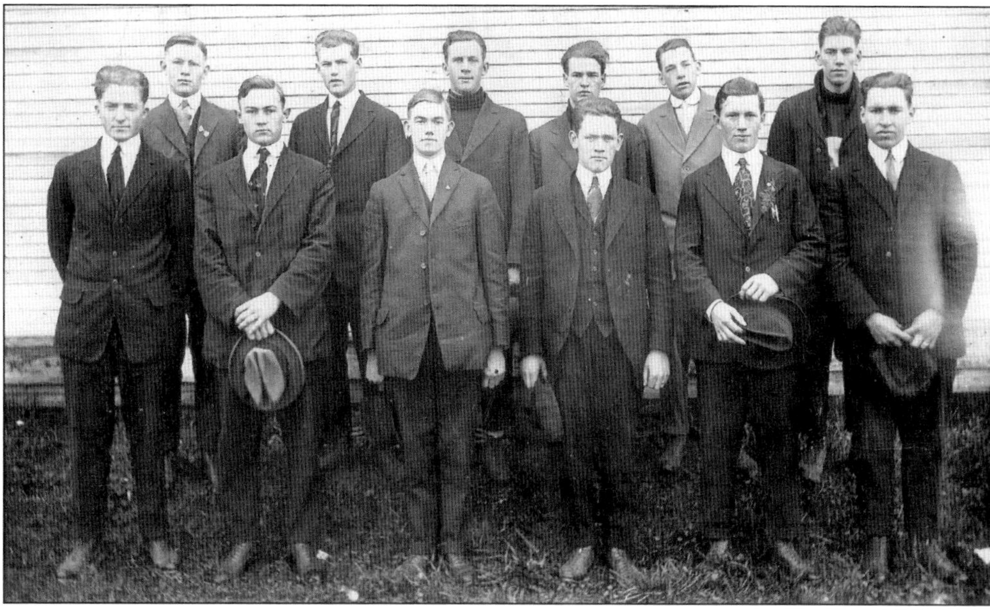

With World War I in full swing, this group of high-school seniors from Washougal enlisted in the Oregon National Guard, Company E, at the Vancouver Barracks in 1917. The young men pictured are (first row, in no particular order) Wallace Weger, Arthur Jones, Walter Strong, Winfield Woodings, Howard Kiser, and unidentified; and, from left to right, (second row) Loren Cochran, Clarence Strong, Ernie Campen, Harland Brock, Cecil Roley, and Lawrence Clark.

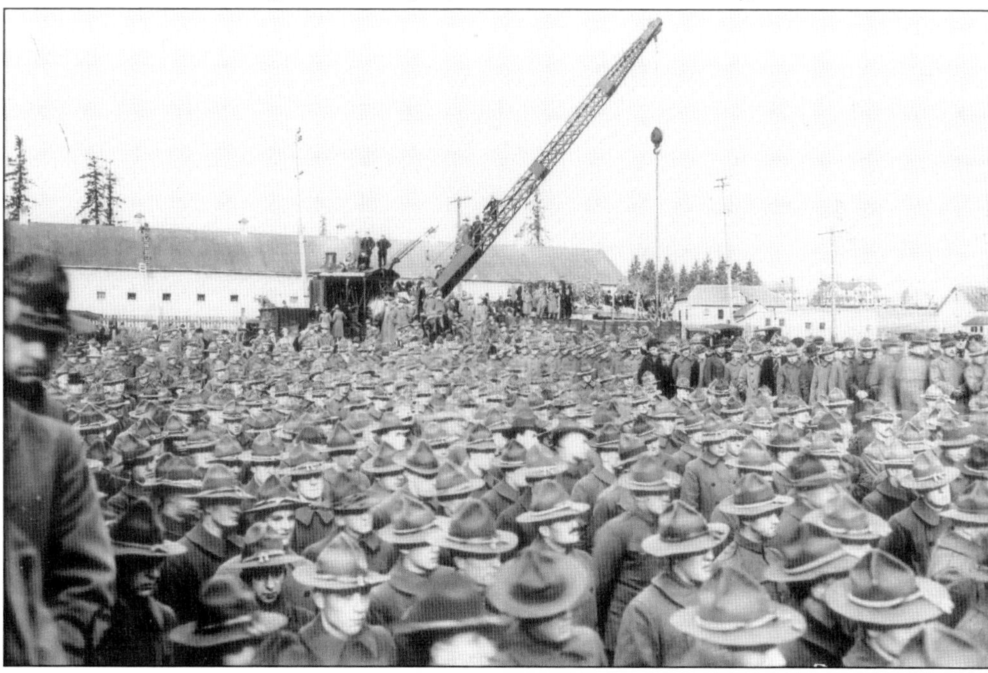

Love of country in Washougal ran deep. Many of Washougal's sons fought during the world wars and in Vietnam, and no small number joined with the throngs of young men gathered here at Fort Vancouver in 1917. Some served overseas, while others rolled up their sleeves on the home front to produce goods the boys at war would need to stay dry and safe so they could return home.

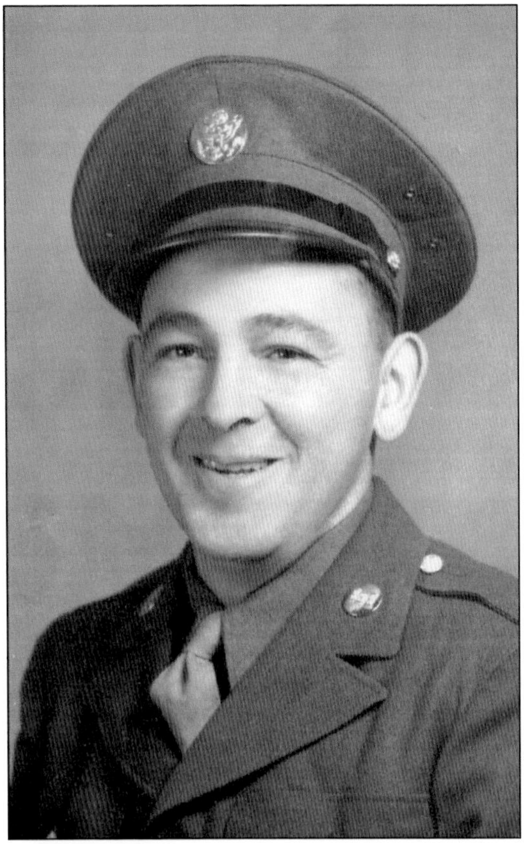

On Monday, May 7, 1945, the *Camas-Washougal Post Record* ran a special V-E Day edition of the paper with the headline "Germany Licked!" Though there was still conflict in the Pacific, Washougal celebrated as they had done in 1918 with word of the armistice. Everyone was hopeful that men like John Ough, pictured here, would soon be coming home.

During World War II, metal was critical to the war effort. America rolled out tanks, airplanes, and munitions, and the citizenry dug up and donated all the scrap metal they could find. Even the cannon outside the Skamania courthouse went for scrap. The army promised to replace the cannon after the war was over, but never did. (Courtesy Skamania County Historical Society.)

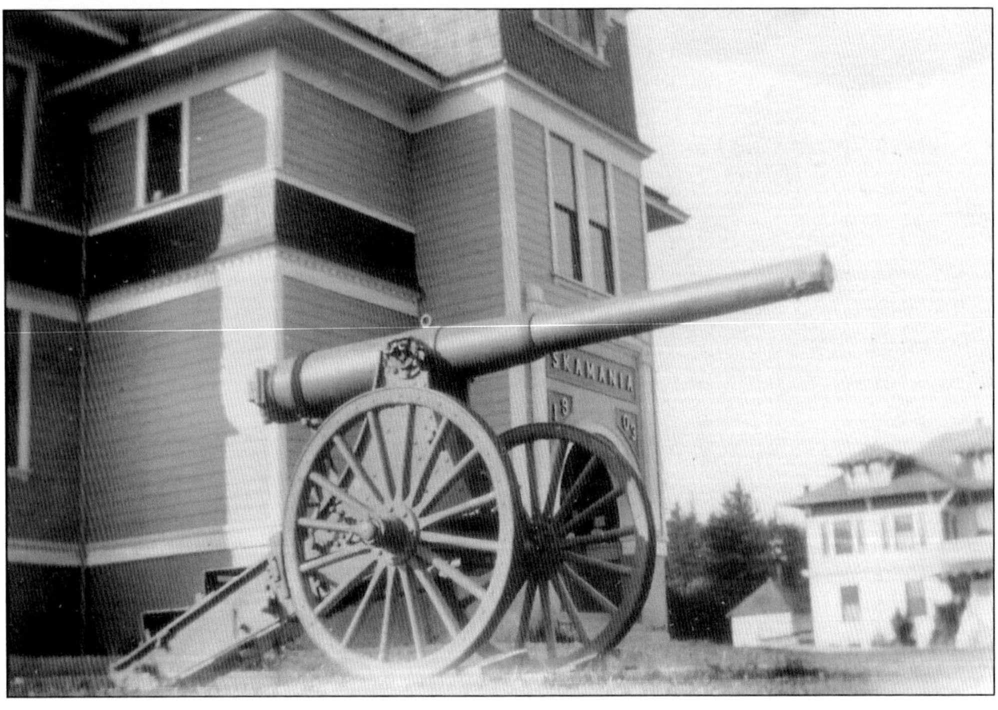

Morris O. Margeson, who drew this autograph in 1945, was 16 years old when he joined the navy. His three older brothers, Jim Jr., Floyd, and Edward, all joined up—and Morris lied so he could, too. Edward and Floyd served as pharmacist mates and Morris served on the USS *Colorado* and saw battle in the Pacific. After the war, Morris became an Alaskan bush pilot.

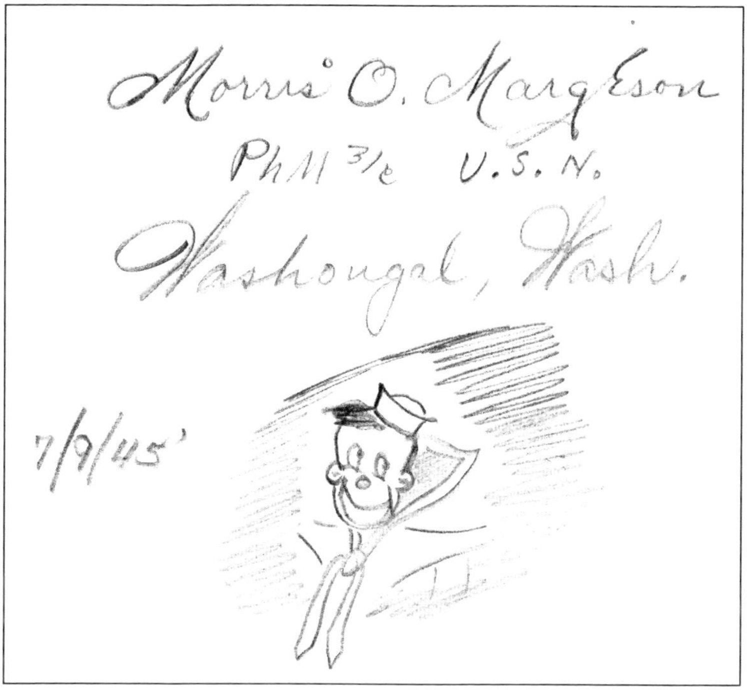

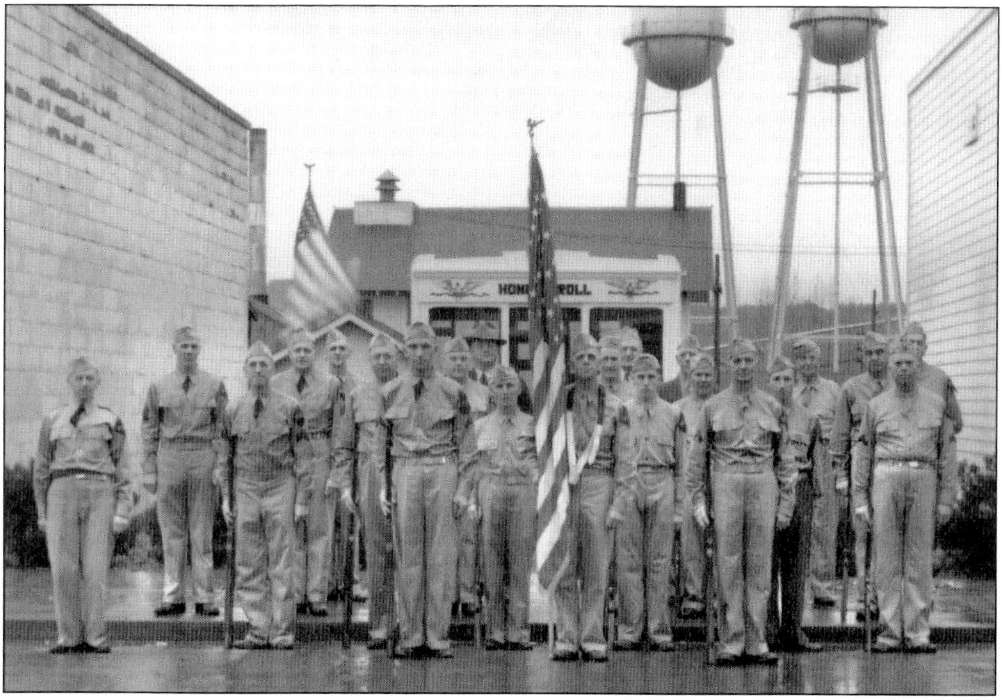

Men stand together in front of this "honor board" on B Street, c. 1943. Though the specifics of this photograph are unknown, occasions like this one provided an opportunity for Washougal to thank its veterans for their service and personal heroism. The men pictured may have included survivors of World War I and perhaps also guardsmen. The civilian is perhaps Washougal mayor Theodore Jenny. (Photograph by Earl Jones.)

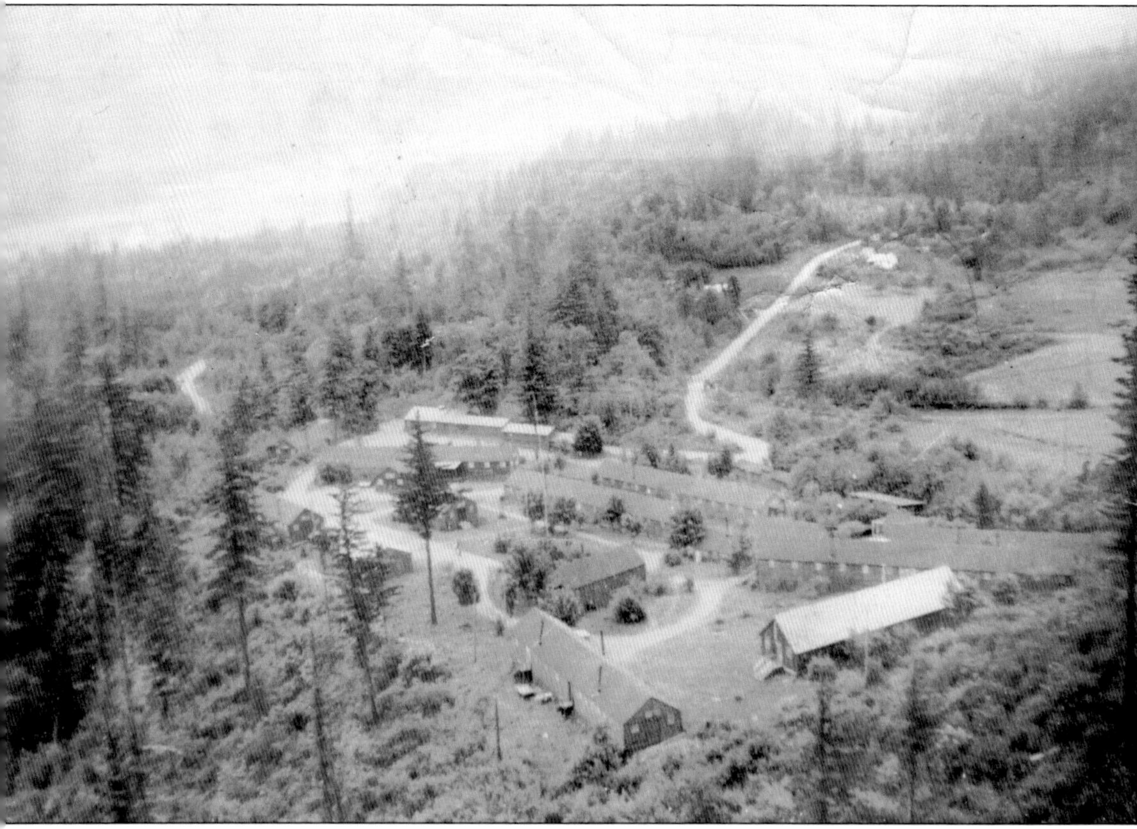

In the aftermath of the Great Depression, Pres. Franklin D. Roosevelt devised plans to lift the country up and put American men and women to work. He developed programs of public work for the public good. One of those was the Civilian Conservation Corps (CCC). In 1933, young men formed into companies began arriving at Fort Vancouver, with many headed for the Gifford Pinchot Forest. Fed and housed by the army, these young men worked hard and earned little, with much of that sent home to their cash-strapped families. The experience would change many of them forever for the better. As they cut trails, planted trees, built roads, and fought fires, they grew up and became men. More than a few married local girls and settled down, becoming part of the communities they helped to build. In the 1930s, camps neighborly to Washougal included Camp Beacon Rock (photographed *c.* 1930), Camp Hemlock at Wind River, Camp Rock Creek at Stevenson, Camp Washougal, and a small camp at Bear Prairie. (Courtesy Skamania County Historical Society.)

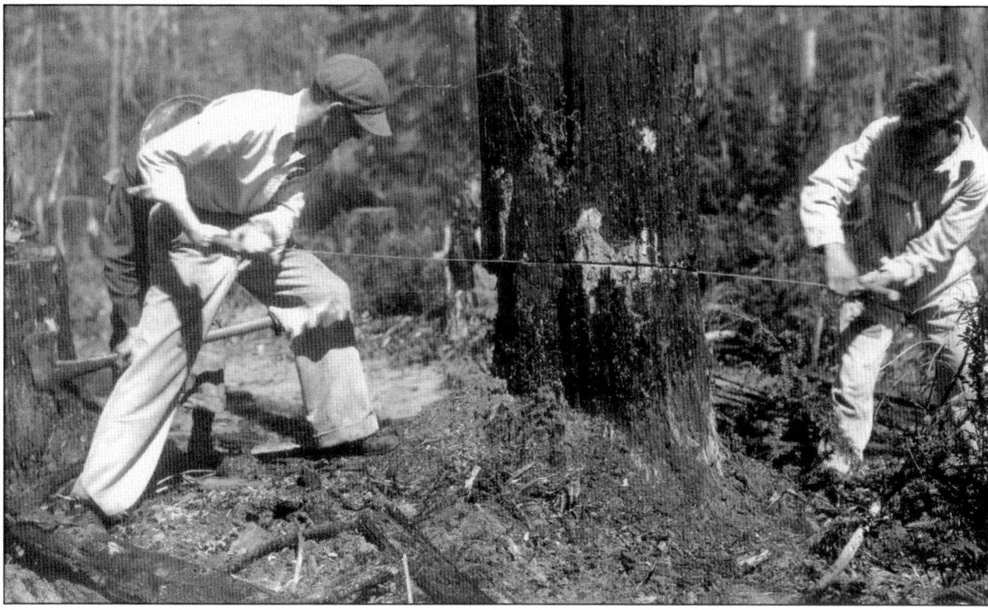

Camp Washougal was unique in that young white men and young black men shared the same camps. Usually they were segregated. Though unsure at first, the camp commander felt things went well. The duties of all the men at Washougal were similar to the work at other camps. These unidentified men of Company 944 from Wind River cut snags to create a fire break. (Courtesy Gifford Pinchot National Forest.)

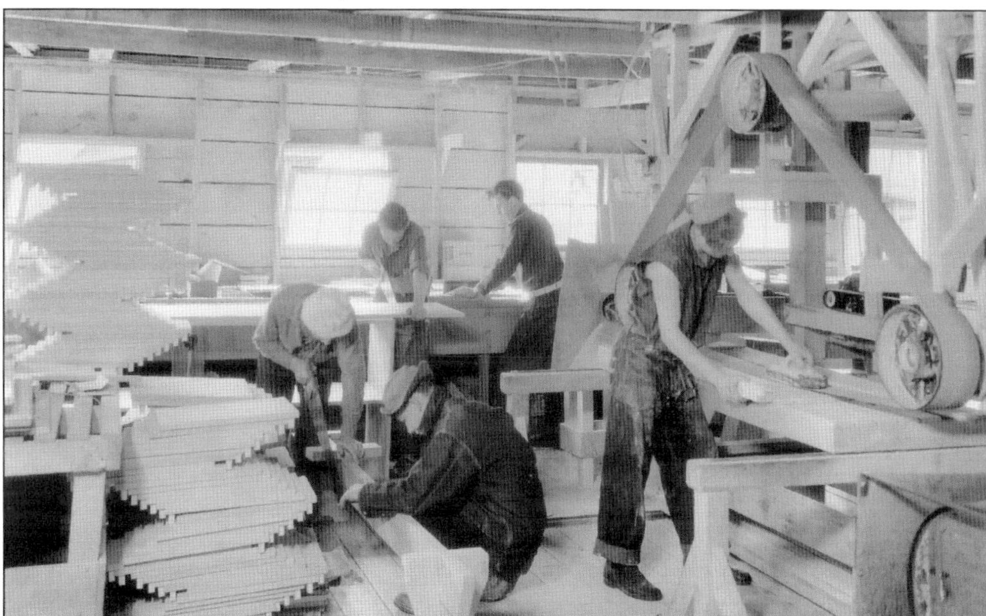

Local CCC men built the concrete dam at Trout Creek and earned reputations as good carpenters and stone masons. They built fire lookouts, strung miles of telephone wire, and built roads extensively through the area. They also replanted hundreds of acres of timberland still scarred from the Yacolt fire in 1902. These men at Rock Creek work at the carpenter shop in 1935. (Courtesy Gifford Pinchot National Forest.)

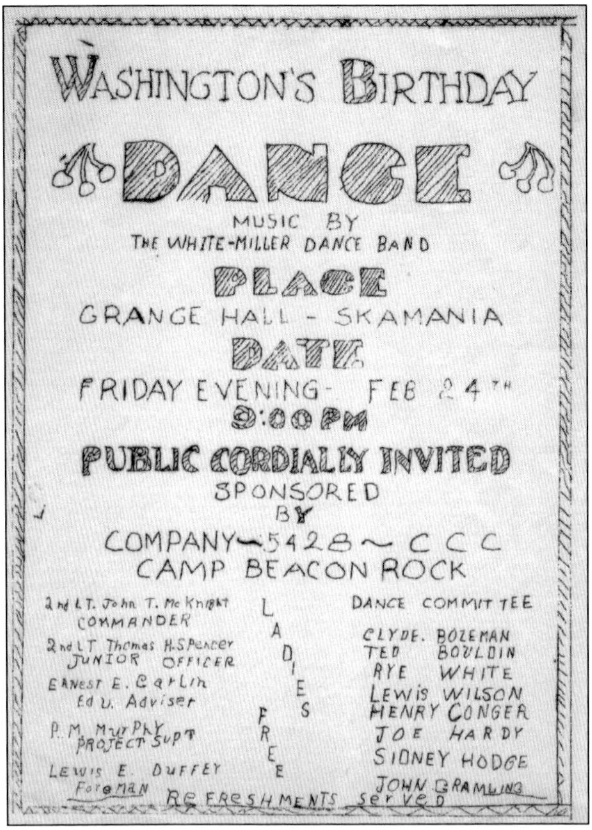

Company 5480 had a baseball team, the Clowns, and recreation, but they still missed their families back home. Mess call was likely an everyday joy, but there is little to doubt that dances were met with an even greater enthusiasm. Beacon Rock even had a dance committee. What the local girls thought of the CCC boys can probably be evidenced by the many marriages. (Courtesy Skamania County Historical Society.)

Men from Company 945 at Rock Creek paint a Forest Service truck in 1935. Though the men were essentially forest rangers, the army handled logistics for the CCC. Gen. George C. Marshall was commander at the Vancouver Barracks from 1936 through 1938, and the camps continued to operate until the start of World War II. (Courtesy Gifford Pinchot National Forest.)

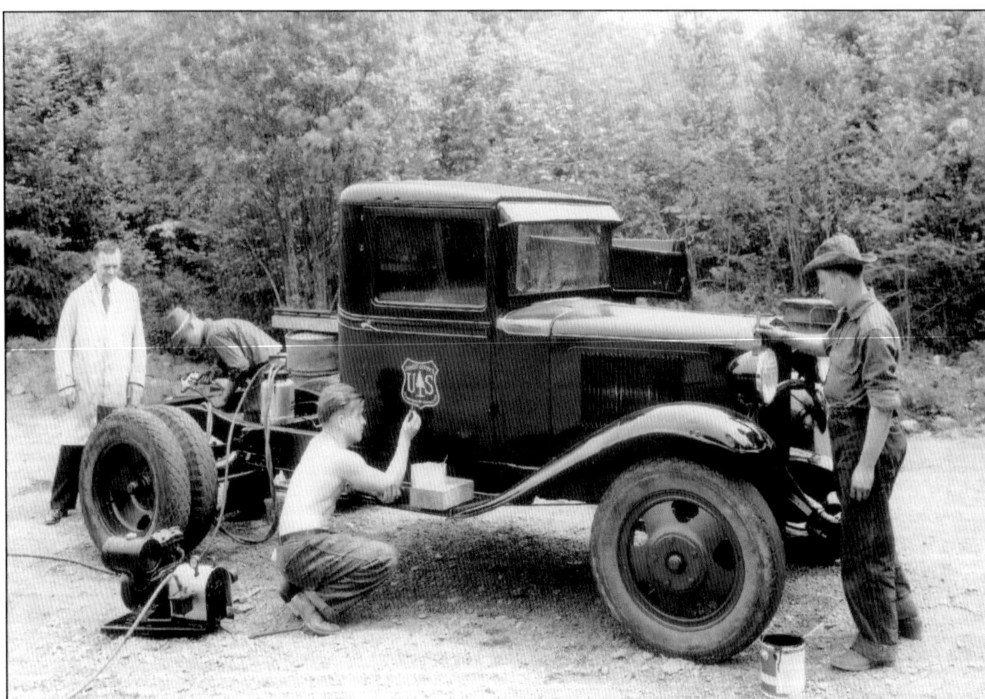

Seven

WASHOUGAL TODAY

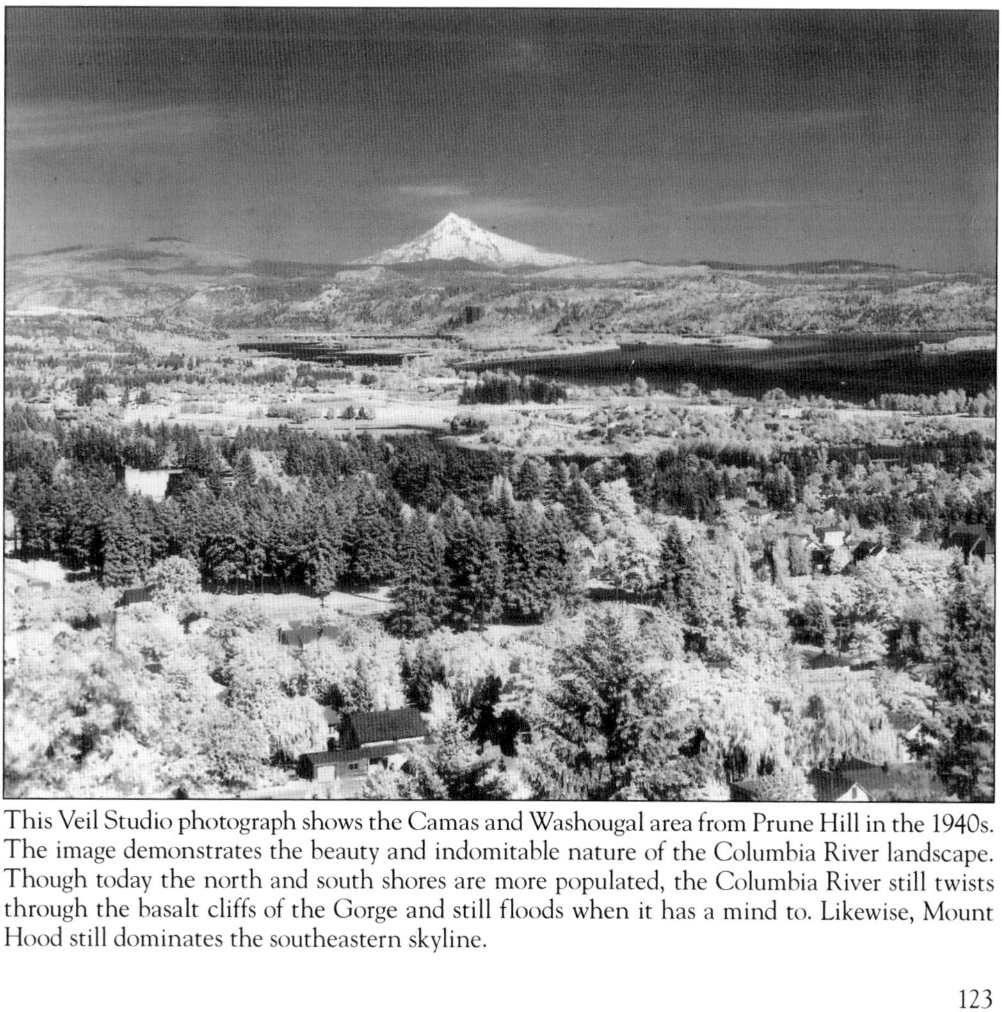

This Veil Studio photograph shows the Camas and Washougal area from Prune Hill in the 1940s. The image demonstrates the beauty and indomitable nature of the Columbia River landscape. Though today the north and south shores are more populated, the Columbia River still twists through the basalt cliffs of the Gorge and still floods when it has a mind to. Likewise, Mount Hood still dominates the southeastern skyline.

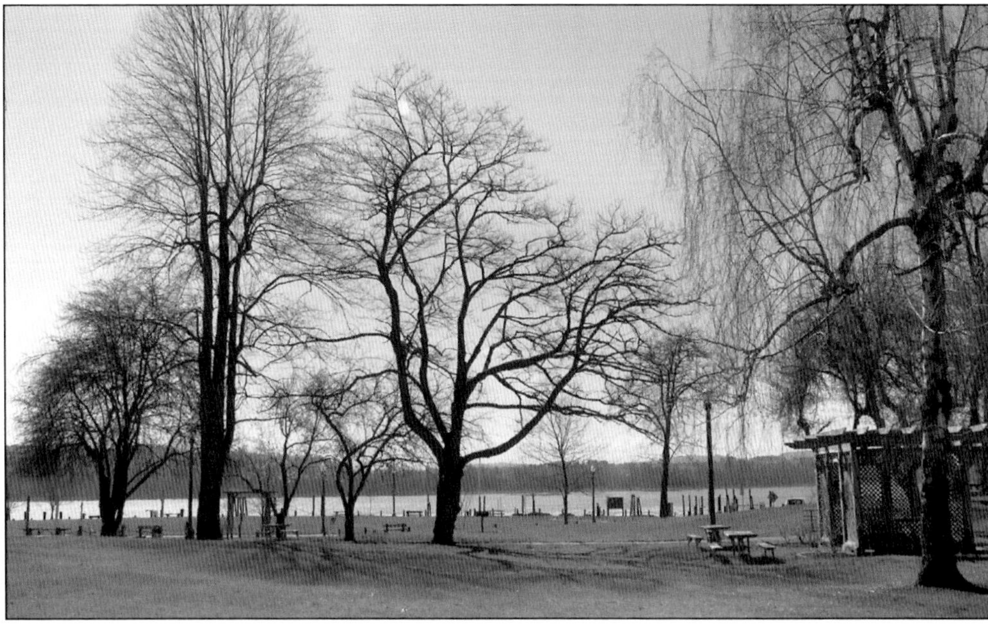

David Clark and Ann Parker were among Washougal's first pioneers, settling on the Columbia River in 1845. Parker built a landing and founded the town of Parkersville, though once Washougal was founded, Parkersville would be abandoned. What remains of the old Parker land claim is now a riverfront park dedicated to Camas and Washougal's pioneers. Shady trees, benches, and picnic tables provide a perfect family setting.

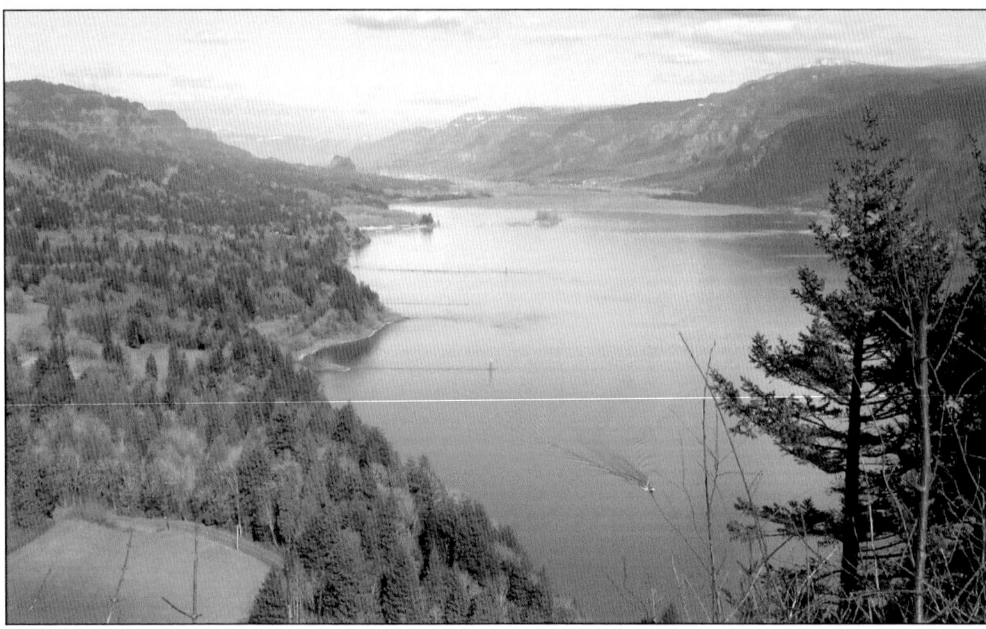

Washougal rests at the foot of the Columbia River Gorge. Forged by volcanics, earthquakes, and the catastrophic Missoula floods, the Gorge is a magnificent geologic landscape that draws volcanologists, campers, hikers, boaters, and windsurfers by the hundreds of thousands annually. The road to the Gorge sweeps through Washougal past Steigerwald Lake and Wildlife Refuge, rising quickly. From the Cape Horn cliffs along Highway 14, the view is absolutely breathtaking.

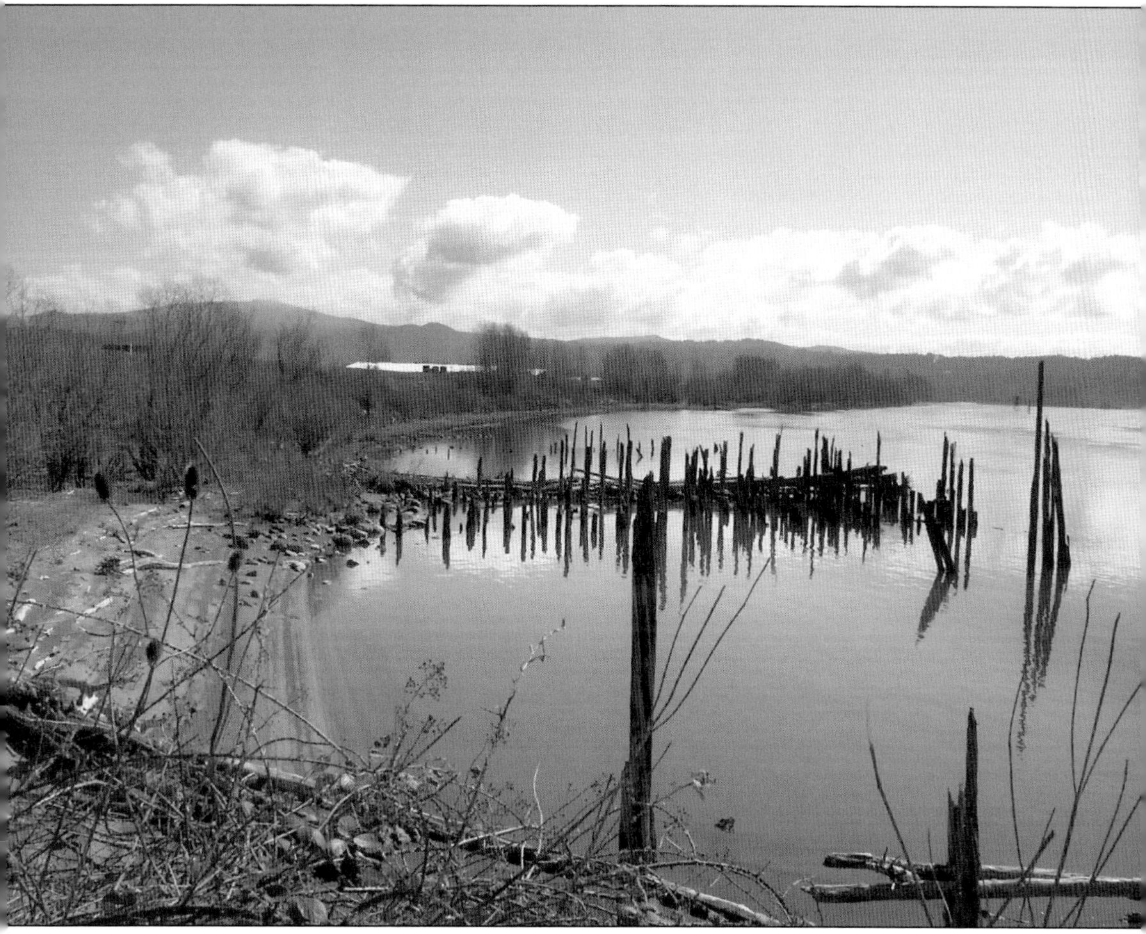

Many of the places Lewis and Clark camped during their trek across America are hard to pinpoint. In 1806, they mention camping at "handsome prairie" east of the "Seal River" and across from the "Quicksand River." Local researcher Roger Daniels was instrumental in putting two and two together, and today it is known that Lewis and Clark's "handsome prairie" is today's Cottonwood Beach, while the "Seal River" and "Quicksand River" are the Washougal and Sandy Rivers. Cottonwood Beach, then, becomes another of Washougal's many historical treasures. Lewis and Clark spent six days at Cottonwood Beach gathering provisions for the journey east. This photograph, taken of Steamboat Landing, shows Cottonwood Beach stretching east toward the Gorge. Steamboat Landing has long fallen to disuse and only remnants now remain of what was once a vital local port. In 1916, the combination of automobiles and railroads pushed the steamboats into obsolescence. For a time in the 1950s, the area was known as Chets Landing and could be used to land pontoon airplanes. It is still a popular local fishing spot.

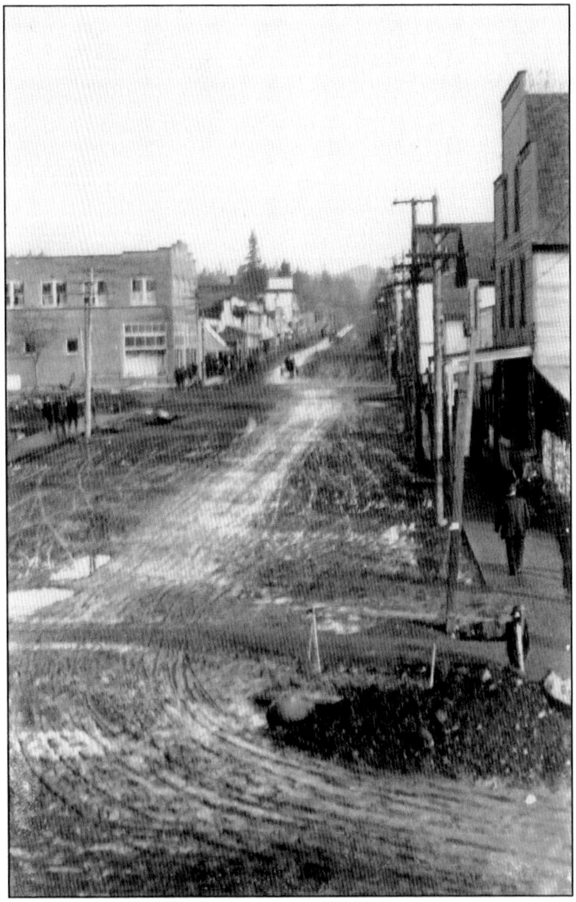

Washougal changed over the years, but B Street has remained a center for small-town commerce, parades, special occasions, and community gossip. This view of B Street in 1901 shows the street awash in mud. Laden wagons churned up the earth and left deep ruts in the road. Horses would have to strain every muscle to pull a heavy wagon through the resulting mud.

This bird's-eye view of Washougal was taken in 1912. B Street runs crosswise through the center of the photograph and is dotted with hotels and boardinghouses. Many boarding rooms were needed as loggers stayed in Washougal though the winter. The Park Hotel is just left of center. Both the Commercial Hotel and Olsen Hotel were likely in operation at the time.

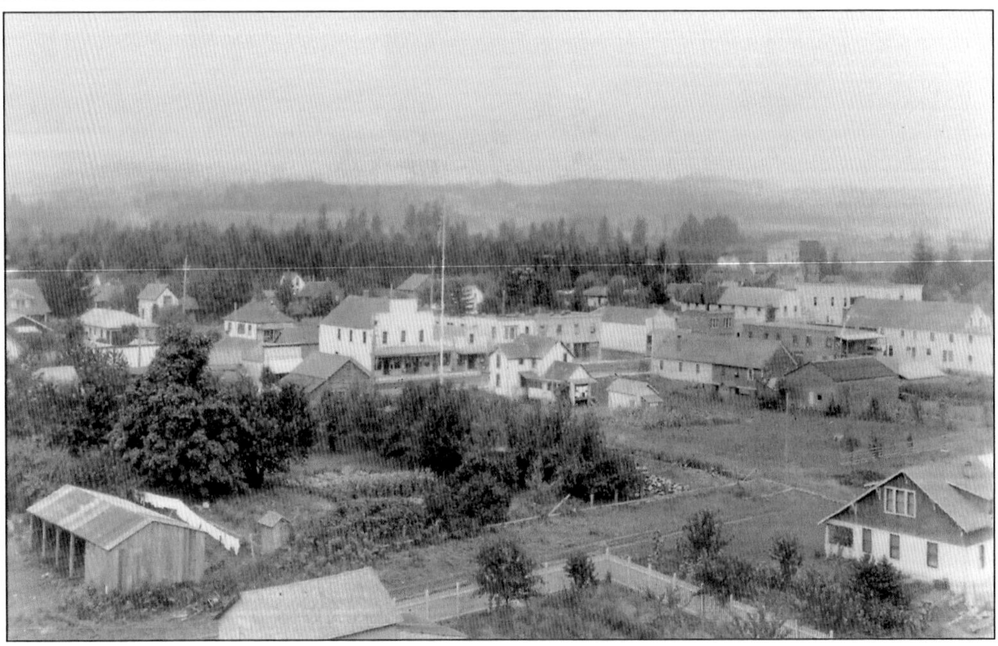

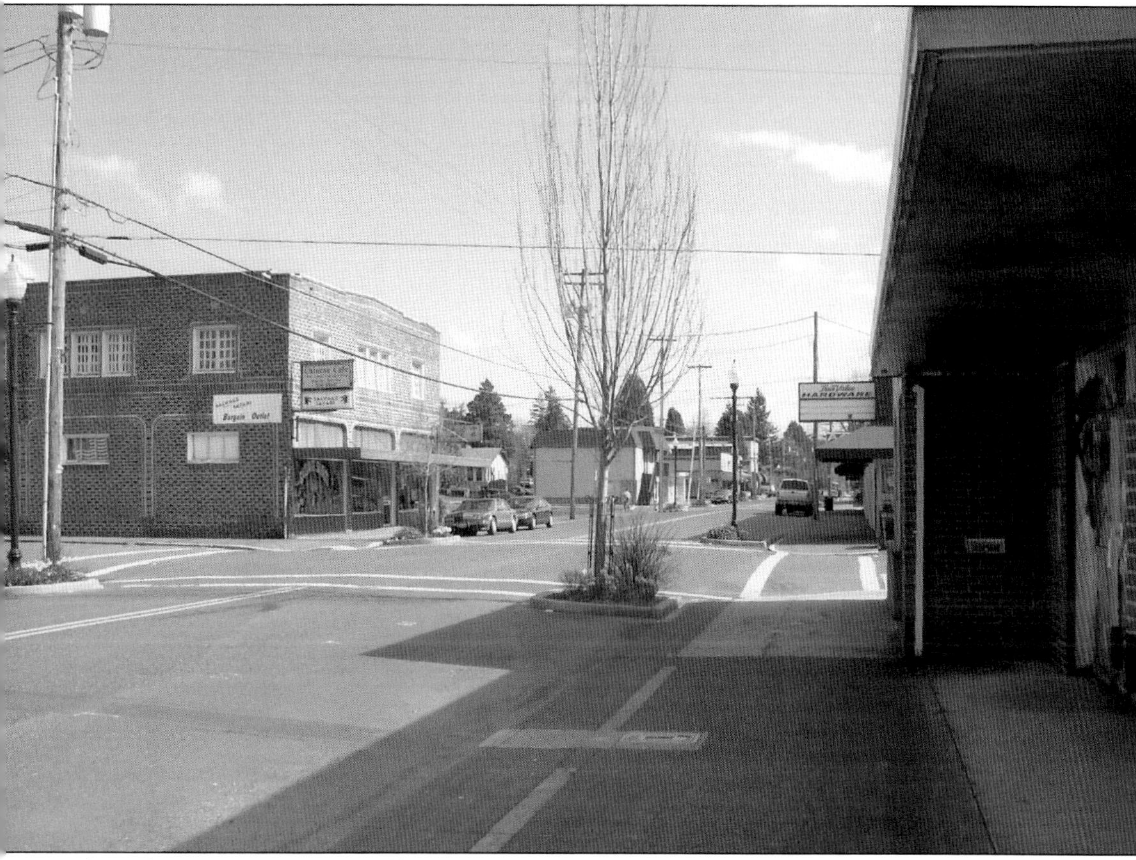

Washougal's B Street in 2006 is still a small-town thoroughfare. Businesses along B Street include the Los Jalapeño Mexican restaurant, the Salvage Safari, and an Arco gas station. The post office and Eagles Aerie are also along B Street. Washougal today is a town perched on the edge of big change. A modern type of settler is moving in. These new residents come in search of a better life, just as Washougal's first families did 200 years ago. New people mean new businesses, and new development will soon change the lines of B Street. Like all transformations, the changes of the future will bring heartbreak for some even as it brings hope to others. But all good things willing, when all is said and done, that which is most precious about Washougal will be part of all that is amazing and yet to come. As to what came before, it will be recorded so no one will ever forget.